Dear Gaim,
Thank you for all
your help!
Sophie ♡

AFRICA UNITED

HOW FOOTBALL EXPLAINS AFRICA

STEVE BLOOMFIELD

CANONGATE

Edinburgh · London · New York · Melbourne

Published by Canongate Books in 2010

1

Copyright © Steve Bloomfield, 2010

The moral right of the author has been asserted

First published in Great Britain in 2010
by Canongate Books Ltd, 14 High Street, Edinburgh EH1 1TE

www.meetatthegate.com

British Library Cataloguing-in-Publication Data
A catalogue record for this book is available on request from
the British Library

ISBN 978 1 84767 658 0
Export ISBN 978 1 84767 778 5

Typeset in Sabon by Cluny Sheeler, Edinburgh
Map copyright © Tim Mitchell, 2010

Printed and bound in Great Britain by CPI Mackays,
Chatham ME5 8TD

For Dree

CONTENTS

AFRICA

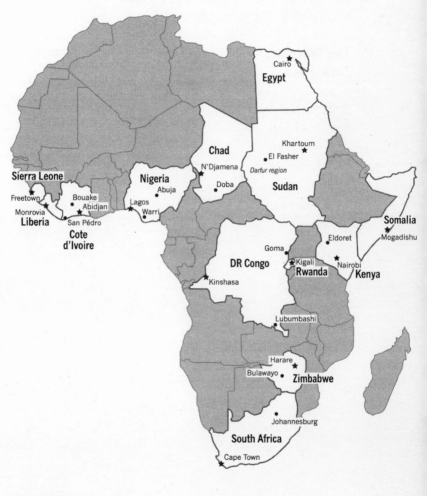

- Cairo ★
- **Egypt**
- Khartoum ★
- **Chad**
- N'Djamena
- El Fasher •
- *Darfur region*
- **Sierra Leone**
- **Nigeria**
- Abuja •
- Doba •
- **Sudan**
- Freetown ★
- Bouake •
- Abidjan •
- Lagos ★
- Warri •
- Monrovia
- **Liberia**
- San Pédro •
- **Cote d'Ivoire**
- **Somalia**
- Mogadishu •
- Eldoret •
- Goma •
- **DR Congo**
- ★ Kigali
- **Rwanda**
- Nairobi ★
- **Kenya**
- Kinshasa ★
- Lubumbashi •
- Harare ★
- Bulawayo •
- **Zimbabwe**
- Johannesburg •
- **South Africa**
- Cape Town ★

Country		**Zimbabwe**
Capital city	★	Harare
Provincial city	•	Bulawayo

0 800 Kilometers
0 800 Miles

PROLOGUE

The bus trundled through the desert, rattling over bumps that threw passengers off their seats. It was crowded and noisy, with more than forty people crammed into a vehicle made for half that number. I sat on the floor, near the back, an old woman with a small child on her lap to my right, a market trader with piles of brightly coloured material – deep blues and rich reds – stacked on his lap to my left.

We had just left Kalma, a vast, overcrowded camp for more than 90,000 Darfur refugees. As the sun began to set, and the bus continued its hour-long journey back to the town of Nyala, I flicked through my notepad and tried to make sense of what I had just seen. A woman raped, a child thrown into a burning hut, a man shot in the back as they fled. Everyone had a story to tell, a horror to relive.

Even in the camps, with international aid agencies providing water and food, few felt safe. The Janjaweed roamed nearby, attacking those who ventured beyond the confines of the camp. The Sudanese authorities were similarly feared – their armed forces had attacked villages alongside the Janjaweed.

As I read, the bus slowed to a halt. Checkpoints along this road were common. Many of the camps like Kalma had become increasingly militarised by rebel groups, and buses like this were frequently searched. From my seat on the floor I could see little out of the windows. I stretched and could just make out the top of a man's head outside and a pair of darting eyes peering in. Everyone on the bus turned to see what he was looking at. It was me.

The man outside was from Sudan's national security agency. He forced his way onto the bus and demanded to see my papers. My passport was handed from passenger to passenger until it reached the front of the bus. Then a copy of my travel permit. Then the original. Then he motioned to me to get off the bus.

I felt calm. I had the correct paperwork. It had taken endless weeks badgering the Sudanese embassy in Nairobi, countless days waiting in air-conditioned offices in Khartoum, and a few hours of drinking tea with local government officials in Nyala, but everything was in order.

My new friend didn't agree. He gestured to the bus driver and pushed me into a small hut. The bus pulled away. It was getting dark, I was in the middle of nowhere and now I was under arrest.

The hut – mud walls and a tin roof – contained an old wooden desk, a white plastic chair and a tatty mattress. Two AK-47s were propped up against a wall. Three other members of the national security agency sat on the mattress. They passed my passport and papers around, each one reading every page, analysing every stamp. I spoke little Arabic, and they spoke little English. The man who took me off the bus, a short, skinny guy with a sneer and sunglasses, knew one word, which he repeated again and again: 'problem'.

'No problem,' I replied, again and again.

The minutes ticked by. Outside the hut the sun was rapidly setting. My mobile phone had no network, so I took out my satellite phone, a hulking blue brick with a long antenna. If I was going to spend the night here, I wanted to let friends in Nyala know what was happening. The man with the sneer snatched the phone out of my hand. 'Problem!' he shouted. 'Problem!'

We weren't getting anywhere. Two of the men on the mattress had started to doze, the third was gently singing to himself, while the Sneer kept going through the passport, one page at a time. It was hot and I was desperately thirsty. Eventually I started to drift off.

I woke with a start. There was a new presence in the hut, towering over me. More than six foot tall and almost as wide, he wore large gold-rimmed sunglasses. He looked far more important than the other men in the hut, so I stumbled to my feet. As I stood up he poked his finger in my chest. 'Problem,' he said. 'No problem,' I wearily replied. He didn't seem to agree. 'Problem. French.'

'No, not French, not French. British. I'm British.'

Suddenly everything changed.

'British?' he asked.

'Yes, British.'

'David Beckham!' he cried.

'Sorry?

'David Beckham. Friend of mine!'

'What?'

'David Beckham! He's my friend!'

'Er, yeah, he's my friend too.'

'Michael Owen! My friend also!'

'Yes, Michael Owen is friends with me too. And Steven Gerrard. We're all friends.'

'Come, come,' said Beckham's friend. He grabbed my arm and pulled me out of the hut. After a couple of minutes a car came into view. He flagged it down and started talking in quick-fire Arabic to the driver.

The only word I recognised was 'Beckham'.

The driver beamed and ushered me into the passenger seat.

'Say hello to Beckham!' yelled my one-time captor, and we sped off back to Nyala.

INTRODUCTION

Africa is a continent in flux. In the first decade of the twenty-first century Africa has been through more changes than at any time since waves of independence swept across the continent fifty years ago.

Africa has experienced record levels of economic growth, which has helped to create a small but increasingly influential middle class right across the continent. The arrival of mobile phones has had a dramatic effect, providing new opportunities to small businesses and connecting even the most rural farmer to the wider world. The spread of mobile phones has also revolutionised the finance industry, giving many people the choice of a wide range of innovative mobile banking services. Internet usage in countries like Nigeria, South Africa, Ghana and Kenya has changed the way young people interact as dramatically as it has in the West.

Africa has become increasingly urbanised, with young people drawn towards the big cities, where there is more chance of finding work. Family structures have also begun to change, with younger generations moving into apartments rather than building a house on the family's plot.

At the forefront of Africa's most positive changes are what the economist George Ayittey has described as a generation of 'cheetahs' determined to overtake the old guard of 'hippos'. They are web designers and civil society leaders, musicians and architects.

But, at the end of the first decade, the hippos are still very much in charge. In those countries which have bothered to have elections that could be accurately described as 'democratic', the competing politicians all tend to be from the same generation of one-time liberation leaders.

While there may be new ways of thinking among younger generations, those in charge tend to stick rigidly to the economic models of the West. Encouraged by the International Monetary Fund, the World Bank and wealthy Western nations, African countries have followed a neoliberal economic growth model. At the 2007 Kenyan elections, the country's president, Mwai Kibaki, was able to point to a steady 6 per cent annual growth. But he remained unpopular because most people had not benefited. Kenya's capital, Nairobi, like a lot of other African cities, has become a series of contrasting enclaves of rich and poor. The rich live in gated communities of new apartment blocks, while the poor are crammed into overflowing slums. The dichotomy of the new Nairobi is summed up by the Westgate Centre, a three-storey mall selling plasma TV screens and soft furnishings. As Westgate's customers, in their shiny 4x4s, queue to get in, small children knock on their windows, begging for loose change.

There is a growing middle class in between, made up of those who live in the smart new apartment blocks springing up in cities across the continent and who can afford an overseas holiday once a year. These middle-class professionals, university educated and comfortably well off, will likely have greater influence as the next decade evolves.

The decade has also been marked by a series of conflicts – some well known, others ignored. An estimated 5.4 million people are believed to have died in the Democratic Republic of Congo during the course of two wars. Most died from diseases which would have been prevented if the country had been at peace. In Sudan, a twenty-year civil war between the Arab-dominated north and the mainly Christian and Animist south ended in 2005, just as a more brutal conflict was taking hold in the country's western Darfur region. Some of the worst fighting has taken place in Somalia, a country of 7 million that snakes around the eastern Horn of Africa. It has been without a functioning central government since 1991 and in the past decade has become one of the world's worst humanitarian catastrophes.

Democracy has taken one step forward and two steps back. Elections in Ghana in 2008 and Sierra Leone in 2007 were heralded as great successes, but those in Nigeria, Kenya and Zimbabwe were marred by blatant rigging and unprecedented violence. There is something deeply wrong in a country where the phrase 'he died during the election' is often used.

Since independence, African leaders' relationships with foreign powers have had far more importance than their links to their own voters. During the Cold War, countries regularly played the two superpowers off against each other, in an effort to gain more money or influence. Although the Cold War has ended, many African leaders are still able to play this game. Since the turn of the century, China has become increasingly influential in Africa. Trade between the two was valued at $2 billion in 1999. By 2005 it had risen to nearly $40 billion, and it has been estimated to soar to $100 billion by 2010, making China Africa's most important trading partner after the USA. China's main interest in Africa has been its minerals – predominantly oil – while in return it has built infrastructure: roads, railways, schools and hospitals. The Chinese have also built football stadiums, from Tanzania's new national stadium in Dar es Salaam to all four of the new stadiums used in the 2010 Africa Cup of Nations in Angola.

Football has been at the forefront of Africa's recent changes. Players such as Côte d'Ivoire's Didier Drogba and Nigeria's Nwankwo Kanu have become global stars. Think of a famous African and the names that come to mind tend to be political leaders or footballers. Mandela and Eto'o. Mugabe and Essien.

Those players have found fame in Africa, but they have made their fortune in Europe. The success of Africa's footballers in Europe reflects the economic difficulties the continent still faces. Few African countries have clubs rich enough to be able to afford the sort of wages that Drogba or Adebayor can earn in Europe. The clubs that do have enough money for this include Egyptian champions Al-Ahly, whose captain we will meet in the first chapter, and Congolese champions TP Mazembe, whose multimillionaire owner and political leader will appear in chapter five.

In most cases, though, African league football is of a poor standard. Despite the continent's love of the game, crowds for local league matches rarely get above a few hundred, particularly if the kick-off time clashes with an English Premier League match on satellite television.

As you will see over the next ten chapters, football in Africa often reflects the political and cultural struggles that a country is experiencing. In Kenya, the divisions within the game's ruling body caused by tribe, power and money, and the debilitating effect these have on the clubs, players and fans, are a microcosm of the country as a whole.

But football can also have an incredible unifying effect. Les Éléphants of Côte d'Ivoire, who we will meet in chapter seven, helped to bring the country together during a time of civil war. Between 2002 and 2007 the country, once the economic powerhouse of West Africa, was split in two. Rebels took control of the Muslim-dominated north, while the government retained power in the south. At a time when the country was divided and issues of nationality and 'true Ivorian-ness' were being fought over, the one thing that still managed to unite the people was football.

Didier Drogba's decision, as captain of the national side, to insist that a World Cup qualifier be played in the north is widely seen as the moment when the country's peace deal, agreed just a few weeks before, looked as if it might stick.

But as we will see in the first chapter, which focuses on Egypt, some governments have taken advantage of the sense of national pride that a successful team can bring. Football diverts people's attention from the reality of their situation, and Egypt's autocratic president, Hosni Mubarak, has become skilled in the art of using that distraction to his own advantage.

The first African football team to make an impact at a World Cup tournament, the Cameroon side of 1990, was similarly used and abused by its country's president, Paul Biya. The star of the Italia '90 tournament was Cameroon's thirty-eight-year-old striker, Roger Milla, but the only reason he was at the tournament was because Biya had insisted.

Throughout the 1980s Milla had been Cameroon's star striker, playing in the team which qualified for the 1982 World Cup and won the Africa Cup of Nations – the continent's premier tournament – in 1984 and 1988.

The 1990 World Cup would be a step too far, though, and midway through the qualifying campaign Milla announced his retirement. Cameroon managed to secure a place in the World Cup without him, beating Tunisia 3–0 over two legs. But as the tournament got closer, Cameroonian football was, not for the first time and certainly not for the last, in turmoil. Competing political factions fought for control of the football federation, while the government, led by the autocratic Biya, interfered at every turn. Bonuses promised to the players hadn't materialised, and fans were starting to worry that the World Cup might be a very public embarrassment.

Biya decided Milla should play for the Indomitable Lions, as the Cameroonian national team is known. The coach, a Russian called Valeri Nepomniachi, who had been appointed by the government as a sop to the Soviet Union, didn't have any say in the matter. The president rang Milla and told him his country needed him. And Milla, like the coach, couldn't disagree.

Biya understood the power of football. The Lions' success was his success. He had come to power in

1982 but had shown a certain level of reluctance to test his popularity by holding elections. The fantastic performance of the national football team in Italy helped to deflect attention away from the less than stellar performance of Biya's government back in Youandé.

Biya eventually allowed elections in 1992, but they were far from free or fair. The opposition protested and called for a national strike on 11 October. But on 10 October the Lions were due to play Zimbabwe in a World Cup qualifier. Victory would guarantee them a place at the 1994 World Cup. And so, with uncanny timing, Biya announced that if the Lions beat Zimbabwe, then the next day would be a national holiday. They did, and the strike was called off.

Cameroon's performance at the 1990 tournament in Italy transformed the way African football was viewed by the wider world.

Egypt had played in the second World Cup back in 1934, but the continent had been forced to wait another thirty-six years before they were allowed to send another team. The refusal of FIFA, football's world governing body, to guarantee an African representative at the 1966 World Cup, held in England, prompted the seventeen African teams that had entered the qualifying competition to pull out. FIFA relented for the 1970 tournament in Mexico, granting a single place, which Morocco eventually claimed. By 1990 FIFA had grudgingly increased Africa's representation to two in a tournament with twenty-four participants, despite the impressive performances in the 1982 tournament of Algeria and Cameroon, both of whom were unlucky not to reach the second round.

African teams were supposed to turn up, play with a bit of heart, let in a sloppy goal or two, then go home. It might have been called the World Cup, but everyone knew it was essentially a tournament between the best in Europe and the best in South America. In 1990 there were no African players in the English league and only a handful in the rest of Europe. Africa was either ignored or patronised.

African football at this time was regularly dismissed as naive. They were energetic footballers, yes. Skilful, definitely. But they couldn't defend. They didn't understand tactics. During Cameroon's first match in Italia 90, against reigning world champions Argentina, the African side were described by ITV's commentator, Brian Moore, as 'a real happy-go-lucky bunch of fellas'. According to his co-commentator, Ron Atkinson, 'they get excitable'. Another commentator described them as 'brainless'.

The facts suggested otherwise. Cameroon's team in 1990 was well organised and strong at the back. In the opening match Cameroon stifled their opponents, barely letting them play, and occasionally hitting them on the counterattack with speed and skill. Things were made even harder for them when the referee sent off the midfielder Kana-Biyik for an innocuous trip on Argentina's blond-haired striker, Claudio Cannigia.

The Lions regrouped, and Biyik's brother, François Omam-Biyik, scored the winning goal, a header straight at the goalkeeper which somehow squirmed through his fingers and over the line. Agentina piled on the pressure and a second Cameroonian midfielder, Benjamin Massing, was sent off. But Cameroon held on.

An African team had beaten the world champions. It was the moment that world football began to realise it could ignore Africa no longer.

The victory over Argentina was no fluke. In their next game, against Romania, Milla came off the bench to score twice and give Cameroon a 2–1 win. Milla celebrated each goal by sprinting to the corner flag, placing one hand in front of his crotch, another above his head, and wiggling his hips. It became one of football's most iconic goal celebrations, repeated in parks and playgrounds across the world.

At the age of thirty-eight, Milla had become the World Cup's oldest goal-scorer. And they weren't just any old goals. He showed the speed and strength of a player half his age, and versatility too – scoring one with his left foot and the other with his right.

Milla's goals took Cameroon into the second round, the first time an African country had made it that far. They weren't done. Two more goals from Milla knocked out Colombia and set up a quarter-final meeting with England.

With seven minutes remaining, the Lions were leading 2–1, and deservedly so. Milla had set up both goals, getting brought down for a penalty for the first, then playing a great through ball for Ekeke to score the second.

England, driven on by Paul Gascoigne, who played probably his best game for his country that night, fought back. Gary Lineker won a penalty and got up to score it, taking the match into extra time. The game remained free-flowing with chances at both ends, until Lineker was brought down for another penalty in the 105th minute, which he duly scored.

The match ended 3–2, and Cameroon were out. The Lions were given a standing ovation by the Italian crowd. England's manager, Bobby Robson, conceded that his team were lucky to win. Never again would an African team be underestimated.

*

I moved to Nairobi in 2006 to become the *Independent*'s Africa correspondent. I was eager to write uplifting, positive stories about a continent I thought had been badly let down by the Western media. The only stories that seemed to come out of Africa were about war and poverty. Surely a continent of fifty-three countries and 800 million people had more to offer than that?

It did, but news doesn't work that way. Most of the stories fitted the 'dark continent' narrative – ethnic cleansing in Darfur, civil war in Somalia, a never-ending war in Congo.

While the world – and I – focused on Africa's ills, there was another side to the continent that tended to get ignored. Africa's economic, technological and cultural renaissance has been ignored in much of the West. The continent is still known more for its dictators and rebels than for its entrepreneurs and artists.

But since Cameroon's triumph in 1990 there is one other thing that Africa has become known for, though: football. There is hardly a single major club in Europe that doesn't have at least one African player. At the 2008 Africa Cup of Nations in Ghana, thirty-four of the participating players plied their trade in the English Premier League. When Barcelona won the UEFA Champions League in 2009, a Cameroonian, Samuel Eto'o, scored one of the goals, while an Ivorian, Yaya Touré, was the driving force in midfield.

Everywhere I've travelled – from the beaches of Freetown to the streets of Mogadishu – young boys and teenagers have been playing football. They don't even need a proper football; a bundle of plastic bags and rags tied together into a roughly spherical shape is enough.

At the weekend bars and shacks across the continent are filled with people watching European football. The English Premier League has become the UK's biggest export to Africa. Ask most football fans in Africa which team they support and they will name an English side rather than a local one. Most fans support one of the big four – Manchester United, Chelsea, Arsenal or Liverpool. No one else gets a look in.

My club, Aston Villa, may have regularly finished in the top six in recent years, but finding a Villa fan in Nairobi is impossible. Twice I've found people wearing fake replica Villa shirts. One was the 1989 pinstripes abomination with 'Mita Copiers' adorning the front; the other was the weird early-90s shirt with string on the V-neck. On neither occasion has the wearer spoken English, let alone known who Villa are.

*

Since 1990, African football has gradually gained more respect. FIFA increased the continent's representation in the World Cup to three in 1994 and then to five in

1998, when the tournament was expanded to thirty-two teams. The 2010 tournament will include a sixth African team.

More importantly, though, FIFA also agreed that it was time that Africa hosted the World Cup. In 2004 South Africa beat Morocco and Egypt to become the first African hosts of one of the world's biggest sporting events.

For decades African footballers have been leaving the continent to play their football. Now the world's best footballers are coming to Africa. The tournament will focus attention on African football like never before. It will also be an opportunity to shine a light on the new Africa. The continent that is constantly viewed through the prism of war, poverty and disease will get a chance to present a different face.

*

Ahead of the 2010 World Cup I have travelled across Africa, from Cairo to the Cape, searching for the stories which put Africa's football in context.

I've chosen thirteen countries, to be covered in ten chapters. They include some of the best on the continent and some of the worst; giants who have appeared at numerous World Cups and minnows that will struggle even to qualify for the Africa Cup of Nations, a sixteen-team tournament held every two years.

This isn't an encyclopaedia of African football. There are great teams that are not covered – Algeria in 1982, Senegal in 2002, Ghana in 2006. But this book is not just about World Cup success. It's not about goals scored and matches won.

It's about how football can rebuild a country, end a war or provide a beacon of light in a time of despair. It's the story of how Africa has been shaped by its football and how Africa is now shaping football.

And it begins in Cairo, the home of Africa's most successful footballing nation, where a crucial World Cup qualifier turned out to be much more than a football match. What happened on the pitch, and the subsequent reaction off it, prompted riots in four cities and created the biggest diplomatic incident in North Africa for more than a decade. Ambassadors were recalled, diplomatic ties were broken, and the son of Egypt's president, Hosni Mubarak, almost started a war.

1
THE PHARAOHS
Egypt

It's after the fifth body search that you begin to feel security might be an issue. Armed police have already taken my water bottle, triple-checked my wallet and raised an eyebrow at my broken phone. There are still two more lines of police to deal with.

'It's always like this for Zamalek fans,' says Ahmad Saied.

'Not for Ahly fans too?' I ask.

He just smiles.

Welcome to Al-Ahly versus Zamalek, the Red Devils versus the White Knights, the new establishment versus the old establishment. The Cairo derby is the biggest club match in Africa. They are the two most successful clubs on the continent: Zamalek have won the African Champions League five times, Al-Ahly six.

This vast metropolis of roughly 20 million people grinds to a standstill on derby day. Everyone, it seems, wants to watch the match. It's the same across the Arab world. Both clubs claim to have millions of fans (Al-Ahly supposedly have 60 million and Zamalek

30 million, although how they work that out I've no idea). When Hamas and Fatah fought each other for control of Gaza in 2007, the only day the guns fell silent was when Al-Ahly took on Zamalek.

It's not a match for the faint-hearted. In the past there have been outbreaks of violence between the two sets of fans, with petrol bombs being thrown and the occasional stabbing, although these days the heavy police presence that I've just navigated helps to keep a lid on things.

The emotion of the game often gets to the players too. Refereeing the derby has become such a gargantuan task that foreign officials have been drafted in to take control, partly because local referees are open to bribes and partly for the safety of the local referees, lest they make a decision one set of fans deems to be wrong.

I've been looking forward to the match all week; Ahmad less so. A self-effacing twenty-something Cairo native who has supported Zamalek all his life, Ahmad had to be cajoled into coming to the match.

'We're going to lose,' he says by way of explanation.

He's probably right. For while the derby maintains most of the animosity and passion that have turned it into a truly international event, the overwhelming success of Al-Ahly in recent years has begun to make it a bit of an anti-climax. Of the last fifteen matches Al-Ahly have won thirteen and drawn one. Their only defeat came in a league match which took place long after Al-Ahly had wrapped up the championship. Most of the first-team players were rested and the manager, a Portuguese called Manuel José, also decided to give it a miss, heading off to the beach and leaving his assistant in charge. The celebrations which greeted Zamalek's 2–0 victory were muted.

As we enter the vast concrete bowl that is the Cairo International Stadium it's clear that many of Ahmad's fellow Zamalek supporters feel the same way as him. While the Ahly end is a loud, volatile, swaying sea of red, here in Zamalek country we've got the pick of the seats. 'Sometimes we put large banners over the seats to hide the empty ones,' Ahmad says. Over the course of the next two hours our end will grow to maybe two-thirds full but clearly the expectation of yet another defeat to a hated rival has kept most fans away.

Al-Ahly's recent domination has won Zamalek some sympathy though, if nothing else. Supporters of Ismaili and Suez, two of Egypt's less famous top-flight clubs, help to pad out the Zamalek end.

The Ahly fans are meanwhile chanting 'one, two, three, four, five, six' in celebration of the most recent embarrassment they have inflicted on their rivals, a 6–1 victory. Two fireworks and a flare are let off in the Ahly end.

'They took my water,' I point out.

Ahmad shrugs. 'Al-Ahly is the government club,' he says.

It wasn't always the case. When Al-Ahly was established in 1907 one of its main purposes was to help student leaders rise up against colonialism. For decades it remained the club of the working classes, while Zamalek was viewed as the club for the intellectuals and the middle classes.

Football and politics have long been interlinked here. The disastrous Six Day War with Israel in 1967 deeply affected the national psyche, shocking a country which had always believed in its own military might. Casting around for reasons for the defeat, the government placed part of the blame on football. The national game had become a 'distraction', they claimed. Football was banned.

The 1960s had been a golden age for Egyptian football. 'Soccer stars were treated like movie stars,' Khaled Youssef, a young film-maker tells me a few days later as we eat dinner at a KFC-style diner that has become popular with Cairo's young and chic.

It took four years before the authorities could be persuaded to allow football to be played again. The revival was short-lived. In its first season back in 1971 violence between Ahly and Zamalek fans marred the Cairo derby. The rest of the season was abandoned.

The political landscape was volatile too. The aftermath of the Six Day War also saw a surge in support for radical Islamist groups, inspired by the teachings of Said Qutb, the founding father of modern-day jihadism, now practised by Osama bin Laden. Anwar al-Sadat, who took over as president following the death of Gamal Abdel Nasser in 1970, tried to gain the support of Islamist groups by emphasising his visits to mosques and peppering his speeches with references to the Koran.

Egypt went to war again in 1973, launching an attack on Israel on Yom Kippur in an attempt to regain the territory lost in 1967. The war lasted seventeen days, and thousands of troops on both sides were killed. Egypt took control of the Suez Canal, but it would require peace talks with Israel before the country was able to take back the Sinai.

Those peace talks, held at Camp David in the USA in 1978, won Sadat a Nobel Peace Prize a year later. But Egypt's Islamist radicals were less impressed.

Demonstrations were held throughout the country condemning the move.

Sadat's government was less wary of football than his predecessor's had been. At a time when national pride was at a low ebb, the government viewed a successful football team as a possible panacea.

Fortunately, the national side was finally showing some promise. Egypt had won the first two Africa Cup of Nations in 1957 and 1959, although neither tournament really counted. Just three teams had taken part: Egypt, Sudan and Ethiopia. After more teams began to enter, Egypt's run of glory came to an end. But during the 1978 World Cup qualifying campaign the Pharaohs were impressive. They beat Ethiopia in the first round before disposing of Kenya in the second and Zambia in the third.

The final round was a group knockout with Tunisia and Nigeria. Each team would play the others twice, home and away, and the winners would be Africa's sole representative at the World Cup in Argentina.

Egypt started disastrously, losing 4–0 away to Nigeria, but they won the return match in Cairo and then defeated Tunisia 3–2 at home a month later.

A point in the final match in Tunisia would see Egypt go through. The government chartered several planes to take fans to Tunis and promised bonuses to the players if they qualified. The World Cup would not just be good for the team, it would serve as an extraordinary boost for the country.

Egypt, though, were hammered 4–1. Tunisia represented the continent in Argentina and went on to become the first African country to win a World Cup match, beating Mexico 3–1 before going out in the group stage.

But despite the failure in Tunis a corner had been turned. Over the course of the next decade Egypt became one of African football's dominant forces. Al-Ahly and Zamalek both won the continental club title twice, and the national team won the Africa Cup of Nations when they hosted it in 1986.

By this time a new president, Hosni Mubarak, had come to power and Egypt had become a far more authoritarian state. The slide from democracy had begun in the last days of Sadat's reign. He had reacted to growing protests against his rule by introducing draconian new laws and arresting hundreds of opposition supporters. But he couldn't arrest them all. On 6 October 1981 Sadat was assassinated by a member of Jama'at al-Jihad while watching a military parade.

*

For all Egypt's success at continental level, qualification for the World Cup finals eluded them. Egypt had played in the second-ever World Cup, the 1934 tournament in Italy, but that had been an invitation-only event. They lost their only match, 4–2 to Hungary.

Once countries had to qualify, Egypt struggled. The rivalry between Al-Ahly and Zamalek didn't help. Players from the two clubs often didn't get on and it seemed they cared more about how many players each club could claim in the national side rather than how well it was performing.

Failure at the 1988 Africa Cup of Nations prompted a fresh bout of introspection. Qualification for the 1990 World Cup, to be held in Italy, was about to begin and few fans believed there was any chance of Egypt breaking their duck.

A new coach was appointed: Mahmoud El-Gohary. 'He was the first proper coach,' Khaled claims. 'He unified the team. For the first time it wasn't about Al-Ahly and Zamalek.'

El-Gohary's strategy worked. Egypt lost just one match and qualified as one of two African teams, alongside Cameroon.

'The mood of the whole nation changed,' Khaled, who is working on a film about El-Gohary's career, told me. El-Gohary's name was chanted at football matches and rallies. Interviews with him instantly boosted the circulation of the new football magazines that had begun to spring up.

Once again the league was cancelled for the good of the nation, only this time it was so that El-Gohary could have enough time to prepare his World Cup squad.

The Africa Cup of Nations, which took place in February, four months before Italia '90, was sidelined. The Olympic team was sent instead so that the main squad could concentrate solely on the World Cup.

Egypt beat Scotland and Czechoslovakia in warm-up matches and headed to Italy in high spirits. They had been drawn in what became dubbed the 'group of death' alongside England, the Netherlands and the Republic of Ireland. Every tournament seems to have one – a group of four teams with no favourite.

The first two matches both finished 1–1: England drew with Ireland, while Egypt came back from 1–0 down to draw with the Netherlands. The second set of matches had the same outcome: England versus the

Netherlands and Egypt against Ireland both finished 0–0.

Going into the final round of matches, all four teams were level. If nothing could separate the teams after three matches, FIFA officials would have to toss a coin to decide which two went through.

Egypt's match against England was the most important in their history. Victory, perhaps even a draw, would take them into the second round.

It was no less important for England. Although that World Cup is now remembered fondly in England (Platt's volley; Gazza's tears; almost, almost beating West Germany in the semis), defeat to Egypt would have been viewed as catastrophic, perhaps as embarrassing as defeat to the USA had been in 1950.

The game was poor. At half-time it was still 0–0 and neither side had really managed to create anything. That changed in the fifty-eighth minute. England won a free kick on the left-hand touchline. Gascoigne whipped it in, Mark Wright rose highest and his flicked header beat the onrushing Ahmed Shobeir in the Egyptian goal.

The 1–0 defeat knocked Egypt out, but their performances against some of the world's best players won the team plaudits at home.

El-Gohary was fêted as one of the country's greatest-ever coaches and there was optimism among the supporters that the team would be able to build on the performances in Italy and qualify in style for the next World Cup in 1994.

Instead, less than two months after the team returned to Cairo, El-Gohary was sacked.

On a rain-soaked pitch in Athens, Egypt's World Cup heroes had capitulated 6–1 in a meaningless friendly against Greece. Back home, though, politicians in Mubarak's ruling party didn't think it quite so insignificant. The defeat had 'damaged the image of Egypt', they claimed, despite the fact that few football fans outside the country were even aware it had taken place. Parliament launched an investigation. Ignoring the first-ever qualification for a World Cup and the impressive performances in Italy, the investigation called for El-Gohary to be sacked. Which he duly was.

In the following twelve years, Egypt had fourteen national coaches. Four of them were El-Gohary. After each new disaster (knocked out in the first round of the 1991 All Africa Games, defeated by Liberia in the 1998 World Cup qualifying campaign) the cry went up 'bring back El-Gohary'. But he struggled to recreate the magic of 1990.

'We were addicted to him,' Khaled says. 'The relationship was complex. He was our father, but he was our drunk father.'

His biggest achievement was the 1998 Africa Cup of Nations victory in Burkina Faso. Mubarak was at the airport to greet the returning champions and El-Gohary was, once again, fêted as the man who could do no wrong.

As African champions, Egypt were invited to take part in the Confederations Cup the year after and initially did well, drawing 2–2 with Bolivia and holding eventual winners Mexico to the same scoreline. Things fell apart though in the easiest match, against Saudi Arabia. Egypt were humbled 5–1 and El-Gohary was sacked for a final time.

*

The year 2005 was the most dramatic in Egyptian politics for a generation. Mubarak's tight grip on power was weakening following a deeply flawed series of elections. At first glance the presidential elections in September had appeared to be a step in the right direction. Previously voters had merely had the chance to vote 'yes' or 'no' to the choice presented to them by parliament. Under pressure from the West to be provided with at least a semblance of democracy, Egyptians were now, for the first time, actually given a choice of candidates to vote for. Not a completely democratic choice, though. The most popular opposition party, the Muslim Brotherhood, was barred from putting up a presidential candidate. And just in case the people didn't decide to give Mubarak an overwhelming victory, his security forces and officials were on hand to ensure the right result. Ballot boxes were stuffed and, in areas where opposition support was high, security forces blocked voters from getting to polling stations, in some cases firing on people trying to vote.

The parliamentary elections in December were just as bad. Mubarak's secular opponent was locked up on forgery charges, while the Muslim Brotherhood's supporters were harassed. Opposition demonstrators took to the streets in their thousands but the security forces managed to prevent them seriously threatening Mubarak's rule.

A month after the disputed elections Egypt was due to host the Africa Cup of Nations. Desperate for something to help boost his popularity and unite the country, Mubarak turned to football. It was a strategy that had started slowly. Mubarak had begun to attend African Champions League finals featuring Al-Ahly or

Zamalek. 'He saw it was popular,' Egyptian journalist Walid al-Hosseiny told me. 'Then he started going to the Pharaohs' training camps, receiving winners at the airport . . . The pro-government media helped to highlight it. They showed it as a boost to the team.'

It reached a peak during the Africa Cup of Nations. Mubarak's regular visits to the Pharaohs' training sessions were headline news and he was careful to attend every match, trying his best to align himself with a team he hoped would be successful.

'The political regime uses football to promote itself,' said al-Hosseiny. 'He is trying to show that he is with the people. It's a constant message.'

Politics aside, the 2006 Nations Cup was to Egypt what Euro 96 was to England. Football, long the preserve of the working classes, became – briefly – a middle-class sport. Stylish young women, with henna tattoos and figure-hugging jeans and tops, were attending matches. Billboards showing stars such as the captain Ahmed Hassan advertising drinks and clothes dominated the main highways.

The team had much to prove. Egypt had, once again, failed to qualify for the World Cup. All five of the African qualifiers, including the team that knocked Egypt out, Côte d'Ivoire, were at the Nations Cup, giving the host nation the perfect opportunity to show their worth.

Egypt breezed through the opening group stage, even gaining a touch of revenge against Côte d'Ivoire, beating them 3–1. They hammered DR Congo 4–1 in the quarter-finals, and a late Amr Zaki goal gave the Pharaohs victory over Senegal in the semis.

The final against Côte d'Ivoire finished goalless after extra time. The tournament would be decided

by a penalty shoot-out. Hassan scored Egypt's first
spot-kick, but Didier Drogba missed the first for
Côte d'Ivoire. Both sides scored, both missed, then
both scored again. Mohamed Abou Treika, the star
of the tournament, stepped up to take Egypt's final
penalty. He scored, Egypt won, and Hosni Mubarak,
Egypt's beleaguered president, was a very happy
man.

*

One glance inside Al-Ahly's training complex suggests
that its reputation as the club of the working classes is
no longer deserved. It's almost ten o'clock on a warm
Cairo evening and training has just begun. The first
team squad jogs gently around the pristine pitch while
the club's members sit around tables on the perimeter,
drinking fresh fruit juice and sodas. All of them have
paid an annual fee of 50,000LE – the equivalent of
£5,500 – to become members of Al-Ahly.

The training session – the last before the derby
with Zamalek – is light. As the players wander off
the pitch an hour or so later, the members finish their
drinks and pay their bills. Their children race round
to the front entrance to wait for the stars to emerge.
Clutching expensive camera-phones, they scream and
yell as each first-team player steps out. The players
dutifully pose for pictures before heading off to the
car park. The loudest screams are reserved for Ahmed
Hassan.

Egypt's captain, Hassan was the face of the
victorious Africa Cup of Nations team in 2006. He's
one of the few Egyptian players who have made a
successful move to Europe and is one of the world's

most-capped players, with more than 160 appearances for the national team.

After more than a decade in Turkey and Belgium, including spells at Besiktas and Anderlecht, Hassan decided to return to Cairo this season. Zamalek and Al-Ahly both fought for his signature, but even Zamalek fans expected him to go to their rivals. Al-Ahly had benefited from a certain amount of stability. In the six years that Manuel José was in charge of Al-Ahly (from 2003 to 2009), Zamalek had no fewer than twelve different managers. Al-Ahly also had more money.

My friend Ahmad Saied knows Hassan well and has arranged for the three of us to meet. Hassan spots us through the crowd and motions towards the car park. He opens the door to a brand-new red Porsche Cayenne, a big jeep-like model with leather seats and built-in TV screens, and we head off.

The whole thing seems faintly bizarre. It's midnight and I'm in a Porsche with Egypt's captain driving around Cairo. We stop outside a rather tired-looking three-storey building in a residential area. Hassan owns a limousine hire company which has its offices here. It may be past midnight but he still needs to finish some paperwork.

We go upstairs to his main office and Hassan switches on the TV. Egypt's coach, Hassan Shehata, is on a discussion show talking about the Pharaohs' victory over DR Congo in Kinshasa the week before. The win, in front of 60,000 pumped-up Congolese fans, gave Egypt a big boost in their quest for World Cup qualification.

'This generation has the best chance,' Hassan says as he puts his coach on mute. 'We have the perfect ingredients of veterans and young players.'

Hassan is now one of the veterans. He has played in six Nations Cups, with Egypt finishing three of them as champions. But his dream has always been to play in the World Cup. He was too young to play in 1990 and has since seen his chance to appear on the world's biggest stage fall apart at the last moment time and time again.

Another North African side has almost always been responsible for Egypt's demise. Tunisia knocked them out in 1978, while it was Morocco that dashed their hopes in both 1982 and 1986. Tunisia again put paid to their chances in 1998 and a combination of Morocco and Algeria saw them miss out in 2002. In 2006, defeat away to Libya certainly didn't help, but they still would have missed out to Côte d'Ivoire.

'Egypt play better when we play in tournaments,' Hassan says. 'Away from home in one-off matches we've been very bad. In the qualifying rounds . . .' He trails off before snapping back: 'We've recently started to get that mentality to win away.'

Having an Egyptian coach has helped. Shehata took over from an Italian, Marco Tardelli, in 2004. Tardelli had won the World Cup with Italy in 1982, scoring one of the three goals in the final before setting off on one of football's most iconic goal celebrations – arms open, fists clenched, shaking his head in disbelief.

But Tardelli struggled, Hassan argues, to understand how to deal with Egyptian footballers.

'The coach now, he knows how to be psychologically with Egyptian players,' Hassan says. 'But if we lose, everyone says, "Ah, we have to have a foreign coach." They are not always the best.'

Hassan is one of the few Egyptian stars to make it in Europe. In the past few years players like Mido, Amr Zaki and Hossam Ghaly have endured a horrendous time in England. Zaki started the 2008–9 season brilliantly for Wigan but ended it dubbed the 'most unprofessional player I've ever worked with' by his manager, Steve Bruce, after he failed to return from international duty with Egypt for a fourth time.

'Egyptian players have our traditions, which contradict with our professions,' Hassan argues. 'We are out all the time. Cairo is always awake. This is why we don't succeed abroad.'

He looks at his watch. 'It's now after midnight. Would you be interviewing an English footballer at this time?'

He has a point. Ahmad Saied and I thank him for his time and head off.

As Hassan said, Cairo is a city that's always awake. It's one o'clock in the morning but the downtown markets are still open. Women haggle for a good price for a bag of oranges; the city's young and cool, wearing sunglasses at night, check out each other as much as the jeans and tops. Despite the time, children run down the street playing with fireworks. Old men sit on plastic chairs along the pavement.

We head to a local restaurant to eat mezes. Most of the tables are full with families and there are children running about. At several tables people are smoking shishas – fruit-flavoured tobacco which is filtered through an ornate metal pot. Egyptians see themselves as Arabs rather than Africans and this certainly feels like an Arab city.

I was told a story, possibly apocryphal, when I first came to Cairo. An Egyptian diplomat, newly appointed as ambassador to Zimbabwe, is greeted at Harare airport by the foreign minister.

'Welcome to Zimbabwe,' the foreign minister says.

'Thank you,' replies the ambassador. 'It's my first time in Africa.'

I understand what the ambassador meant. Cairo appears more modern, more developed, more Western than any African city I've been to. There are flyovers and eight-lane highways, pavements and working streetlights. There are shiny new branches of Nokia, Nike and HSBC, while McDonald's and Pizza Hut are here too – and they deliver.

It's a sprawling metropolis of bungalows and apartment blocks and slum huts and mansions, spreading for mile after mile along and away from the banks of the Nile. Satellite dishes, beaming in bad American movies, Italian gameshows and Arab news networks, litter the rooftops. From my hotel room, fourteen floors up, I can count more than 150 dishes.

Smart new coffee shops on the banks of the Nile have free Wi-Fi. The Internet has taken off in a big way, and Ahmad Saied is one of those who has benefited. He writes for a football website called filgoal.com, which covers Egyptian and European football in both Arabic and English. The stories are far more interesting than those found in the daily newspapers, and thanks to a sponsorship deal with a mobile phone company Ahmad's pay is better too.

He's a big Arsenal fan, and we spend an hour or so over dinner discussing their chances of winning the Premier League ('not good'), Zamalek's odds of winning anything ('really not good') and Egypt's chances of qualifying for the World Cup.

'We will be fine,' he says, 'so long as we aren't drawn in the same group as another North African side.'

When the draw for the final qualifying round is made a few months later, I wince. Egypt have to play Zambia, Rwanda and Algeria. Only the top team will make it to South Africa.

The campaign starts badly with a defeat against Algeria. After the match I get a text from Ahmad. 'It's always the North African teams,' he writes.

*

In the summer of 2009, with Egypt's qualification for the World Cup looking precarious, they get an opportunity to test themselves against some of the best teams in the world. The Confederations Cup, held the year before every World Cup, is contested between the six continental champions, the World Cup winners and the next World Cup hosts.

Egypt, representing Africa, are drawn in the same group as South American champions Brazil, World Cup winners Italy and North and Central American winners the USA. They play brilliantly against Brazil in the first game, losing 4–3 to a last-minute penalty, before shocking Italy in their second game, winning 1–0.

Victory against the USA – a team far weaker than Brazil and Italy – will put Egypt into the semi-finals. A draw might also be enough. In the end even a 2–0 defeat will see them go through, since Brazil beat Italy in the other game. But Egypt lose 3–0.

Later that summer Al-Ahly are invited to London to take part in a pre-season tournament at Wembley.

For the other three teams involved – Barcelona, Celtic and Tottenham – it's a chance to prepare for the new season. For Al-Ahly, though, it's another opportunity for Egypt to prove its football deserves to be taken seriously on the international stage. It's just a pity no one told the players.

Al-Ahly come to Wembley as African champions, having beaten Coton Sport of Cameroon in the final of the African Champions League the previous November. The team isn't at full strength but still includes Ahmed Hassan and one of Africa's most creative forwards, Mohamed Abou Treika, who is playing in England for the first time.

Wembley Stadium isn't even a quarter full by the time Al-Ahly and Celtic kick off. I'm keen to see how Abou Treika performs and have hyped him up to friends at home. Al-Ahly start well and Abou Treika is at the centre of every half-decent attack they put together. But it doesn't take long to realise this isn't going to be pretty. Some slapstick Ahly defending presents Celtic with the lead midway through the first half, a lead which they double shortly afterwards when the goalkeeper gives away a penalty. A third, fourth and fifth follow far too easily in the second half.

The second match against Barcelona two days later isn't quite so embarrassing. Yes, Al-Ahly lose 4–1, and yes, the Barca team is mainly made up of teenagers, but for the first half at least Al-Ahly play some good football. Abou Treika again shows some nice touches, although nothing to suggest he's the best player in Africa, as the BBC claimed earlier in the year.

After the second match I meet up with Hossam al-Badri, the new coach of Al-Ahly. After seven years Manuel José has moved on. Al-Badri was José's assistant, but the transition has not been smooth. 'He is difficult to follow but we will do well,' he says. 'Our team today was not full – we had many injuries,' he adds. 'You saw the Confederations Cup. You can see that we can perform.'

He's right, but the same Egypt side which played so well against two of the best teams in the world made a disastrous start to their World Cup qualifying group. With just four games remaining the Pharaohs' World Cup campaign is in a mess. They win the next three, setting up a crucial final match with Algeria in Cairo.

A 3–0 win would send Egypt through, while a two-goal victory would leave both sides level on points and with the same number of goals scored and conceded. A play-off in Khartoum would be required to separate them. If Egypt won 1–0 or failed to win at all, then Algeria would go through.

★

It's four and a half hours before the match kicks off but Cairo International Stadium is already full to capacity. Over-capacity, in fact. Having fought my way through a huge crush at the gate, while armed police looked on impassively, I try to find a seat. No luck – I have to make do with perching on a step in the gangway. Officially, there are 75,000 people in the stadium. Unofficially, estimates range from 90,000 to 120,000.

'Football represents a malfunction in our society,' Ahmed Hassan has told me. 'People are so interested in football it diverts attention from their reality, from the social and economic problems.'

In the run-up to the crunch match with Algeria, the Egyptian government has done its best to divert attention. Mubarak, now eighty-one, is widely believed to be considering stepping down at the next election, scheduled for 2011. The man expected to take over from him is his son, Gamal. Taking a page out of his father's PR handbook, Gamal has visited the Pharaohs' training camp a few days before the match. It was the day's top news story.

Opposition groups have begun campaigning against Gamal's expected coronation, and there appears to be little popular support for him on the streets, but the criticism stopped as the match got closer. 'This week no opposition will talk about elections or the grooming of the president's son or prices rising,' says al-Hosseiny. 'There will be no criticism. If we win it will be the same up to the World Cup. The only thing Egypt will talk about is football.'

After Egypt won the 2006 Africa Cup of Nations, food prices – controlled by the government – rocketed. It was the only time the government thought they could get away with it – and they were right.

For the Algeria match the Egyptian government has also been able to call upon decades of resentment between the two countries. Few rivalries in Africa are as fierce as this one. A qualifier for the 1984 Olympics ended in a riot, while a World Cup qualifier in 1989 led to fighting in the VIP area, with Algerian players throwing pot plants at FIFA officials. Algeria's one-time African player of the year, Lakhdar Belloumi, was accused of smacking the Egyptian team doctor in the face with a bottle, blinding him in one eye. An Interpol arrest warrant for Belloumi was dropped in 2009 only after a personal request was made by Algeria's president.

For days before the match Egyptian television has been endlessly screening short films showing slow-motion shots of Egypt scoring against Algeria in previous matches, flag-waving Egyptian fans and an applauding President Hosni Mubarak – all set to emotional music.

Another film reminds Egyptians of the debt Algeria still owes them for helping to win their independence. Grainy footage shows Egypt's former president Gamal Abdel Nasser being cheered by crowds in Algiers and Algerian troops being trained by Egypt.

Despite the foreign ministers of both countries appealing for calm and organising 'peace' concerts featuring Algerian and Egyptian artists, the atmosphere in the lead-up to the match has been increasingly febrile. Abuse flows in newspapers and on Internet forums. An Algerian newspaper prints a picture of the Egyptian team with their heads replaced by those belonging to Egyptian actresses. An Egyptian rival responds by printing pictures of the Algerian team dressed as belly dancers. The rivalry also affects marriages. An Egyptian woman leaves her Algerian husband after the couple have an argument about the match.

Algeria went to great lengths to ensure the team was able to prepare properly. Fearing food poisoning in the team's hotel, they brought their own chefs, ingredients, even a team of waiters. A hotel was chosen deep within the airport complex to prevent Egyptian fans playing music and blaring car horns outside to stop the team sleeping before the match.

The fevered atmosphere almost inevitably turned to violence. As the coach carrying the Algerian team left Cairo International Airport, a group of Egyptian fans pelted it with rocks. They smashed the windows and hit four of the players, cutting two of them badly on their heads. The Egyptian FA tried to argue it hadn't happened. A police spokesman told reporters the Algerians had smashed the windows from the inside, a bizarre claim backed up by the bus driver, who was interviewed on television recounting how angry Algerian players had wanted to yell at the Egyptian fans but couldn't open the windows. Neither the police, the bus driver nor Egypt's television commentators could explain how the Algerian players got their injuries, though.

*

The roar which greets Egypt's first goal is deafening. Amr Zaki, the former Wigan striker, has given the Pharaohs the lead after two minutes. Mohammed, the KPMG accountant who has very kindly allowed me to share his small patch of concrete with him, jumps up and down and turns to hug me. The Algerian players look in shock, as well they might. Two of them, the defender Rafik Halliche and the midfielder Khaled Lemmouchia, are still nursing head injuries sustained in the attack on the team coach. The febrile atmosphere they face in Cairo International Stadium is intimidating. Every time an Algerian touches the ball a cacophony of boos and whistles rings out.

Egypt need a second goal to force a play-off, a third to win outright. But as the match progresses they struggle to break down Algeria's strong defence.

For most of the second forty-five minutes Algeria do not venture out of their own half. The crowd is getting restless. A roar rises every time a cross is flung into the penalty area, replaced by a groan when yet again the Algerian defenders head it clear.

Mohammed is chain-smoking, anxiously glancing at the clock on the scoreboard every few minutes. Before the match he predicted a 2–0 win – now he's not so sure. 'We're not creating any chances,' he says, between puffs.

As the clock ticks down, Algeria begin to waste time. Every time the ball goes out of play another Algerian player falls to the ground demanding treatment. It's little surprise that the referee chooses to add on six minutes.

Egypt need all six. The match is in its final minute when the ball comes to Sayed Moawad, on the left-hand side of the penalty area. His cross is deep, for once evading Algeria's big centre-back Madjid Bougherra. Egypt's substitute, Emad Moteab, rises to meet it at the far post, heading it back across the goal and towards the far corner. The ball seems to trickle slowly towards the goal line. The goalkeeper can't reach it. Egypt have done it.

I've never heard a roar as loud as this. All the pent-up emotion of the last ninety minutes, the last month of build-up, the last twenty years of World Cup failure, is released at that moment.

The goal sparks a pitch invasion by Egypt's bench and everyone else whose route to the players isn't blocked by a fence: ball boys, stewards and photographers. Around me in the stands grown men are weeping. A dozen firecrackers go off and smoke drifts across the pitch.

Half an hour after the final whistle, the stadium is still full. 'How much is a flight to Khartoum?' Mohammed asks me.

★

After the euphoria of Cairo, where the celebrations came to an end only when the sun rose the next day, comes the crushing anti-climax of Sudan. The Egyptian and Algerian governments each chartered dozens of planes to fly thousands of supporters to the play-off match in the Al-Merreikh Stadium in Omdurman, Khartoum's twin city on the opposite side of the Nile. The tickets had been split between Algerians, Egyptians and locals, although judging by the green and white flags the majority of locals were supporting Algeria.

Whether it was the lack of support from the crowd or tiredness from the previous match, Egypt were poor. Algeria took the lead at the end of the first half, and despite dominating possession in the second half Egypt struggled to create many chances. When they did, Algeria's young goalkeeper was in the way. At the final whistle Egypt's players sank to their knees. After all that, Egypt were out.

The political repercussions overshadowed the football. Egypt had failed to qualify for the World Cup because they weren't good enough. But this fact did not fit with the Mubarak regime's narrative. Luckily for the president, there was a very convenient enemy to blame, one that many Egyptians could unite against: Algeria.

After the first match in Cairo the Algerian media had claimed, wrongly, that eight Algerians had been killed in Cairo. Fans in Algiers attacked the offices of EgyptAir and an Egyptian phone company. The Algerian government then accused the phone company of failing to pay taxes.

Sudan had provided 15,000 police, many of them armed, to keep the two sets of fans apart at the stadium. But after the match there were clashes, and the Egyptian media reported claims that Algerians had attacked Egyptians with knives while the Sudanese police looked on.

Egypt recalled its ambassador from Algiers, Algeria threatened to do the same with its man in Cairo, while the Sudanese also became embroiled, demanding an explanation from the Egyptian ambassador to Khartoum for the negative press stories about Sudanese security.

There was something fundamentally depressing about all of this. The road to South Africa had brought a country together. But that unity had been hijacked by the country's regime. Unemployment in Egypt, particularly among the young, is incredibly high. While the country's GDP has grown steadily over the past decade, thanks to the liberalisation of the economy encouraged by the IMF and the World Bank, the vast majority of Egypt's population have not got richer. Prices have continued to rise, leaving millions across the country in poverty. There's no real democracy. In 2008 thousands rioted over the price of bread. In a rare moment of people power the government lowered the price. But that victory has not encouraged more demonstrations. There's a simmering anger and resentment in the country, particularly among the young, and at the moment football is one of the only outlets for it.

'The Egyptian national team is the only thing that all Egyptians are unanimous about,' said al-Hosseiny. 'There are always two sides to everything else – politics, religion . . . Football is the only thing that unifies us.'

There was a moment when I wondered whether the crowds, the hundreds of thousands who had taken to the streets to celebrate Egypt's victory, might take their anger out on their government. It wasn't hard to find someone to say something bad about the government. Quite the opposite. In public squares and tea shops across the city I heard only negative words about Mubarak and his regime.

As Egypt's captain, Ahmed Hassan, had said to me: football diverts attention from reality. The football might have been over, but Algeria was still the enemy. As the rhetoric between the two countries increased, Mubarak's elder son, Alaa, went on television.

'We have to take a stand,' he said. 'This is enough. That's it! This is enough. Egypt should be respected. We are Egyptian and we hold our head high, and whoever insults us should be smacked on his head.'

That night a crowd of 2,000 attacked the Algerian embassy in Cairo, throwing stones, bricks and petrol bombs.

2
THE DESERT HAWKS v. THE SAO
Sudan v. Chad

As coup attempts go, the attack by a group of Darfur rebels on Sudan's capital, Khartoum, in May 2008 was pretty pathetic. Around 2,000 men, teenagers and boys – some as young as ten – drove more than 600 miles across harsh, unforgiving desert. They arrived in Omdurman, Khartoum's twin city on the opposite bank of the Nile, in the early afternoon.

Some of the old Toyota pick-ups they'd travelled in had broken down; others had run out of petrol. The rebels hadn't brought enough food or water. They limped into Omdurman and stopped at some stalls at the side of the road to buy bananas, honey and water.

Refreshed, the leaders then tried to solve their next problem: working out where they were supposed to go. Armed with Kalashnikovs, M16s and rocket-propelled grenade launchers, they got out of their trucks and wandered up to bemused residents. 'Which way is it to the presidential palace?' they asked.

The directions were irrelevant. The rebel convoy had been tracked by Sudanese military officials as it made its way across the country. By the time the rebels had worked out which way they were going, Sudanese tanks were blocking the two bridges which linked Omdurman and Khartoum across the Nile.

The fighting lasted several hours and was brutal. Hundreds died on both sides – as well as more than one hundred civilians. By the following morning Sudanese forces had regained control and Sudan's president, Omar al-Bashir, was claiming victory.

*

I arrived in Khartoum on a blisteringly hot summer afternoon, three days after the attack on Omdurman. My fixer, an indefatigable middle-aged taxi driver called Al Siir, took me to the main road where the fighting had taken place. The city still showed evidence of the battle. Several holes had been blown in the side of the military hospital. Billboards along the bridge were riddled with bullets.

Al Siir had been driving customers to Omdurman when the fighting began. He spent the evening cowering in an alleyway, hoping he wouldn't be found and praying for the shooting to stop. 'I thought I was going to die,' he said, his voice shaking.

We drove further on, towards Souq Libya, the sprawling market in Omdurman where hundreds of Darfuris own stalls. The atmosphere was tense. Khartoum's security forces, under pressure to ensure there was no repeat, had begun a crackdown against what one Sudanese official described to me as the 'fifth column'. The Darfuris in Omdurman, the official said, could not be trusted. In the days since the attack more than 1,000 had been rounded up, including nearly one hundred children. Some of the adults had been summarily executed. One friend told me she saw two teenage boys pulled off a bus and shot in the head.

Diplomats and analysts I spoke to in Khartoum were still trying to work out how a Darfur rebel group had been able to launch such a daring raid. The group, called the Justice and Equality Movement (JEM), had close ties with Sudan's neighbour, Chad, and the finger of blame was now being pointed in their direction.

The governments of Chad and Sudan have long had a testy relationship. Chad's president, Idriss Deby, came to power in 1990 following a coup which al-Bashir had helped to finance and support. But once Deby became president the two men quickly fell out.

Relations had soured further with the Darfur conflict, which had begun in 2003. Deby had given Darfur rebel groups, including the JEM, weapons and logistics support, as well as allowing them to set up bases in eastern Chad, close to the border with Sudan. Rebel groups would cross the border to carry out raids on Sudanese government forces in Darfur, before scurrying back to the safety of Chad.

Al-Bashir had responded by providing similar levels of support to Chadian rebels that wanted to depose Deby. In February 2008 these rebels managed to get as far as the presidential palace in Chad's capital, N'Djamena, before Deby (with the help of Chad's former colonial power, France) fought them off.

To many, it made sense to suspect Deby's hand in the attempted attack on Khartoum. One senior Western official described a meeting that had taken place in N'Djamena just a few months before. Deby, flush with oil money, had provided up to £30 million to three Darfur rebel groups and had promised to give them logistical support for any attacks outside Darfur. Until this moment the rebel groups had, by and large, restricted their military manoeuvres to the Darfur province. Deby, the Western diplomat told me, was now encouraging them to look further afield.

When the Khartoum attack failed, President al-Bashir immediately placed the blame on Deby. He portrayed the incident as a great victory for Sudan over Chad. A massive outdoor celebration was organised where jubilant soldiers showed off the military vehicles and weaponry they had captured from the rebels. Thousands of Sudanese turned up for the opening ceremony. Children jumped on top of captured tanks, old men danced next to a cache of grenades, and al-Bashir made an appearance, waving his stick in the air and saluting his soldiers.

As well as the weapons, Sudan's military showed off Chadian army badges which they claimed had been ripped off the rebels' clothing. The badges looked suspiciously clean and new – as if they had just been pulled out of a packet rather than off a shirt worn by a rebel who had just spent three days crossing the desert.

For those who attended the rally, though, it didn't matter. All everyone could talk about was the victory against Chad. A group of young soldiers danced in front of a set of gory enlarged photos of alleged rebels killed on the battlefield. One of them waved his gun at me and said: 'We will beat them again! We will beat them again!' Everyone cheered as the soldier pointed over my shoulder towards the Omdurman National Stadium.

★

The result on the battlefield had been a rather bloody draw (Chad claimed victory in N'Djamena in 2007; Sudan won in Khartoum in 2008), but both countries would soon have the chance to prove their superiority in a much less violent arena. Chad and Sudan had been drawn in the same qualifying group for the World Cup. Just three weeks after the Omdurman attack, which took place in the shadow of the National Stadium, the first match was due to take place.

In the days leading up to the match, football overtook the rebel attack as the main topic of conversation in Khartoum.

Taxi drivers and government officials, businessmen and expats working for aid agencies – it seemed like the whole of Khartoum was planning on going to the match.

The same enthusiasm couldn't be found in Chad. With diplomatic relations between the two countries officially broken off (Chad even banned the playing of Sudanese music in N'Djamena's cafés), the Chadian football association was reluctant to send a team to Khartoum. Just two days before the match was due to take place, FIFA announced it would be postponed for four months.

Sudan cried foul, insisting that the Chadians would be safe in the city. FIFA officials, perhaps having paid a visit to the 'museum of Chadian aggression', thought otherwise. Sudan responded by refusing to travel to N'Djamena for the return match. Neither side wanted to give up on the chance of going to the World Cup, though, so a compromise was reached. The games would be played back-to-back in a neutral venue, Cairo.

An uneasy truce was established and for the next four months neither country tried to attack the other.

*

By the time the two teams arrived in Cairo, their World Cup campaigns were in jeopardy. Both had won one game and lost two, leaving them joint bottom of a four-team group where only the group winners were guaranteed a place in the next round. Both Sudan and Chad needed to win the two matches in Cairo to stand any real chance of progressing.

Such a task would be easier for Sudan, it appeared. Their record was not great – a single Africa Cup of Nations victory in 1970 – but compared to Chad they looked like giants. Chad had never qualified for the Africa Cup of Nations, nor had they ever looked likely to. In the four matches that the two countries had played against each other, Sudan's Desert Hawks, as the team were known, had won three and drawn one.

That record isn't so surprising when you consider that Chad is the seventh-poorest country in the world. What little wealth it has is concentrated in its capital, although even there most people live on less than sixty pence a day.

Chad's government had a chance to turn a corner when they discovered oil in the late 1990s. The World

Bank helped to finance a pipeline which would take the oil from landlocked Chad through neighbouring Cameroon and on to the Atlantic Ocean.

Wary of the damage that oil wealth had caused in other African countries, the World Bank insisted that 72 per cent of the government's share of the oil revenues should be spent on schools, hospitals and infrastructure. A further 10 per cent would be placed in a 'futures fund', saving up for the day when the oil ran out. An additional 5 per cent was also promised for Doba, the southern region where the oil had been discovered. Chad only had to glance at its next-door neighbour, Nigeria, to realise how disastrous it can be when the region which produces oil gains nothing from it – militant groups in the Niger Delta, furious at the lack of investment the central government placed in the region, had sparked off Africa's first 'oil war'.

When I visited Doba in early 2007, it was clear that not everything had gone to plan. Exxon Mobil had built a few school buildings as a thank-you gesture, which doubtless looked good in their annual report. But the education problems in Doba had nothing to do with the lack of buildings. 'Children don't get their education because there are not enough qualified teachers and there's not enough equipment,' a local aid worker told me. Exxon, it seemed, hadn't bothered paying for any teachers or any equipment. So the buildings, brightly painted and with a prominent 'Esso' sign in front of them, lay empty and unused.

It wasn't just that oil had failed to bring improvements. The discovery had actually had a detrimental effect. The lucky few who found jobs in the oilfields were, on the whole, brought in from other parts of the country. The oil workers, with salaries far higher than the locals, drove up prices. In less than a year the price of a bag of millet, the main staple food in Doba, had doubled.

As for government spending, the residents of Doba were to be disappointed. They were hoping for a health clinic, maybe some teachers, perhaps some streetlights. They got a football stadium.

Why does Chad need a football stadium in Doba? I asked friends when I got back to N'Djamena. I couldn't work out why they would want to play football in the south, so far away from the capital. It's not for football, they said, rolling their eyes. It's so that Deby can go there and make big speeches.

★

The conflict in Darfur didn't stop at the border. For generations nomadic tribes had crossed freely from Sudan into Chad and back again. The governments in N'Djamena and Khartoum had little influence over their lives, and most saw themselves as Zaghawa or Dajo rather than Chadian or Sudanese.

Around 250,000 Darfuris had fled into Chad, most of them living in bleak refugee camps similar to those I'd seen in Darfur. Built from a combination of sticks, rags and tarpaulin, the huts that families were crammed into provided little in the way of shelter. Some were better than others and there was a sense of order to the construction – paths, junctions, space for a market – but it was still a depressing sight.

International aid agencies had established the camps and were trying to provide basics like water, food and shelter. This sometimes led to tension between the refugees and those living in nearby villages who were similarly destitute thanks to the callousness of the Deby regime in N'Djamena.

Violent attacks had taken place on this side of the border too. Around 100,000 Chadians had fled their homes in the past year after attacks that sounded eerily familiar. Sudan's Janjaweed forces had crossed the border armed with Kalashnikovs and RPGs. They had razed villages, raped women and killed men. Groups of Chadian Arabs, who had long lived peacefully with non-Arab tribes, had joined them.

One morning I toured one of the camps and met a woman who had buried her two-month-old baby the night before. Fatuma had been heavily pregnant when her village was attacked. At least eighty people were killed, and the remaining 200 women and children set out the next day to find safety elsewhere. On their way the group was attacked again, and Fatuma was thrown to the ground and beaten. Although she was still able to give birth, her baby was not strong enough to survive.

While those in the camps waited for some sort of international protection force to arrive (an EU force was eventually sent two years later), the men took matters into their own hands. Abdul Karim and Aballi Ibrahim, two wiry young men, established a self-defence force. Their home-made bows and arrows would be no match for the Janjaweed's AK-47s, but what they lacked in weaponry they hoped to make up for in determination.

Aballi demonstrated his somewhat limited prowess with the bow and arrow before boasting that he had killed ten Janjaweed fighters as well as ten of their horses. This was a part of the world where law and order and a sense of jutice had completely disappeared.

*

The problems were not just limited to Chad and Sudan. Bordering the two countries to the south is the Central African Republic (CAR), a country that few people would be able to place on the map even with the hints in its name. The CAR had also been affected by the conflict. Rebels, bandits and rampaging government forces had turned large swathes of the north of the country into a danger zone.

Thousands of people had begun to cross from the CAR, the sixth-poorest country in the world, into Chad, the seventh-poorest. A solitary metal signpost indicated the point where the CAR meets Chad. Beyond the border the wide, dusty track, framed by wild bracken and a smattering of trees, extended to the horizon. Half of the stone bridge which crossed the dry river basin below had collapsed, the rubble scattered over the sand.

Standing by the border post, I watched as Fadimatou Fanta and her four sons, the family's entire belongings strapped to the back of three donkeys, skirted around the collapsed bridge and scrabbled up the embankment to safety. They had walked for seven days. An hour later, sitting under the shade of a mango tree while her boys shared a bowl of cooked maize, Fadimatou explained why her family had left the CAR. In the past few months, a succession of armed men – some aligned to the government, others to the rebels – had come to her village about 150 miles from here. Each group had been a menace, threatening to rape women and kidnap boys. 'I don't want my children to be killed by rebels,' she said. 'All the women are leaving my village with their children.'

Bordering Chad and Sudan to the north and the Democratic Republic of Congo to the south, the CAR has had a turbulent history since gaining independence from France in 1960. The country's diamond and timber wealth has made power a valuable prize and a succession of military dictators have taken control by force. In the past decade there have been eleven attempted coups and mutinies, including the one in 2003 which brought the current president, General Bozizé, to power. His government struggled to exert much power outside the capital, Bangui, allowing various armed groups to try their luck. The breakdown of law and order in neighbouring Sudan hardly helped matters. Both rebels and Sudanese government forces were thought to be venturing into the CAR to regroup and plan attacks. The Darfur conflict had not just brought devastation to Sudan; it had made the entire region unstable. Back in N'Djamena I met a Western diplomat who painted a doomsday scenario. There had been whispers about a fresh coup attempt against Deby, and he thought it was likely. 'If Deby goes, so does Bozizé (in the CAR). Deby protects him. Civil wars in Chad and the CAR will undermine Cameroon to the west and Sudan to the east. We could have failed states from the Atlantic to the Indian Ocean.'

He was wrong, as it turned out. If there was a coup attempt it was silent and unsuccessful. But the fears he expressed underlined the fragile nature of the region and how easily it could all fall apart.

★

The Chadian and Sudanese teams arrived in Cairo in September 2008 for their long-awaited double-header. While most Egyptians had little idea the matches were taking place, there were thousands of Sudanese in the city who had been looking forward to seeing the Desert Hawks in action. Over the past two decades Egypt has become home to millions of Sudanese, many of them refugees from the country's long and brutal civil war in the south. Cairo is also home to tens of thousands of Sudanese students who have left home to study at a better university.

So Cairo shouldn't really have been a neutral venue for the match. Talking to Sudanese refugees in the days leading up to the game, I got the impression that everyone was going to it.

On the night of the first match I met Ehab Ali outside the stadium. Ehab liked to describe himself as Sudan's biggest fan. An engineering student who had lived in Cairo for the past year, he had a plastic bag full of small Sudanese flags, which he thrust into the hand of everyone who passed. His two nephews, seven-year-old Mohammed and Modther, fourteen, stood quietly by his side. It was their first football match.

Considering the heated rhetoric between the rival governments, the atmosphere outside the ground was relaxed. Hundreds of armed Egyptian police lined the streets, but there was little for them to do. Most of those milling around were Sudanese. Every now and then a Chadian supporter would wander along, yellow and blue flag in hand. There was no animosity.

Thousands of Sudanese had turned up but nowhere near enough to fill the stadium's 55,000 seats. Chadian supporters, meanwhile, numbered

200 at most. The main stand – the cheap seats where I sat with Ehab – was a microcosm of Sudan. Tall Dinkas from the south dressed in baggy dark blue jeans and basketball T-shirts sat next to old Arab men in pristine white djellabas. Women from Khartoum in brightly coloured headscarves stood and clapped and sang alongside refugees from Darfur. For a country that has rarely had a day in its history when it hasn't been at war with itself, it was an unusual sight.

Ehab quickly got to work, running up and down the stand, jumping over the old plastic seats, to hand out his flags. He handed out red, green and white Sudanese flags to all and sundry, stood on his seat singing at the top of his voice and implored all those around him to do the same. He was remarkably successful. Often I'd notice another pocket of fans in a different part of the stand suddenly break into song – Ehab would be at the heart of it, singing the loudest and waving his flag.

This would be easy, Ehab assured me. Sudan were the best team in Africa, he insisted. The record said otherwise. But Ehab could point to a victory the month before in a friendly match against Egypt, the current African champions. President al-Bashir had invited the Egyptians to Khartoum following their Africa Cup of Nations victory earlier in the year. At a lavish ceremony al-Bashir had handed over envelopes stuffed with cash to each member of the Egyptian squad, congratulating them on their success. The next day, the Egyptian players showed just how grateful they were by rolling over and getting hammered 4–0.

For all Ehab's hyperbole, he was right – this was going to be a walk in the park. And for the first half-hour it was. Sudan, playing a 3–5–2 formation, dominated possession and caused Chad's flimsy back line all sorts of problems.

Ehab started a chant: 'North, south, east, west, Sudan is always best!' which was soon being bellowed by thousands.

But despite creating chance after chance, Sudan's strikers caused the Chadian keeper few problems.

Then the inevitable happened. With Chad's first attack they scored, Mobin Meryouz heading home a cross from the right wing. Away to my left a small band of around 200 Chadians celebrated, while the Sudanese end fell silent in disbelief. Chad held on until half-time, by which time Sudanese disbelief had turned to outrage.

'I am very angry! Very angry,' screamed Ehab. 'They had one attack and scored – we have had many!' All around the stand discussions had broken out among fans about what was to be done. The consensus appeared to be that Sudan's number ten, Haitham Tambal, needed to be replaced, and the star of the recent victory against Egypt, Mudathir El Tahir, was on the substitutes' bench. Whenever he had stood up and run down the track to keep himself warm, the Sudanese had cheered him.

But when the teams came out for the second half, Sudan's coach, Mohamed Abdallah Mazda, had decided not to make any changes.

Again Sudan were the stronger team, carving out a host of chances for the two strikers, Faisal Ajab and Tambal. 'Impossible!' exclaimed Ehab after another terrible miss. As the minutes counted down, the atmosphere in the crowd became angrier. Misplaced passes were greeted with catcalls and the chants for substitutions became louder.

The equaliser came eventually, scored by the much-maligned Tambal. Sudan poured forward, searching for the winner. But Chad countered and won a free kick on the edge of the penalty area. It was hit straight and low, and shouldn't have been a problem, but the keeper couldn't hold on to it. Hassan Diyallu poked it home.

The goal sucked the life out of the game. Having invested so much energy in getting the first equaliser, the Sudanese players looked spent. Chad tried to waste as much time as possible. Their goalkeeper faked an injury which took three minutes to be treated. A couple of substitutions were made, the players being replaced walking off as slowly as possible.

Around me people started to wander silently home. By the time the full-time whistle blew, half the stand had emptied. The Chadian players celebrated jubilantly in front of their small but enthusiastic band of supporters. The Sudanese looked at each other in amazement and trudged down the tunnel to the dressing room.

Outside the ground buses pulled up to take fans home. A handful of Chadians were waving flags and dancing on the pavement. Some Sudanese fans shook their hands as they passed.

Little Mohammed looked on the brink of tears. I told him they'd win the next match. Ehab agreed, but his usual enthusiasm was missing. We arranged to meet again in four days' time, when the second match would take place. He wandered off into the night, holding Mohammed and Modther on either side.

★

The first time I worked in Sudan I learnt a very valuable lesson. People are happy to talk to you if you just turn up at their door. Al Siir had taken me from office to office, house to house, without so much as a phone call to warn that we were on our way. And so, a couple of days after the first match, with Al Siir's lesson burned into my brain, I started knocking on doors in the Sonesta, a five-star hotel near the airport that the Sudanese team were staying in.

Ahmed on reception thought the coach, Mazda, was in room 612. He was. Dressed in only a towel. Somehow I couldn't imagine Fabio Capello answering his hotel door with only a small piece of white towelling to protect his modesty.

Once dressed, Mazda was happy to talk. He could be forgiven for being a little stressed. The defeat to Chad had gone down badly in Khartoum. Newspapers were blaming him, asking how a team that had thrashed the African champions just a few days earlier had now lost to one of the continent's minnows.

Worse still, President al-Bashir was blaming him too. The president had just rung Mazda to tell him in no uncertain terms that he would not be welcome back in Sudan unless his side beat Chad convincingly in the second match.

The coach was still trying to work out whether to pass on the president's threat to the players when I had knocked on his door.

For a man unsure whether he'd ever be allowed home Mazda was remarkably relaxed. 'These things happen,' he said. I struggled to agree. It was one thing being threatened with the sack, but being made *persona non grata* in your own country seemed a bit excessive to me. 'We must make sure we win then,' Mazda said with a smile.

*

I went to the second match with two doctors, Hussein Yousef Ali and Ahmed Hasab. The two men were friends, studying at the same college in Cairo, but they came from very different parts of Sudan. Hussein was from Khartoum, Ahmed from Gereida, a town in Darfur.

Their views on the conflict, though, were similar. 'It's all politics,' Ahmed said, as Hussein nodded. 'The rebels only want power, the government has power. No one is blameless.' He had supported the rebels when the war started in 2003. Darfur had been marginalised for decades. Before Sudan gained independence in 1956, Britain ignored Darfur, making little effort to develop the region's economy. Education and health care were non-existent, and there was no railway linking Darfur to the rest of the country. Successive governments in Khartoum continued to marginalise Darfur, refusing to spend money there.

Ahmed's father hadn't gone to school, and there were few jobs. Darfur's political leaders had done their best, Ahmed said, but it wasn't until the two original rebel groups, the Sudan Liberation Army (SLA) and the Justice and Equality Movement (JEM), had been launched that Ahmed felt there was anyone looking out for him.

Rebels from three main tribes in Darfur began the insurgency in February 2003 with a daring attack on Sudan's air force stationed in Al-Fashir, the capital of

North Darfur. Khartoum responded by unleashing a bloody counterinsurgency, arming Arab militias – known as Janjaweed – and destroying village after village. The Janjaweed, fighting alongside Sudanese armed forces and with the support of air strikes, tore a path through Darfur, razing villages to the ground, pillaging and raping as they went.

Khartoum's tactics were no surprise. Over the previous two decades the northern government had waged a similar war against the south, again using proxy militias to do much of the dirty work. Approximately 2 million people had died before a peace deal was finally struck in 2005.

The conflict in Darfur was different, though, if only for the international attention it attracted. The US government accused al-Bashir's regime of genocide. While a subsequent UN investigation stopped short of using the word 'genocide', it did accuse the Sudanese government of committing 'crimes against humanity'.

In the first three years of the conflict an estimated 200,000 people were believed to have died. Most of those deaths were from war-related diseases caused by mass displacement and a lack of food, water and health care. Nearly two and a half million people were forced from their homes, prompting the world's largest humanitarian operation, with around eighty international agencies employing 14,000 aid workers. Most of those who fled ended up in makeshift, squalid camps near Darfur's main towns.

A small African Union force had been established to monitor an early peace deal, but as the conflict continued they were reduced to the role of note-takers. Their mandate didn't enable them to prevent attacks, not that their limited resources would have made it possible.

Fresh peace talks were launched in Nigeria's capital, Abuja, in 2006. By this time the first divisions had appeared within the rebel movements, with the SLA splitting in two. The breakaway faction, led by Minni Minnawi, decided to sign a deal with al-Bashir. Minnawi was awarded with a government position. Abdul Wahid, who led the main group and enjoyed more popularity within Darfur's camps, refused to sign, as did the leader of the JEM, Khalil Ibrahim.

Later that year the UN Security Council voted to send a joint UN–AU force to Darfur, but without a peace to keep it was unclear exactly what they could do. The hazy mandate turned out to be the least of the force's problems. To great fanfare the AU troops took off their green helmets and put on blue UN headgear at the start of 2008, but that was all that changed. The promised extra troops hadn't turned up, nor had the helicopters they needed to patrol an area the size of Spain.

There weren't even enough blue helmets. When I returned to Darfur in June 2008, many of the troops I met had been forced to buy blue paint in the market to recolour their own helmets. Some had even used blue plastic bags fastened on with string.

The nature of the conflict had begun to change dramatically. Janjaweed-led attacks on villages were now rare – most of those they wanted to clear had already been attacked. The splits in the rebel groups had continued. What had begun as a rebellion by three Darfur tribes against marginalisation by the Arab-dominated Khartoum government had escalated into a complex multilayered conflict. Some former

Janjaweed militias had switched sides, as had some of those once aligned with the rebels. Intertribal fighting had also broken out. Desertification had increased tensions – between everybody – as tribes fought to gain control over precious water points. Sudan's government was ready to arm any group prepared to attack anyone connected with the rebels. The conflict was now far less about ethnic cleansing and much more about power.

There has been a complete breakdown in law and order, creating a free-for-all which only encouraged more groups to take up arms. By one analyst's reckoning, by 2008 there were more than thirty different armed groups across Darfur.

In the midst of it all was General Martin Luther Agwai, the head of the joint force (known as UNAMID). General Agwai was one of the most experienced soldiers in Africa. A former chief of defence staff in Nigeria, Agwai had also taken on a senior role in the UN force in Sierra Leone. He was well-liked by his men and by his bosses in New York.

But he faced an almost impossible task. He was expected to keep a peace that didn't exist and had to do it with half the manpower and few of the resources he had been promised.

Logistically too, the mission was near impossible. At the UNAMID headquarters in Al-Fashir he showed me a map of Darfur. It was taking several months to get equipment from Port Sudan, 1,200 miles away. 'You look at this map and you will see roads,' he said, pointing out the red lines between towns. 'They are not roads. They are just tracks! A distance of twenty miles takes three or four hours – and that's not even in the rainy season. It makes the deployment very difficult. People find it very difficult to understand.'

Even finding a place for his troops to be based had been a problem. 'Any land you touch in Darfur, somebody owns it, though you see it is desert. If you're not careful you have the land very far away from a source of water. In some of our camps people leave and go five or six miles just to get water. Instead of performing the mission we are just running around trying to fend for ourselves.'

On several occasions in the past few months he had wondered whether he had made the right decision to come here. UNAMID had been criticised by activists in the West as well as some of the political leaders who had called for the force but done little to provide it with resources.

'It becomes discouraging when there's no appreciation of what hours, days you are spending for the mission and nothing positive is coming out. Nobody is even giving you a pat on your back, they are just criticising.'

He considered resigning, but after talking to his family and reading a self-help book – *How to Stop Worrying and Start Living* – he decided to stick it out. 'It helped me a lot. I feel a lot better about it now,' he said.

By the time the Sudan v. Chad matches were taking place Agwai had received a few more troops, but the political situation in Sudan had become more volatile. Luis Moreno-Ocampo, the chief prosecutor at the International Criminal Court, had decided to charge al-Bashir on ten counts of war crimes, crimes against humanity and genocide.

While this had pleased activists in the West and some of those in Darfur's camps, humanitarians worried that it would lead the government to kick them out, and some analysts warned it would make a peace deal harder to negotiate. Al-Bashir played a canny game, claiming Moreno-Ocampo's decision was part of an international plot led by the Americans and 'Zionists' to overthrow the regime and steal the country's oil. He rallied support from the opposition and cast himself as a selfless nationalist protecting Sudan from 'Western imperialists'.

*

There was some support for al-Bashir in the Cairo crowd. As I took my seat next to the two doctors, a young man in a white djellaba a few rows behind us waved a picture of al-Bashir above his head and started to chant, 'Sudan, Sudan! Up, up, up!'

Ahmed Hasab turned to look at the poster. 'Not all of us support him, you know. We are here to support our country. That's different.'

Ahmed's family still live in Gereida and he tries to speak to them once a week. 'It's difficult being here knowing what is going on,' he said, as we took our seats. We were in the Sudanese end, surrounded by thousands of other Sudanese. There were others here from Darfur, Ahmed said, and pointed out a group of young men who he knew away to the left waving a flag.

'Don't you want to support Chad?' I asked, half-jokingly. Ahmed looked at me as if I was crazy. 'Why?' he asked. 'I'm Sudanese.' 'Well, because of the war,' I stuttered, losing confidence in my point, 'and Chad supporting the rebels.' Ahmed just looked at me. 'I'm Sudanese,' he repeated, as if I hadn't heard the first time. 'This is still my country.'

'You see how we don't fight the Chadians,' he said, referring to the few hundred fans at the opposite end of the ground singing loudly and waving their flags. 'It's all politics.'

I told him what Mazda had said about al-Bashir refusing to let him back in the country unless they won. Ahmed and Hussein laughed.

Whatever Mazda had decided to tell his players had had an immediate impact. Within five minutes, Sudan were ahead through Ahmed Adel. And for the next half-hour Sudan played like a team that could beat the African champions. They passed and moved with ease, slicing apart Chad's ropey back line. The crowd loved it. Ehab, once again, was at the centre of things, starting chants and chastising those who weren't waving their flags vigorously enough.

But just like in the first match, Sudan's finishing – Adel's goal aside – was woeful. Chad's first chance came in the thirty-fourth minute. The ball dropped outside the penalty area, just in front of Leger Djime. His volley was perfect, searing into the bottom right-hand corner. The Sudanese crowd fell silent as Djime celebrated with a series of backflips.

It was a nervous half-time in the stands. I couldn't begin to imagine how bad it was in the Sudanese changing room. As things stood Sudan were on their way out of the World Cup and Mazda was about to apply for asylum in Egypt.

Ahmed and Hussein were calm though. We spent the fifteen-minute break talking about the English Premier League and Aston Villa's chances this season.

Ahmed was a fan of our winger, Ashley Young. 'He should be in the England team,' he said. I agreed.

Ehab wasn't so calm. 'This is a disaster,' he shouted. 'A disaster!' He ran off to find a glass of water for young Mohammed, who must have been starting to wonder what the point of football was. His team had lost the first match he'd ever been to and had now thrown away a lead in the second. I tried to explain that this is what football is like for pretty much everyone who doesn't support Chelsea or Manchester United. He said he was a Chelsea fan. I decided he didn't need my sympathy after all.

Loyal to a fault, the fans cheered the team as they made their way out for the second half. 'We will be okay,' said Ahmed. 'I feel we are a stronger team.'

He was right, they clearly were. But in the match and a half so far they had gone out of their way to mess things up.

Within five minutes of the restart the Sudanese defence was once again making mistakes. With the ball bouncing in their own area, two Sudanese defenders and the goalkeeper left it to each other, leaving the Chadian striker, Djime, with an open goal. Except, somehow, he managed to miss.

This let-off seemed to fire up Sudan. Seconds later the ball was up the other end, Tahir had been brought down, and a penalty was awarded. If Faisal Ajab was nervous it didn't show. The lanky Sudanese striker, who had been responsible for more missed chances than anyone else in the two games so far, stepped up to take it.

Faisal held his nerve and calmly stroked the ball past the outstretched hand of the Chadian keeper to put Sudan 2–1 up. Half the Sudanese team sank to their knees in prayer. The crowd, and Ehab in particular, went ballistic. 'Where is the third? Come! Come!' cried the crowd. It didn't take long. A few minutes later Faisal stroked a delicious through ball to Saifeldin Ali, who slotted in the third.

And that was how it stayed. There was still time for a Chadian player to get sent off for a nasty tackle, but most of the steam had already been taken out of the game by then.

Later that night, back in the team hotel, Mazda was beaming. He admitted he'd been putting on a brave face when we'd spoken earlier. 'I couldn't have my players see me nervous,' he said. 'They needed to have confidence.' The president, he was told, had watched the match on television and was happy with the result. 'I think my job is safe,' he grinned. 'For now,' I said. Mazda laughed. 'Insha'Allah!' (God willing).

*

A few months later I was back in Darfur. It was my fourth trip in two years and each one was more depressing than the last. The camps had the feel of permanence. Mud-and-wattle structures had been replaced by brick houses. Markets were thriving. People still talked of one day going home, but few seemed to think it would happen any time soon.

In Abu Shouk, one of Darfur's squalid refugee camps, I chatted to a group of young men standing under the shade of a neem tree. They felt like prisoners, one of them, a short guy called Ahmed, said. Half a dozen of them had tried to leave the camp the day before but had been robbed by a group of men on horseback. 'Janjaweed,' Ahmed spat.

The conversation moved on to football. They were Chelsea and Manchester United fans, and they joked good-naturedly about their teams' chances in the Premier League. What about the Desert Hawks? I asked. They were torn. Ahmed wanted the national team to do well; one of his friends pointed out there were no Darfuris in the team.

'One day maybe we will have a Darfur team,' Ahmed smiled. Until then, he said, he would cheer for Sudan.

After the victory against Chad, Mazda had managed to squeeze his side into the final qualifying round for the World Cup and Africa Cup of Nations. A 2–0 victory against Congo-Brazzaville in Khartoum was enough to make the cut.

The national side had been the only East African side to make it to the 2008 Africa Cup of Nations, and Mazda now had an opportunity to repeat the feat in 2010. World Cup qualification would be beyond them, but third place in a four-team group would take them to Angola for the Africa Cup of Nations. If he succeeded, it would be the first time Sudan had qualified for two successive tournaments.

But Mazda never got a chance. A week after I left Darfur, he was sacked. The team had lost to Tanzania in a fairly meaningless match. The minister for sport claimed the defeat was 'unacceptable'.

There was one consolation for Mazda. The match against Tanzania had been in Sudan – at least no one could stop him going home.

3

THE OCEAN STARS

Somalia

We didn't have long. The car screeched to a halt at the side of a deserted road. Bashir looked in the rearview mirror and waited for the car behind us to stop too. It did, and four gunmen jumped out and fanned out across the road, Kalashnikovs at the ready, safety catches off.

'Okay,' said Bashir, opening the car door, 'let's go.'

We got out – me, Bashir and Farah – and stood at the top of the hill looking out across the ruined city of Mogadishu.

It was late afternoon. The equatorial sun was rapidly falling, casting an orange hue across the city. Within the hour, the sound of a thousand muezzins calling worshippers to prayer would echo across the city's whitewashed, bullet-pocked walls.

Away to the right lay the national stadium. Once one of the most impressive stadiums in East Africa, it had been built in 1978, when Somalia was a country at relative peace. Now it looked as devastated as the rest of the city. Football was no longer played there.

Instead, it had become home to a battalion of the Ethiopian army, which had swept into Mogadishu a month before.

After a couple of minutes of silence, Bashir motioned to us to get back in the car. The gunmen got back in theirs and our convoy sped off again.

It had been like this all week. We'd drive around, blacked-out windows hiding the fact that a *gaalo* – an infidel – was in the car, stopping for two minutes here, five minutes there. It was just enough time for me to get out and quickly interview a market trader, look at a destroyed building and get a tiny sense of the city. At every point the gunmen – my gunmen – would fan out around me, creating a bizarre little cocoon that in hindsight probably made me even more of a target than I already was.

On the occasions when we arranged interviews in advance, Farah made it clear we could only stay fifteen minutes at each location. It was just long enough to get something useful, but hopefully not long enough for word to get around that a *gaalo* was inside. During one interview, a snatched ten minutes with a leading Islamist, Farah suddenly appeared at the doorway frantically signalling for us to leave. The Islamist had another visitor who, like us, had arrived with a team of heavily armed gunmen. The three groups of armed men (mine, the new visitor's, the Islamist's) had started arguing. Now they had started waving their guns at each other. I made my apologies and headed quickly for the door.

★

Mogadishu was in the midst of yet another bout of violence. The city and its residents had been battered relentlessly for twenty years, as a mix of warlords and militias fought for control of every street corner. The last functioning central government, the military regime of Mohamed Siad Barre, was overthrown in 1991. Numerous attempts to form a fresh government failed as rival warlords' factions fought for control.

The divisions were mainly based on Somalia's complicated clan structure, which consists of five main clans (Darod, Dir, Hawiye, Isaaq and Rahanweyn), each with their own sub-clans and sub-sub-clans. Rival clan-based militias made alliances and enemies, often switching between the two. There's a Somali proverb I heard on one of my first trips here which always seemed to sum up Somali politics pretty well: 'Don't love your friend too much because tomorrow he could be your enemy; don't hate your enemy too much because tomorrow he could be your friend.'

Within a year of the fall of Siad Barre, Somalia faced a famine. Prompted by images of emaciated children and babies with distended bellies, US president George Bush Snr, one month before handing over to Bill Clinton, sent 30,000 US troops to help deliver food aid.

The mission began to shift, though, as it became clear that some of Mogadishu's warlords – in particular Mohammed Farah Aideed – refused to abide by an international agreement on a new Somali government. The US decided it was time to take out Aideed, but their initial efforts ended in failure. An attack on a supposed safe house resulted in the deaths of seventy-three clan elders who were meeting to discuss ways of persuading Aideed to back down. It was a costly mistake which merely helped to harden Somali support for Aideed and turned many against the US operation in the country.

Four months later a team of US special forces launched a fresh attack on Aideed. Two of their Black Hawk helicopters were shot down, and in the resulting battle eighteen Army Rangers and an estimated 1,000 Somalis were killed. President Clinton, who had inherited the operation from President Bush, swiftly pulled the USA's remaining troops out, and the UN operation soon came to an end.

During the next decade UN conferences tried and failed repeatedly to set up new governments. However, the West only got involved when its own interests were at stake.

Those interests came to the fore in 2005. President George W. Bush's administration believed that the men accused of orchestrating the 1998 US embassy bombings in Nairobi and Dar es Salaam, which killed 240 people, were hiding in Somalia. The CIA funded a handful of warlords, hoping they would capture the suspects. Instead, this set off a series of events which turned Somalia into a crucible in the war on terror; a country where both the USA and al-Qa'ida believe it's vital they gain influence.

The Bush administration's fear of al-Qa'ida threats – real and make-believe – led it to destroy Somalia's best chance for peace in nearly two decades. A loose coalition of Islamist groups, known as the Islamic Courts Union (ICU), took control of Mogadishu in 2006, ousting the last of the US-backed warlords. They brought a semblance of peace and security to the city that Somalis hadn't experienced in nearly two decades.

There were disagreements within the ICU between moderate leaders like Sheikh Sharif Sheikh Ahmed, whose main priorities were bringing law and order to the country, and more extreme leaders like Sheikh Hassan Dahir Aweys, who wanted to build a greater Somalia, annexing parts of Ethiopia and Kenya.

The USA, encouraged by Ethiopia, focused on the extremists. President Bush's top African diplomat, Jendayi Frazer, accused the ICU of being run by an 'East Africa al-Qa'ida cell'.

With the tacit approval of the USA, Ethiopia invaded Somalia on Christmas Day 2006. Three days later the ICU crumbled, its leaders fled south and their fighters took off their uniforms, hid their guns and melted back into the city. The Ethiopians, with US advisers working alongside them in Mogadishu, installed a UN-backed transitional government, which had been nominally running the country from Nairobi since 2004. The government had moved inside Somalia, to a town called Baidoa near the Ethiopian border, a few months earlier, but until Ethiopian tanks rolled into Mogadishu it had been too dangerous for them to enter the capital.

*

I arrived in Mogadishu four weeks after the initial attack, just as the hardline remnants of the ICU, known as al-Shabaab, announced the start of an insurgency against the Ethiopians and the Somali government they had helped install.

I was wary about coming. Somalia has never been a good place for Western journalists. A BBC producer, Kate Peyton, had been killed coming out of her hotel in 2005, while a Swedish cameraman, Martin Adler, was shot dead while covering a rally a year later.

Several of my colleagues in Nairobi had gone in with the Ethiopians and spent a couple of weeks at the optimistically named Peace Hotel, which was owned by Bashir. They came back to Nairobi, a mixture of bravado and relief flowing through their stories of spending the days driving around the city with armed guards and the nights on the hotel roof drinking wine and eating lobster. I was jealous.

My foreign editor at the *Independent*, Leonard Doyle, was keen for me to go if I thought it was safe enough, but didn't place me under any pressure. The only pressure I felt was from myself. It was a big story, in my patch, and other journalists were going. A couple of colleagues warned against it, but I'd already made up my mind. If it was safe enough for others it was safe enough for me. It wasn't the most logical decision I've ever made.

Mogadishu is a seaside city and the approach into the airport is stunning, flying directly above golden orange beaches and sand dunes. The Indian Ocean lapping the shore is an emerald green. Unlike most of the Kenyan coast there are no hotels or beach houses – unsurprisingly, few people think Mogadishu a city worth investing in – just mile after mile of unspoilt, undeveloped coastline.

It was a different story once we had landed. As we drove through the city, there appeared to be barely a single building which was not scarred in some way. Most had been so badly damaged they could hardly be called buildings any more. Entire streets were lined with nothing but piles of rubble. A thin layer of grey dust covered everything, from donkey carts to telegraph poles. It looked like the aftermath of a shock-and-awe bombing campaign, but this damage had been caused gradually, year by year, battle by battle, by AK-47s, RPGs and mortars.

The Peace Hotel felt like a fortress, although in truth there was probably little that could have been done if either the Ethiopians or the insurgents had decided to attack it. To run the hotel and protect his guests, Bashir had to employ a small unit of gunmen. Apart from the four who accompanied me, whenever we drove outside the hotel compound there were several others permanently on guard, both inside the grounds of the hotel and outside the gate.

There were two other Western journalists staying at the hotel as well as a couple of aid workers. At night we would dine on the roof, eating seafood and drinking white wine. Occasionally, gunfire would ring out. 'Somali music,' said Farah with a smile.

Farah was in limbo. Like so many other Somalis he had fled the country shortly after the fall of Siad Barre. His final destination was Finland, where he now lived with his wife and two small children. He worked nights as a caretaker at seven schools in Helsinki, driving between them checking all was well.

A few months earlier he had decided to pack in the job and return to Mogadishu. He was not alone. Ever since the ICU took control of the capital, thousands had been returning every month looking for business opportunities. Farah had come to check out an idea he had for a seafood restaurant. As I could now confirm, Mogadishu had some of the best seafood in the world. His wife and children had stayed in Helsinki while he worked out the logistics. But then the Ethiopians came, the insurgency started and everything was on hold.

When the fighting broke out over Christmas, Farah was helping out Bashir at the Peace. Farah's mother, who lived in a more dangerous district, had told him to stay with Bashir, a family friend, until things calmed down. Meanwhile, I was in need of a fixer, someone who spoke good English and, most importantly, wouldn't take any unnecessary risks. Farah was perfect.

*

The insurgency began the day after I arrived. I was drinking sweet cinnamon tea at the café beside the Peace Hotel when a man came round handing out leaflets. He solemnly handed one to me, then turned and left.

The leaflet was written in English, not Somali. 'Heavy warning,' it said, above a picture of two AK-47s leaning against each other. It claimed that the Ethiopians, who they referred to as 'colonialists', would 'face new insurgent operations and attacks'. Those working alongside them, referred to as 'stooges', were also threatened.

Later that day Farah and I went to see the owners of Mogadishu's Coca-Cola factory. In a city where most major buildings displayed some sort of war damage, the Coke factory was pristine, the familiar red logo perfectly painted onto the outside of the whitewashed compound walls. Inside the factory, uniformed staff stacked cases of the hourglass bottles, ready to be transported to hotels, shops and restaurants across the city.

Bashir Mohammed had been running Somalia's official Coca-Cola franchise for the past three years. The concentrate was delivered from a Coca-Cola factory in Swaziland, and Mohammed sent daily reports to the company's headquarters in Atlanta. Business had been good under the Islamic Courts. Checkpoints which had littered the city when it was run by warlords had forced Mohammed to take several armed guards and pockets full of US dollars every time his lorries crossed the city. The Courts abolished most of the checkpoints. Now, though, they were back. 'When the Islamic Courts were here, there was peace in Mogadishu,' said Mohammed. 'If there is no peace, we cannot work. We will have to close the factory.'

While the Coke factory was the most visible example of the USA's influence in Somalia over the previous two decades, there was a far more painful symbol hidden away in the suburbs.

One morning Farah took me down a winding dusty track, past cactus trees and chickens pecking at the rubbish piled up against rusting corrugated iron walls. In a dirt-floored shack Khalid Abdullahi lived with more than twenty brothers and sisters, aunts and uncles, nephews and a niece.

Khalid was nine the day his father died in 1993. 'We were sitting here in this room when we heard this big noise,' he says. The 'big noise' was the sound of an American Black Hawk helicopter being shot down and crashing into Khalid's house.

Propped up against the wall, hidden behind a mattress, was the nose cone of the Black Hawk. Khalid pulled it out and placed the piece of black fibreglass in the middle of the room. 'The Americans said they were helping us,' he said. I asked him whether he thought they had. Khalid just smiled and didn't answer.

A five-minute walk away – out of his house, back down the track and on to the main street – lay the rusting remains of two UN tanks. Children scrambled on top of the dust-covered shells. A couple of goats next to one of the tanks searched in vain for something green to chew on.

In many ways Mogadishu had some of the ramshackle charm that many other African towns have. Goats and donkeys plodded along dusty, rubbish-strewn streets. Shiny new 4x4s, doubtless owned by the many businessmen who made money however bad the war was, shuffled past the animals. There was a bustle to the city, the sound of shouting and laughter, markets and street traders and hawkers selling everything from rusty car parts and T-shirts to spaghetti and shoes. A mangle of telephone wires hung low between each pole, dozens of them criss-crossing streets and working their way up the sides of houses.

There was one thing that was missing. Children playing football. It was a staple of every African city, town, village and refugee camp I had ever been to. But here, there was nothing.

'Does anyone play football here?' I asked Farah. 'Of course,' he said. 'Down by the beach. We'll go one day.'

*

Football was one of the few things that managed to survive the two decades of violence. Playing football in such an environment wasn't easy, but somehow the

Somali Football Federation had managed to hold the league together, arranging matches when it was safe to do so.

Somalia had once been an Italian colony, and the country still bore its imprint. I had enjoyed a great espresso every morning at the café in the grounds of the Peace Hotel. Somali football had also maintained an Italian influence, if not in style then at least in name: the top division was called Serie A.

The league had been cancelled by the time I arrived in Mogadishu. Hardline elements of the Islamic Courts took a dim view of football, viewing it as 'un-Islamic'. During the 2006 World Cup, shortly after the Courts took control of the capital, gunmen stormed the run-down video shacks where hundreds had gathered to watch satellite coverage of the tournament. At least two people were killed, and the makeshift cinemas were closed down across the city.

The children who Farah said played down by the beach stayed indoors.

The Federation, perhaps foolishly, still wanted the national team to compete in the upcoming Central and East Africa tournament, called the CECAFA Cup, which that year was due to be held in Ethiopia. A squad was picked and a few training sessions were organised, but the Courts still hadn't given them permission to go.

The players were called to the Global Hotel, a run-down establishment on a deserted street protected by two roadblocks. A delegation of ICU clerics was there to meet them. The clerics were uneasy about allowing a team of Somalis to play a tournament in the home of the enemy, but the squad could go on one condition: if they played Ethiopia they had to win. And should the unthinkable happen, the players must resort to unconventional tactics to prove Somalia's superiority. 'Destroy them before they leave the stadium,' one of the clerics, Sheik Nur Shuuriye Hussein, said.

Fortunately, Somalia were placed in a separate group to Ethiopia. They played Rwanda, Uganda and Sudan, losing to all three and failing to score a single goal.

The end of the ICU's reign in the final days of 2006 should have made things easier for football. But it didn't. The war made training almost impossible. Just getting to the practice ground in the morning required getting up before dawn in order to avoid the roadblocks that would spring up across the city.

The Somali Federation had no funding, no offices and nowhere to play. They didn't give up, though. Every year a squad of players – some from Mogadishu, others from the Somali diaspora – would be cobbled together to appear at the CECAFA Cup. They knew they probably weren't going to win any matches, but that didn't really matter. What was important, as Ahmed Nur Abdulle, the cheery vice-president of the Federation, told me when we met in Uganda at the start of the 2009 tournament, was 'flying the flag'.

The CECAFA Cup was the only thing Somalia had to play for. Their World Cup campaign hadn't lasted long. In fact, it was the shortest, most dismal World Cup campaign any country had endured. The worst six teams in Africa had to enter a preliminary qualifying round, with only three teams making it through to the first round proper. Somalia were drawn against Djibouti. They were supposed to play two legs, one in Somalia, the other in Djibouti, but because it wasn't safe enough to play anywhere in Somalia, the tie became a single match in Djibouti.

Somalia lost 1–0. Their World Cup was over in ninety minutes. To put this into context, the results of Djibouti's qualifying matches after the victory over Somalia were: Malawi 8–1 Djibouti, Djibouti 0–4 Egypt, Djibouti 0–6 DR Congo, DR Congo 5–1 Djibouti, Djibouti 0–3 Malawi and Egypt 4–0 Djibouti.

In the CECAFA Cup Somalia were drawn in the same group as Tanzania, Rwanda, Zanzibar and the hosts, Uganda. Judging by their previous results, Somalia would be lucky to get a point. The squad had been hastily put together over the previous few weeks. Ahmed Nur had scoured the diaspora, picking players from the USA, Canada and the UK, as well as a dozen from inside Somalia.

None of the diaspora players were professionals. One of the Brits, a centre half called Guled Adan, played for Hanwell Town in the British Gas Southern League. Guled's team-mates in London had been surprised when he told them he was about to become an international footballer. So too were his employers: Guled spent his nights as a bouncer at the Trocadero in Leicester Square.

I watched the team train at the Mandela Sports Complex a few miles outside Kampala. Gelle, the head coach, was a Somali institution. He had been coaching the national team on and off for most of the past two decades. He appeared to get his points across by shouting. If that didn't work, he'd shout a bit louder and sometimes shove a player in the direction he wanted him to go.

When I spoke to him after training, though, it was clear he had the utmost respect for his players. 'If we had clubs and a league we could compete,' he said. 'We will try our best.'

Some of those he'd picked last time around hadn't made it for this tournament. It wasn't because of injury or loss of form, though. Gelle described his first team meeting at the training camp he'd held in Djibouti a few weeks earlier, when he realised players were missing. 'Osman is here? No, he fled. Oh, Mohamed is here? No, he fled. Everyone has fled.' Since the Ethiopians entered Somalia at the end of 2006, more than a million people had been forced to leave their homes. Mortars, bombs and gun battles had become an almost daily occurrence. Mogadishu had turned into a ghost town.

Some of the players still lived there, although it wasn't out of choice. A young defender, Hassan Ali Roble, who played at centre back alongside Guled, had been offered a contract by a club in Yemen, but he wouldn't have been able to bring his family. His son was one and a half, his daughter was a newborn. 'I cannot leave them behind,' he said.

Getting to training was fraught with difficulties. Roadblocks, gun battles and roadside bombs had to be avoided. Some nights, when the fighting was particularly fierce, the players didn't bother trying to get home after training. 'If you try to move when the Ethiopians are around,' Hassan said, 'you might go to jail or be shot.'

Hassan knew only too well how thin the line between life and death was in Mogadishu. His friend, Omar Hassan Ali, was an eighteen-year-old right back with a bright future. He had trained with the national team and had been pencilled in for the CECAFA Cup squad. Ali arrived home one day after training to find a policeman outside his house. The policeman wanted money. Ali said he didn't have any. The argument became heated. The policeman said he would shoot him. 'How can you shoot me? You don't have a gun,' said Ali. The policeman stared at him, then turned and left. Half an hour later, the policeman returned with a gun, burst into the house and shot Ali in the head.

'Playing football is our only hope,' said Hassan. 'It is the only thing we have now.'

*

Somalia's first match was against Zanzibar. Zanzibar is part of Tanzania and doesn't normally have a separate national team. The only time they play on their own is in the CECAFA Cup. Only one member of the Zanzibar side was considered good enough to make the Tanzania side, so this was undoubtedly Somalia's best chance for a win.

They lost 2–0.

I watched the second match with Ahmed Nur. He had been a player in the 1980s, although by his own admission he had never threatened to set the world alight. In the late 1980s, after retiring from playing, he became a referee, but, like so many Somalis who had a bit of money, he and his family left the country in 1989 as war broke out. 'Football has gone since the civil war,' he said.

The only reason it has survived is because of men like him. He helped to fund a club called Elman FC, sending them balls and kits from London, but it wasn't until 2003 that he felt it was safe enough to return to Mogadishu, where he got involved with the Somali Football Federation, eventually becoming its vice-president.

Appearances were important for Ahmed Nur. Every day he was dressed smartly, always wearing his Somali Football Federation blazer. 'They don't think we are professionals,' he said, referring to some of the other Federation presidents and officials at the tournament.

We took our seats in the VIP area at the front of the main stand in Kampala's run-down Nakivubo Stadium. Somalia were about to take on Tanzania, a match that, it's fair to say, hadn't really grabbed the attention of Ugandan football fans. The ground was almost empty, save for about a couple of hundred Somalis, most of them refugees who lived in the nearby Kisenyi slum.

Somalia looked shaky at the back. Guled and Hassan were failing to deal with the high balls which Tanzania pumped towards them. But although Tanzania were dominating possession, they were struggling to create any chances. And while neither of the Somali centre backs seemed particularly competent in the air, they still towered over Tanzania's rather short forwards.

Somalia seemed to be playing for a draw. Every time one of their players was fouled, they would stay on the ground for as long as possible. Sometimes they'd go down even if there hadn't been a foul.

Midway through the first half, Somalia won a free kick on the left-hand side, about forty yards out. It was played in high towards the far post. Cisse Abshir, Somalia's only professional player – who plied his trade for Lillestrøm in Norway – had time to take it down on his chest. The ball dropped and he hit it on the half-volley. The ball flew into the far corner. Somehow, with their first chance and completely against the run of play, Somalia had taken the lead.

Ahmed Nur and the rest of the Somali delegation were understandably ecstatic. Oblivious to the condescending glances from the other football association heads and Ugandan ministers gathered in the VIP box, Ahmed Nur danced a jig and yelled at the top of his lungs. 'Please, please, let us hold on,' he said, more to himself than me, as he struggled to contain his nervousness. The whistle went for half-time, and Ahmed Nur rushed out of his seat and down towards the dressing room.

Holding on to the lead would be almost impossible. It was more than twenty-five years since Somalia had beaten Tanzania, and today they were up against a fast-improving Tanzanian side. Their Brazilian coach, Marcio Maximo, had taken the Taifa Stars from 162nd in the world rankings up to 99th. All the players were professionals, and they had come very close to reaching the final qualifying round for the World Cup, grabbing a draw at home to Cameroon, one of the African giants.

Within five minutes of the restart it became clear what Somalia's tactics would boil down to: wasting as much time as possible. Almost every time the ball went out of play a Somali would go down clutching one part or other of his body. The goalkeeper was the most impressive, if impressive is the right word. On one occasion I timed four minutes between him hitting the floor and the match restarting.

Maximo was, somewhat understandably, getting rather agitated on the sidelines.

The Somali keeper redeemed himself a few minutes later, acrobatically flicking the ball over the top from a close-range header. From the resulting corner Tanzania hit the bar. A Tanzanian cross flashed across the six-yard box, just missing three onrushing forwards. Somalia were hanging on by the skin of their teeth. So the goalkeeper rolled around on the floor a bit more.

Five minutes of added-on time were signalled by the fourth official. Ahmed Nur was gripping the sides of his seat. Tanzania couldn't find the breakthrough. The final whistle blew and the Somali players collapsed on the pitch. Some were praying, some crying, others just knackered. Ahmed Nur raced down onto the pitch to hug those who could still stay upright. In the stands the Somali contingent, which had grown to almost a thousand by the end of the match, waved their light-blue flags with the single white star.

The Tanzanians, who had harboured hopes of winning the tournament, looked shell-shocked. When I met Maximo the day after, he admitted that no one in the squad thought Somalia would pose much of a challenge.

*

Somalia lost their remaining two games. Injuries and suspensions weakened a squad that was already suffering from playing so many games in such a short space of time. By the time Somalia's final match took place against Uganda, they could barely muster eleven fit men.

It didn't matter. HornAfrik, a popular independent radio station in Somalia, had broadcast commentary of the Tanzania match. After the final whistle people had come out onto the streets in Mogadishu. For the first time in a long while there had been something to celebrate in Somalia.

'We flew our flag,' Ahmed Nur said when we met up after Somalia's final match. We were sitting on plastic chairs in the courtyard of the team's simple hotel. It was their last night in Kampala before flying back to Djibouti. From there, the players would head to their various homes. It was impossible to keep the team together. Somalia, out of the World Cup and Africa Cup of Nations qualifiers, wouldn't have another match until next year's CECAFA Cup. 'We will try and get them all back again,' said Ahmed Nur, 'but it will not be easy.' Those living in the West had to take several weeks off work to come to Djibouti and Uganda. Much as they loved playing for their country, many of them knew they wouldn't be able to do the same next year too.

As for those still living in Mogadishu, the question of how many would still be there in twelve months' time was left hanging in the night air.

Ahmed Nur finally felt able to relax. He had spent the past six months travelling halfway across the world, watching players in Minnesota and Toronto, London and Helsinki, trying to assemble a squad that could compete. Even once the team was together here in Kampala, he had problems to sort out. The organisers, he said, treated Somalia like second-class citizens.

'Every other team has rested for three days. We are the only team playing four games in seven days.' Nor was he particularly impressed with the organising committee's decision to issue the Somali team's tickets home for the day after their final group match. No one expected Somalia to make it through to the semi-finals, not even Ahmed Nur and his players, but he felt it was a bit much to give them their tickets home before they had even played a single match.

Now though, under the dim yellow lights in the courtyard, bottle of Coke in hand, he was smiling and joking. The players sat around playing cards and listening to music, while coach Gelle and Ahmed Nur reminisced about Somalia's glory days. During the 1980s, when there was still a functioning government in Mogadishu, the league had been strong. 'We had ten teams in the league,' said Gelle. 'Really good teams. The national team was strong.' Not strong enough ever to qualify for the African Nations, or even threaten to, but certainly strong enough to win the odd match and attract tens of thousands to the national stadium now occupied by Ethiopian troops.

Ahmed Nur was upbeat about the future. Peace talks between the government and the opposition were ongoing in Djibouti. Ethiopian withdrawal was on the table; so too was the possible resignation of the president, Abdullahi Yusuf, whose militias were just as guilty of war crimes as the Ethiopians and al-Shabaab. Optimists hoped that the election of a new, more moderate, more popular president, along with the withdrawal of the Ethiopians, could signal a new dawn for Somalia. Al-Shabaab, who had insisted they were fighting for the country's liberation, would get their wish.

'As soon as the Ethiopians leave we can restart Serie A,' Ahmed Nur said. 'We will be ready to go.' The stadium would need some work. Trees and thorn bushes had grown in the middle of the pitch. The standard of football would also take some time to improve. Too many of their top players had been forced to leave the country or had been unable to train properly for too many years. Ahmed Nur and Gelle were confident, though, that if they were able to restart the league, they could assemble a stronger national team for next year's tournament. 'Maybe I could get the players together for four months beforehand,' Gelle mused.

*

A couple of months later, when I was back in Nairobi, I met up with Ahmed Nur, who was there looking for a job with the UN. The UN's enormous aid operations in Somalia were run from neighbouring Kenya because it was too dangerous for any foreigners to work inside the country. Ahmed Nur's hopes of getting a job were slim, though. 'If you're Somali, you have to go inside the country,' he said. Right now, that was the last thing he wanted to do.

His dreams of restarting Serie A had been dealt a blow. As expected the peace conference in Djibouti had resulted in the withdrawal of Ethiopia's forces and the election of a new president, Sheikh Sharif Sheikh Ahmed.

Sheikh Sharif was a popular choice. A softly spoken former geography teacher and a respected Islamic scholar, he had also been the nominal head of the Islamic Courts Union which had ruled Somalia during the second half of 2006. Many of those now part of al-Shabaab had once been fighting on Sheikh Sharif's behalf.

Not any more, though. Since the disintegration of the ICU there had been a split between the two major leaders, Sheikh Sharif and Sheikh Hassan Dahir Aweys. Aweys took a far more hardline approach and dismissed Sheikh Sharif as a 'Western puppet'. He encouraged al-Shabaab to continue their insurgency.

The fighting, yet again, was brutal. Every day there were mortars, roadside bombs and gun battles in the streets. Somalia's ridiculously overstretched hospitals couldn't cope with the number of civilian injuries and casualties.

Playing football in such an environment was impossible. And to make matters worse, the stadium was once again out of bounds. Within days of the Ethiopians withdrawing their troops from the stadium, al-Shabaab took it over.

'Maybe it will get better soon,' Ahmed Nur said.

It didn't. A few months later I met up with some of the players, including Hassan, the centre back. CECAFA's annual competition for club champions was due to take place in Khartoum, and Somalia had entered a team despite the fact that it had been three years since the last Serie A. Benadir Telecom, the last champions, came to Nairobi for a few days of training uninterrupted by bombs and mortars.

They looked unfit, huffing and puffing around a barely grassy pitch that the Kenyan side, Mathare United, normally trained on. The situation in Mogadishu was as bad as ever. Despite Sheikh Sharif introducing sharia law, one of al-Shabaab's demands, the insurgency had continued. Tens of thousands were once more fleeing Mogadishu. Al-Shabaab had also started targeting footballers.

After training, Hassan, wearing a yellow Chelsea away shirt, came over to speak to me. 'It's more dangerous now,' he said. 'If the Shabaab suspect you of being a footballer, they will kill you immediately.' He'd had another offer to move abroad but, again, wasn't able to take his family with him. Every day, he said, he feared something would happen to his children. 'Playing is our only hope,' he said.

Yet again, Somalia's footballers saw the chance to play in an international tournament as an opportunity to remind the world that they existed. Journalists from HornAfrik and Radio Shabelle would be accompanying the team and broadcasting live commentary.

This time there was no victory. The tournament started promisingly with a 2–2 draw against Prisons of Tanzania. Then things unravelled. Benadir were embarrassed in their second game, losing 8–1 to TP Mazembe, a Congolese side bankrolled by a very rich governor, before losing their final match 5–1 to Kampala City Council. The results were not unexpected. Both TP Mazembe and KCC had appeared in that year's African Champions League, something Benadir could only dream of.

*

On one of my last afternoons in Mogadishu in 2007, I was lying on my bed in the Peace Hotel, the ceiling fan whirring away. A couple of hours earlier we'd had a hairy journey back from Medina Hospital. Ethiopian troops were 500 yards down the road, apparently looking for groups of gunmen. 'If they see our guards, they'll start shooting,' Farah said. We jumped in the car and sped out of the hospital gates. As we raced through the streets, swerving past donkeys and pedestrians, Farah looked nervously over his shoulder out of the back window. It probably took only five minutes to get back to the safety of the Peace, but it had felt like a lot longer.

There was a knock on the door, disturbing my sleep. It was Farah. 'One more trip,' he said. The last thing I wanted to do was go back out. I was already thinking of dinner on the roof. Bashir had told me this morning that his chef had bought some fresh lobster.

'One more trip,' Farah insisted. 'I want to show you something.' He was excited but wouldn't say why. We drove towards the beach, past some of Mogadishu's once-beautiful but now destroyed art deco ruins. Before the Second World War Italian architects in Somalia had constructed one of Africa's most stunning cities. Continual civil wars had had a devastating effect on the architecture, but it was still possible to make out beautiful whitewashed arches and ornate balconies.

The car stopped outside the concrete shell of an abandoned building. Farah led me inside, up the stairs and into a large, bare room overlooking the sea. The wind ripped through the gaps where plate-glass windows had once stood.

'When Mogadishu is safe again,' Farah said, 'this will be my restaurant.' He had spoken to the owner of the building and agreed a rent. It would serve the finest fresh fish and seafood to the Mogadishu elite and the battalions of aid workers and foreign businessmen that Farah hoped would all one day return to the city.

We stood at the open window, staring out at the golden sand beach and the emerald-green sea stretching out below us. It didn't take much imagination to realise this was once a beautiful city.

'We could do it together,' he said, turning to me. I laughed, and instantly regretted sounding so rude. It was such a ridiculous idea, though. I'd needed four gunmen to protect me, and even then we weren't safe. There was no way, no way, I was ever going to move to Mogadishu and set up a seafood restaurant.

'When it's safe,' Farah said. 'It won't be,' I muttered. 'Yes, it will,' he insisted. Farah didn't want to go back to Finland. Didn't want his kids growing up in a cold, dark place thousands of miles from home. Didn't want to be a school caretaker for the rest of his life. This was his home and this restaurant was his dream.

We stood there, the wind howling. We'd need to do something to protect the diners from the wind, I thought. 'Okay,' I said. 'When it's safe.' Farah grinned and we shook hands. We turned and walked down the stairs, back towards the street. There was a strange noise outside. We stepped out of the restaurant (I was mentally picturing the colour we could paint the lobby walls) and found dozens of boys playing football.

It was the first time I'd seen something like this in Mogadishu. There were several games going on at once, at intervals along the street. We stood and watched, the early-evening sun bathing the players in a soft orange light.

One of the footballs – the usual rolled-up plastic bag affair – bobbled towards me, a group of five boys hurtling after it. I controlled it with my left foot and chipped it over the onrushing gang. Some of the other boys laughed and cheered. It would be getting dark soon. The sun was rapidly disappearing over the horizon, but for a few minutes we joined in. A small boy in a fake yellow and blue Arsenal shirt, the name 'Henry' and the number '14' on his back, slipped the ball through my legs and raced past me before I could turn. Farah nodded his head. We'd been here too long and the guards were keen for us to move on. It was just as well – I was about to take the game too seriously.

4

THE HARAMBEE STARS

Kenya

'Oliech! Odinga! Obama!' roared the crowd. 'Oliech! Odinga! Obama!' The chant raced around the concrete bowl of Nyayo Stadium in the heart of Nairobi's city centre. The capacity was just 35,000 but there were at least 50,000 Kenyans crammed into the stands, pressed up against each other, raising their arms in the air and joining in the cry. 'Oliech! Odinga! Obama!' Thousands more had been locked out an hour before the game as police struggled to keep out those without tickets. They had moved on to bars across the city packed full with fans watching the match on television.

On the pitch Dennis Oliech, Kenya's star striker, had just scored the Harambee Stars' second goal, sealing a convincing 2–0 victory against Zimbabwe. Raila Odinga, the country's new prime minister, celebrated in the VIP box. And across the Atlantic Ocean, Barack Obama, the son of a Kenyan goatherd, had just become the Democratic Party's nominee for president of the USA.

At last there appeared to be something for Kenyans to celebrate. The Oliech-inspired victory against Zimbabwe would all but secure Kenya's place in the final qualifying round for the Africa Cup of Nations and the World Cup. Odinga's presence was a reminder that Kenya had been on the brink of civil war just a few short months ago but had stepped back from the abyss. And the hope of Obama's campaign was felt as strongly in Nairobi as New York: a son of a Kenyan could become the most powerful man on the planet.

But as the fans continued their chant, the police stepped in. There had been a heavy police presence throughout the game, with hundreds of officers armed with tear gas canisters, Kalashnikovs and batons patrolling the ground. Now they began to fire tear gas into the crowd. For a moment it looked like there could be a riot. But the fans stopped singing and the police stopped firing, and an uneasy truce held until the end of the match.

The reason for the violence – the reason for so much of the violence throughout Kenya's troubled history – was politics. The chant was not just an expression of national pride: it was about the success of the Luos.

Oliech, Odinga and Obama all hail from Luo families in Kenya's western Nyanza province. Kenya is a country of forty-two tribes, and in much of the country people identify themselves by their tribe first and their nationality second. Much of the fault lies with Kenya's politicians.

After independence, land and jobs had been divided up and handed out on the basis of tribe. When most of the white settlers left in 1963, Kenya's first president, Jomo Kenyatta, gave much of the land in the Rift Valley to his fellow Kikuyus, rather than to the Kalenjins that it had previously belonged to. A majority of civil service jobs went to Kikuyus, as well as key positions in the armed forces and security services.

Daniel arap Moi, who succeeded Kenyatta in 1978, followed a similar path, rewarding friends in his own Kalenjin tribe.

Mwai Kibaki, who was elected in 2002 as Kenya's third president, had vowed to be different. But as his government became increasingly ethnicised, it merely proved to voters that you would only get something if your man was in charge.

The Luos had long considered themselves Kenya's most maligned tribe. Raila Odinga's father, Oginga Odinga, had been vice-president under Kenyatta following independence from Britain in 1963, but the pair soon fell out and Odinga found himself sidelined.

Raila was jailed three times under Kenya's second president, Moi, spending a total of nine years behind bars. Other prominent Luo politicians suffered more serious fates. Tom Mboya and Robert Ouko were both murdered and their killers never brought to justice.

Football has been just about the only national stage where Luos have dominated. The Luo club, Gor Mahia, was arguably the best in Kenya in the 1960s and 1970s, and enjoyed a great rivalry with AFC Leopards, the Luhya club from Western Province. The majority of the national team has always come from western Kenya, and the present side is no different. On the day when Oliech completed the victory against Zimbabwe, eight of the eleven Kenyans on the pitch had Luo heritage.

The reaction of the crowd, and the over-reaction of the police, served to underline the ethnic problems which six months earlier had threatened to take the country into civil war.

*

On 27 December 2007 Kenya went to the polls. It was only the second time in the country's history that people were able to choose their leaders in a free and fair vote.

I spent the day in Kibera, the largest slum in Nairobi and one of the biggest in Africa. Around a million people live in a patchwork of iron shacks and market stalls, surrounded by rubbish-strewn dirt paths and open sewers. Kibera, like all of Nairobi's slums, is a melting pot of different tribes. When people moved to the big city to find work, they usually ended up in places like Kibera – and people had come from everywhere.

The election was going to be tight. Odinga, the opposition leader, was up against President Kibaki. The two had once been close allies. Kibaki had come to power in 2002 in the country's first truly democratic election, beating Uhuru Kenyatta, the son of Jomo and the protégé of Moi. Odinga was a leading member of Kibaki's coalition, an alliance carefully calibrated to include influential members from all of Kenya's major tribes. Kibaki had promised to change the constitution, creating a post of prime minister which Odinga would fill.

The days of tribal politics would come to an end, Kibaki promised, as would grand corruption.

Moi's rule had been dominated by corruption scandals, which further enriched his allies at the expense of ordinary Kenyans. He and his ministers had brazenly looted from the state, and the culture of corruption had trickled down to the lowest levels. It was impossible to move anywhere or do anything without having to hand over *kitu kidogo* – something small – to a police officer or a civil servant.

Kibaki promised that his government would have 'clean hands'. It didn't work out like that. Kibaki's anti-corruption czar, John Githongo, unearthed fresh corruption scandals which had enriched members of Kibaki's new government. The president chose to ignore the reports from Githongo, who began to receive death threats. He fled to London and released a dossier detailing the allegations which Kibaki had refused to act on.

It soon became clear as well that Kibaki, once in power, wasn't so keen to hand any of it over to Odinga, as he had promised. Plans for a radical new constitution were quickly shelved. Odinga quit the government and started an opposition group, the Orange Democratic Movement (ODM).

Odinga styled himself the 'people's president' and built his own coalition of leaders from other tribes. Kibaki was increasingly surrounding himself with Kikuyus like himself, so much so that the Kibaki government had been dubbed the 'Mount Kenya mafia', after the area in Central Province where he and his closest advisers were all from.

In the run-up to the 2007 election, some of the comments by politicians on both sides were alarmingly tribal. Other signs that should have set off alarm bells were either ignored or insufficiently analysed.

Nakumatt, the leading supermarket chain, reported suspicious sales of *pangas* (machetes). Young men were buying dozens at a time. A car belonging to an assistant minister was stopped on the way to Kisii. Police discovered a haul of weapons inside. Just before the election Kibaki unilaterally appointed several new electoral commissioners, ignoring an agreement with the opposition to appoint them together.

But few people read the signs, journalists like myself included.

The day after the election, as the results began to pour in, it was clear that something seismic had happened. Cabinet ministers were losing their seats. The vice-president had gone, so had the foreign minister. Moi's three sons had all been vying for parliamentary seats, but all three lost, as did his former right-hand man, Nicholas Biwott. The voters had had enough, and it appeared as if that would mean a change at the top as well. By the evening Raila Odinga was more than one million votes ahead of Kibaki. One British newspaper wrote that it would 'take a miracle' for Kibaki to win.

Overnight that miracle began to happen. At the Kenya International Conference Centre (KICC), an iconic tower in downtown Nairobi where the count was taking place, Kibaki's people were stealing the vote.

The next morning the ODM declared that their man had won. Kibaki's party, the Party of National Unity (PNU), said they had won. The official results had still not been announced. The following day it became clear what was going on. Votes from Central Province, the predominantly Kikuyu region which was Kibaki's stronghold, had been falsified. European

Union observers who had been present at the polling stations there reported one set of figures, but the supposedly impartial head of the electoral commission, Samuel Kivuitu, was on stage announcing far higher votes for Kibaki.

ODM supporters tried to stop Kivuitu announcing the vote. Paramilitary police stormed in, batons raised, and hustled Kivuitu out of the room. They returned a few minutes later to throw everyone – politicians, election agents, observers and journalists – out of the building. In a small room on the third floor, in front of a state television cameraman, Kivuitu announced that Kibaki was the winner. Within half an hour the riots had begun.

*

It was a sombre New Year's Eve. When the clock struck twelve, we all raised our glasses, but it was hard to raise a smile. A couple of dozen of us, expats and Kenyans, had come to a small Nairobi bar, but there was little to celebrate. The wishes of 'Happy New Year' were muted, the clinking of glasses half-hearted.

Kenya was burning. Riots had broken out in the slums. Mobs were burning down houses and setting up roadblocks in the Rift Valley. People who had lived next to each other in peace for years were now attacking each other with machetes. There were rumours of an imminent coup.

The Kenyans in the group began to sing the national anthem. At a time in their country's history when politicians were busy stoking a tribal conflict, a group of friends from several different ethnic groups stood together and sang:

O God of all creation
Bless this our land and nation
Justice be our shield and defender
May we dwell in unity
Peace and liberty
Plenty be found within our borders.

Let one and all arise
With hearts both strong and true
Service be our earnest endeavour
And our Homeland of Kenya
Heritage of splendour
Firm may we stand to defend.

Let all with one accord
In common bond united
Build this our nation together
And the glory of Kenya
The fruit of our labour
Fill every heart with thanksgiving.

As we drank beers and hoped for a peaceful new year, I told a story to my friend David about a man I'd met in Mathare, one of Nairobi's slums, earlier that day. The man told me his name was Elvis. After he told me what had happened to him, I asked for his surname. 'Just Elvis,' he said. Then I asked who he had voted for. 'My vote is secret,' he insisted. Then I asked where he came from.

'You want to know my tribe,' Elvis retorted. He was right. I felt ashamed and embarrassed but at the time it seemed important. His back straightening, Elvis looked me in the eye and said: 'My tribe is Kenyan.'

David sat back, thinking. 'We should get that on T-shirts,' he said. Odinga had called for a mass rally in three days' time. 'We'll get it on T-shirts and hand them out at the rally,' David said.

While tribe was clearly still a major issue in rural areas and in parts of the slums, there was a new generation of Kenyans to whom it meant very little. David is a Luo and his girlfriend Juliet is Kikuyu. It hadn't been until the election that I realised they were from different tribes.

'It has never been an issue for us,' said David. 'We went to school with people from different tribes. Now we are trying to build our businesses, forge our careers. Tribe doesn't come into it.'

At this stage no one knew how bad things were going to get. The next afternoon we found out.

The worst of the violence took place in the North Rift Valley, one of the most beautiful and fertile parts of the country. It was also one of the most volatile. There had been land clashes at elections in 1992 and 1997, both of which had been marred by extensive rigging, which had kept Moi in power.

Ahead of the 2007 election prominent busi-nessmen and politicians in the Rift Valley had begun to organise militias. Investigations by local and international human rights groups later revealed that the violence which followed the election result was premeditated. Kalenjin leaders saw the election as an opportunity to finally purge Kikuyus from their land.

On New Year's Day a gang of Kalenjin men surrounded a small church in the village of Kiambaa, where hundreds of Kikuyu women and children had gathered for safety. The men locked the doors, stuffed mattresses and leaves against the walls, covered the church in petrol and set it on fire.

I was in Nairobi at the time, covering the riots which had broken out in the capital, and spoke on the phone to a Red Cross volunteer at the church who was helping those trying to put out the fire. Through the smoke he could see piles of bodies. 'So many children,' he whispered. 'So many children.'

When I reached Kiambaa the next morning, the Red Cross were carrying the charred remains of more than a dozen bodies out of the ashes and rubble. There was little trace of most of those who had perished in the fire. Doctors eventually confirmed that at least thirty-six people had died.

The patch of grass outside the nearest hospital, a few miles away in Eldoret, was full of families forced from their homes. Men shot in the back with arrows, women with enormous burns down the sides of their faces. Inside the hospital every bed in every room was occupied. Doctors and nurses struggled to cope – many of their colleagues had also been forced to flee.

Within days Kikuyu gangs were taking revenge in other parts of the country. The Mungiki, a gang financed and organised by prominent Kikuyu politicians, sent militias to Nakuru and Naivasha to carry out revenge attacks on those who had voted for Odinga.

On the shores of Lake Naivasha, just outside the luxurious country club, a crowd of armed men and women waved machetes, axes and wooden poles at hundreds of men, women and children huddled on the other side of the road. A thin line of no more than a dozen police officers tried to hold them back.

Naivasha had been one of Kenya's most cosmopolitan towns. People from all over the country had flocked here to work at the many flower farms which dotted the lake, producing cut roses and tulips which were flown to Europe and sold in supermarkets.

Now the Mungiki were driving everyone else out. 'They killed our people,' said one of those waving a machete, a twenty-three-year-old called Francis Mbogo. 'So now we will do likewise. We are just revenging.'

Kenya was becoming increasingly Balkanised, with convoys of families living in the 'wrong' province criss-crossing the country and heading back to their 'ancestral homes'.

It took the intervention of an African elder statesman, former United Nations Secretary General Kofi Annan, to bring an end to the killing. Urged to go to Nairobi by the African Union, Annan spent forty-four days in the capital wrestling with Kibaki's and Odinga's negotiators before getting the two men to agree to a power-sharing deal. Kibaki would remain as president but a new role of prime minister would be created, which Odinga would take. It was far from perfect – and the underlying issues which had laid the ground for the violence remained – but it was enough to create an uneasy truce.

*

'There is more intrigue and more politics and more problems in Kenyan football than there is in Kenyan politics,' Gishinga Njoroge told me. We were sitting on white plastic chairs behind one of the goals at Kampala's Nakivubo Stadium, watching a fairly dire match between Rwanda and Zanzibar during the CECAFA Cup. In a forgettable first half, the ball had come far closer to hitting us than the back of the net.

As we ate grilled chicken bought from the side of the road, Njoroge, a former sports journalist who now worked for the Kenyan Premier League, took me through a potted history of Kenyan football incompetence and corruption. It was a story of stolen gate receipts, missing FIFA funds and institutional match-rigging. Senior figures in the football administration had been charged with corruption but Kenya's notoriously creaking justice system had failed to prosecute anyone.

Football was not just seen as a money pot; it was a route to political power. Kenneth Matiba, chairman of the Kenyan Football Federation (KFF) in the 1970s, had used his platform to become a prominent politician, standing against Moi in the 1992 elections. Several MPs elected in 2007 had also been deeply involved in football administration, using the sport as a support base to further their political ambitions.

The mix of money and power led to a succession of rows over who should control football, arguments which have had a terrible effect on the game itself. In 2004 and 2006 FIFA banned Kenya from international football because of political interference from the government.

By the time of the 2007 election there were two rival camps which claimed to run football in Kenya – the discredited leadership of the KFF and a new body set up with FIFA's blessing called Football Kenya Ltd (FKL). FKL was established after FIFA decided that the KFF was beyond saving. Countless corruption scandals had destroyed its reputation and ruined both the league and the national team. But many of the figures involved in FKL had also been accused of corruption and those who ran the rival KFF could still rely on the financial support of a number of prominent government ministers.

'It is a question of which poison is less lethal: KFF or KFL,' Bob Munro told me. Munro, a Canadian ice hockey fan, got involved in football when he moved to Kenya in 1985. He knew little about the game but believed that sport had the power to change lives.

Mathare, the slum where Munro chose to establish a sports association, is the sort of place which needs all the help it can get. Set in a valley just a stone's throw from the elite Muthaiga Golf Club, Mathare is one of the poorest areas of Nairobi, and is home to around half a million people.

The Mathare Youth Sports Association (MYSA), which Munro established in 1987, has become one of Africa's most amazing football projects and arguably Kenya's greatest social institution. It has 1,600 youth teams with more than 23,000 players but it is about much more than football. Each team is required to carry out tasks in Mathare, like clearing rubbish and cleaning drains. Teams get points in their league for their actions both on and off the pitch.

Munro set up a professional club, Mathare United, in 1994, which was made up entirely of graduates from MYSA. They rose swiftly through the ranks to reach the National Super League, one step below the top flight. That's when the problems began.

The fight against corruption in Kenyan football has required some unusual tactics. Mathare United tended to win their home matches, but the away games were a different matter altogether. Dubious penalties, phantom offsides and fouls that didn't exist became common. Corrupt local referees were ruining Mathare's chances of winning promotion to the Premier League.

'We had to do something,' Bob Munro told me. 'So we borrowed a video camera.' In their second season Mathare's team manager spent every away game running up and down the touchline, filming the referee. The camera was actually broken. Nothing was ever filmed. But the tactic worked, and Mathare won promotion.

Fighting corruption in the Premier League was a lot harder. Few of the clubs were happy with the way football was being run, but there seemed little they could do about it. The Premier League teams toyed with the idea of setting up their own tournaments and began with the Transparency Cup. Organised with the help of John Githongo, Kibaki's anti-corruption czar who would later flee to London, it was the first corruption-free football tournament anyone could remember being held in Kenya.

Major companies flocked to sponsor it. They desperately wanted to be associated with football, but the game's authorities had such bad reputations that few companies had previously been prepared to have anything to do with them.

For Githongo, cleaning up football was about far more than improving the national sport. To him, it was as much about politics.

'Everyone knew football was corrupt,' Githongo told me. 'Everyone also knows that politics is corrupt. If we could prove that you could clean up football then we could prove that you could clean up politics.'

Mathare United paid for their public stance against the football authorities. Their officials were threatened, money they were owed was never paid and referees were told to make sure they lost.

'I told the players, you guys are going to have to train harder than any other club,' Munro said.

But the fight paid off. In 2007 the clubs established a private company which would run the Premier League independently from FKL.

The Kenyan Premier League is now owned and managed by all sixteen clubs, something which has not only prevented corruption but has also 'detribalised' top-flight football. Now that teams compete on a level playing field each club ensures it picks the best players it can, regardless of where in the country they come from.

Ending the corruption which surrounds the national team, the Harambee Stars, has not been so successful. Kenya's football officials have managed to ruin Kenya's best-ever chance to qualify for the World Cup. It was a slim chance, but it was a chance nonetheless.

*

In the wake of the post-election violence the Kenyan football authorities were skint. The government, struggling to deal with more than 300,000 internally displaced people, could not provide any funding. FKL feared they wouldn't be able to put together enough money to allow the Harambee Stars to compete in the World Cup qualifiers.

The Kenyan Premier League, financially stable following a TV deal with the South African satellite broadcasters Supersport, offered to loan FKL the money they needed. In return, the league would have a major role in the running of the team.

The first task was choosing a coach. For the first time, Kenya's national team coach would be picked on the basis of talent, rather than tribe. The sixteen clubs voted for Francis Kimanzi, the thirty-three-year-old coach of Mathare United.

Kimanzi was born in Mathare and grew up in MYSA. He had been groomed for leadership from an early age, taking on the role of chairman of one of the junior sides when he was just thirteen. An attacking midfielder, he had been a crucial part of United's rise into the Premier League, but at the age of twenty-five, when most footballers still have their best years ahead of them, Kimanzi quit playing. He was already Mathare's assistant coach and a director of MYSA. Munro suggested he was now mature enough to become head coach.

Under Kimanzi's leadership Mathare performed well, culminating in three great seasons in 2007, 2008 and 2009, in which they managed three consecutive finishes in the top two. The greatest success was in 2008, when the team of slum boys managed to win their first-ever title.

Kimanzi had also found time to take coaching classes in the Netherlands, gaining his UEFA C and B licences, and had plans to return to take his A licence – the premier coaching badge in Europe.Under Kimanzi the Harambee Stars won three of their qualifiers – including the home win against Zimbabwe – and drew one. It was enough to earn them a spot in the final qualifying round.

Kenya were drawn alongside Mozambique, Tunisia and Nigeria. While the latter two were clearly favourites, Kenya were playing confident football and had proved in their victories over Guinea and Zimbabwe that they could beat middle-ranked teams. Tunisia and Nigeria would be a step up, but it was one that Kimanzi thought they were capable of making.

'Too many sides in Africa do not play like a team – they are just a bunch of individuals,' Kimanzi told me. 'My team plays like a team.'

When I watched him take a training session during the CECAFA Cup in neighbouring Uganda, it was clear that he had the respect of the players. Many of them were almost the same age, but it didn't seem to matter – he was the boss.

Kimanzi hoped to do well in the CECAFA Cup, but it was merely a warm-up for the final World Cup qualifiers. Kenya played well, though, reaching the final, in which they played the hosts, Uganda.

Played in front of 20,000 Ugandan fans at the Nelson Mandela Stadium on the outskirts of Kampala, the final was an entertaining match. Kenya lost 1–0, but it had been an even contest.

A narrow defeat to the host nation was not a disaster, and Kimanzi had been able to take stock ahead of the vital World Cup qualifiers.

But days later Kimanzi was sacked. Football Kenya had arranged a friendly match against Egypt for the following weekend. It was a crazy decision, motivated purely by the money which the Egyptian FA were offering. Kimanzi's men were tired after playing five matches in twelve days. What's more, they were due back at their clubs in Kenya, where the Premier League season was about to start.

Kimanzi told FKL that he wouldn't be able to take a decent side. 'It would have been the third- or fourth-string players – you'd never use them in a village tournament.' If Kenya were defeated, which is what happened, vital FIFA ranking points would be lost.

Under Kimanzi, Kenya had finally broken into the world's top seventy for the first time. This was crucial. It was all but impossible for players to get work permits to play in Britain unless their national team was consistently in the top seventy. Kenya had two stars in Europe – McDonald Mariga at Parma and Dennis Oliech at Auxerre – but if they could manage to stay in the top seventy, there was a chance that some of their other players could make it in England.

Kimanzi stood his ground and refused to go. So FKL got rid of him.

There was another reason too, according to Titus Kasuve, the secretary general. Prime Minister Odinga had decided that Kenya needed a foreign coach to take them to the next level. Like many other politicians, Odinga saw football as a way of building popular support, but at least he had a record in the game. He had played football as a child and had been aligned to the Luo club, Gor Mahia, since the 1960s.

Odinga, Kasuve told me, thought a German coach would be best. Odinga had studied in East Germany, spoke German and still had close links to the country.

'The prime minister had been very adamant,' Kasuve said. 'He knew the second round would require someone more qualified. Africans have their own way of doing things. He wanted someone who could connect to the players.'

The new coach was a man called Antoine Hey. Odinga himself announced the appointment at a press conference. Hey had experience of coaching in Africa, having previously been in charge of Lesotho, Gambia and Liberia.

None of them had been a success, though. He had failed to win a single match.

★

Antoine Hey's regime got off to a bad start. Ignoring FIFA rules ensuring that international football doesn't interfere with national leagues, he demanded that Premier League players report to a Harambee Stars training camp one month before the first qualifier against Tunisia. Some of the players, not wanting to miss important league matches, refused. Hey ended up suspending eleven players, including several from Mathare United. The impasse was eventually resolved, but it was a bad first impression for both parties.

If Kenya were to have any chance of qualifying for the World Cup, they would need to do what they did in the last round and win all their home matches. Tunisia and Nigeria were strong sides but were definitely beatable away from their raucous home crowds. Hey hoped that a capacity crowd at Nyayo Stadium could spur his players on.

They made a terrible start, going behind to an Ammar Jemal goal after just six minutes. But the Harambee Stars fought back and scored a deserved equaliser in the seventieth minute through Dennis Oliech. Nine minutes later though, Tunisia got the winner.

Preparations for the second tie, away to Nigeria, were chaotic. Hey had been in the job three months, but he'd yet to receive a pay cheque. Fearing he might never get one if his side lost heavily to Nigeria and he was sacked, Hey insisted that he wouldn't board the plane to Abuja until he was paid.

'Oh,' said Football Kenya, 'didn't the sports ministry pay you?'

'Oh,' said the sports ministry, 'didn't the German embassy pay you?'

'What?' said the German embassy. 'He's your coach, not ours.'

The sports minister, Helen Sambili, tried to claim that the German embassy had agreed to pay Hey's salary – something the German ambassador vigorously denied. By the time the flight to Nigeria was supposed to leave, Hey had still not been paid. The plane left without him. Realising he really wasn't bluffing, and fearing the embarrassment of losing their coach the day before a World Cup qualifier, the sports ministry rustled up a cheque. Hey took the next flight out.

The 3–0 defeat in Abuja was not unexpected. Nigeria's first team all played for top European clubs; Kenya's didn't.

I went to watch the next home match against Mozambique with some of the friends I'd shared New Year's Eve with back in 2007. Two of the group, David and Juliet, were among the first people I had met when I moved to Nairobi in 2006. Juliet was a journalist and David was a businessman. They had been going out for a few years and David had finally proposed a few months earlier.

We met up at Fifi's, a small bar near the Kasarani Stadium in the north of the city. Previous matches had been held at Nyayo Stadium in the city centre, but after one security incident too many FIFA had insisted they be moved to Kasarani, a far larger stadium set back from the main road and a lot easier to police. They also limited the capacity to 35,000, meaning a sell-out would still mean 40 per cent of the seats would be empty. They needn't have bothered. Security problems had persuaded a lot of fans it wasn't worth going to football matches any more. Last time around, Juliet and her friend Alice had watched a group of men get mugged right in front of them. We parked the cars at a nearby hotel and left wallets and mobiles in the glove compartments.

The Harambee Stars' performances in the last two matches hadn't helped attract fans either. Defeat today against Mozambique would probably end their hopes of reaching the Africa Cup of Nations.

On the way to the stadium there were the usual hawkers selling hats, scarves and flags, but even with half an hour until kick-off it didn't look like many people had decided to turn up. Inside, the stadium was probably four-fifths empty. 'It's so sad,' said Alice. 'This place would be full if we were doing well.'

The juju man, face and body painted in the red, green, white and black of Kenya's flag, performed a blessing on the pitch. 'He should be fired,' said David. 'We're losing.'

The teams came out and the anthems were played. It was the first time I had heard it sung since New Year's Eve. This time it was bellowed out with a sense of joy.

Kenya got the best possible start. Julius Owino attempted a cross from the right, but it wasn't very good. The ball looped up towards the goal, catching the keeper unawares. He backpedalled furiously but could only push it into the net as he fell. Kenya were one up.

'Eh! Eh! Eh! Ole! Ole! Ole!' the fans chanted.

Kenya started playing with confidence, although it sometimes stretched into the realms of cockiness with little flicks and tricks. The Mozambique goalkeeper, having already gifted one goal, was having a torrid time. 'Blunder! Blunder!' yelled Alice as he tried and failed to deal with a back pass.

The Mozambique coach decided he'd seen enough. We were less than halfway through the first period, but the goalkeeper was being substituted. He looked crestfallen as he walked off the pitch behind the goal before crouching on the floor with his head in his hands.

'I think he's crying,' said David.

Photographers crowded around him before someone from the Mozambique bench came over and ushered him out of the stadium.

The score was still 1–0 at half-time. We bought cold drinks from a hawker, who had hopped over the divide between us and the stand to the right, as the substitutes warmed up on the pitch. One of them, Taiwo Atieno, attracted more attention than most. Taiwo, who played his football in a minor league in the USA, had been hyped up in the Kenyan papers for the past few months. He had taken out Kenyan citizenship just so that he had a chance of playing for the Harambee Stars, an act that had already endeared him to the fans.

For the second half Hey had made a change, but not the one the fans wanted. Oliech, who had looked tired in the first half, had been replaced by

Allan Wanga, who played his football in Angola. As Wanga was announced, the fans chanted for Taiwo.

'Has anyone actually seen this guy play?' asked Juliet. 'Good point,' replied David.

Kenya started the second half slowly, ceding far too much possession to Mozambique. The crowd started to voice its frustration. '*Twende!*' they roared. 'Let's go!' It didn't help. Mozambique got their equaliser after the keeper, Arnold Otieno, failed to hold a shot. Domingues knocked in the rebound.

The chants for Taiwo increased. Instead, Hey brought on Victor Mugabe, the brother of McDonald Mariga. Mugabe looked impressive, taking players on down the left-hand side. After one run he was brought down about thirty yards out. The free kick was swung in by Mariga, and Robert Mambo, the centre half, headed it home. It didn't count, though – the linesman on the near side had raised his flag. Bottles were thrown in his direction as whistles rang out.

Kenya had looked a lot better since Mugabe had come on, but they were unable to find a way through. Some of the fans started to turn on the coach, chanting 'Hey out!'

Kenya's salvation – Hey's too – came a few minutes later. Mariga burst past two defenders and was brought down in the box. He got up to score the penalty.

The game was as good as over. And with a couple of minutes left on the clock, Hey turned to Taiwo. He ran around like a headless chicken and touched the ball once (a mistimed header from a goal kick). Still, he'd got his debut.

It hadn't been pretty, but Kenya had three points. 'A win is a win,' said David with a shrug.

The sun was still shining as we walked back towards Fifi's. It was crowded but peaceful. No one tried to mug us. Even the police were smiling. 'They've done well today,' Alice said, referring to the police. 'This is so much better than last time.'

*

Three months later David and Juliet got married. It was a burning hot Nairobi afternoon and the church doors had to be flung open to keep everyone cool. Several months had passed since the rains had last fallen and Kenya was turning brown. A drought in the northeast was spreading across the country, and cattle were beginning to die in large numbers. Aid agencies were warning of a humanitarian crisis, while the government estimated that around 10 million people were in need of food aid. There had been water rationing in Nairobi, followed by regular electricity cuts as the hydroelectric dams which powered the country ran dangerously low.

The service took place in a large church in Nairobi's Kileleshwa suburb. *Matatus* – the minibus taxis which are the main form of public transport – had brought in family from Nyanza and Central, and the church was packed with around 200 friends and relations. Even more turned up for the reception, held on the lawn at the Royal Nairobi Golf Club. A marquee had been set up, festooned with black and yellow fabric. As the speeches began, dark clouds rolled in overhead. Much was made of the different backgrounds of the bride and groom. Referring to the coalition government which had been established between Kibaki and Raila, several speechmakers joked that this was a 'coalition wedding'. Everyone knew it would be more successful than the political one – unlike the politicians, David and Juliet actually wanted to be together.

There was a patter on the marquee above. It got louder and louder until everyone was looking outside. It was finally raining.

Rain on a wedding day may not be a good omen in the UK, but that wasn't the case here. Women ululated. Speeches were peppered with references to the 'blessings' which the wedding had brought. David and Juliet stood there beaming. It was a happy day.

5

THE WASPS v. THE LEOPARDS

Rwanda v. DR Congo

It's hard to think of a way that things could have gone worse for the first sub-Saharan team to reach the World Cup finals. Zaire had qualified in style for the 1974 tournament, which was held in West Germany. But they lost all three matches, scoring none and conceding fourteen. A team which had come to West Germany as African champions and full of promise left broken and humiliated.

The nadir appeared to be the defeat to Yugoslavia in the second game. Midway through the first half, with Zaire already losing 3–0, the goalkeeper, Mwamba Kazadi, was substituted. Zaire's coach, Blagoje Vidinić, would later reveal he made the change on the orders of the sports ministry officials sitting in the stands. It made little difference. The new keeper barely had a chance to touch the ball before Yugoslavia scored their fourth. A fifth and sixth followed before half-time; a seventh, eighth and ninth in the second half.

But worse, far worse, was to follow in the final match against Brazil.

The world champions were already 3–0 up when they won a free kick on the edge of the Zairean penalty area. As Rivelino stood over the ball, the Zairean defenders in the wall edged closer to him. As the referee blew his whistle and Rivelino prepared his run up, Mpewu Ilunga, one of the defenders in the wall, suddenly broke free and sprinted towards the ball. Ilunga beat Rivelino to it and, to the astonishment of the Brazilians, the referee, the crowd and Ilunga's teammates, he blasted the ball halfway down the pitch.

It was a moment that would be replayed endlessly – a moment that suggested that not only were African teams not very good at football but that they didn't even know the rules.

The truth was rather more complicated. Months earlier, Zaire's dictator, Mobutu Sésé Seko, had hailed the players as heroes when they qualified for the World Cup by beating Morocco 3–0 in Kinshasa. He invited the players to his presidential palace and awarded them houses, cars and envelopes stuffed with $100 notes. But while Mobutu basked in the reflected glory of a successful football team, he feared failure at the World Cup would heap embarrassment on his country and, more importantly, his leadership.

Following the humiliation against Yugoslavia Mobutu sent some of his presidential guards to West Germany to give the players a message: lose by four goals against Brazil and you can't come home. Ilunga's apparent act of madness was more an act of desparation. The team was prepared to do anything to restore some pride and escape Mobutu's punishment.

*

Zaire was originally known as Congo. One of the largest countries in Africa, it stretches for more than 1,800 miles from the Atlantic Ocean in the west to the shores of the Great Lakes – Tanganyika, Albert and Kivu – that border Uganda, Rwanda and Tanzania in the east.

It was carved out as the personal fiefdom of King Leopold II of Belgium, who plundered Congo's rubber and ivory. King Leopold's reign cost the lives of an estimated ten million Congolese between 1885 and 1908, one of the worst acts of barbarism the world had ever witnessed.

The 'winds of change' which Harold Macmillan said were sweeping across Africa in the late 1950s were felt in Congo too. Belgium's rule was increasingly unpopular in Congo and independence was finally granted on 30 June 1960.

At the ceremony marking the handover, King Baudouin foolishly referred to his great-uncle, Leopold II, as a 'genius'. Patrice Lumumba, the charismatic and popular liberation leader – who had just been made prime minister – angrily turned to the king. 'We are no longer your monkeys,' he said.

Belgium had greatly benefited from Congo's vast mineral wealth. Not letting the small matter of independence get in its way, within a fortnight of the ceremony thousands of Belgian troops had helped to annex Katanga, the province in southeastern Congo that was home to most of the country's minerals.

Lumumba, frustrated at a perceived lack of support from the United Nations, turned to the Soviet Union for help. It was the height of the Cold War, two years before the Cuban Missile Crisis. The USA was not about to let Congo 'turn red'. They found a willing ally in Mobutu, then the Chief of Staff to the Army.

By the start of 1961 Lumumba was dead and Mobutu had carried out a coup. He kept the figurehead president, Joseph Kasavubu, in office until 1965, when, with the full support of the CIA, he finally decided to take power for himself.

Mobutu had been born Joseph-Désiré Mobutu, but in 1972 – a year after he switched Congo's name to Zaire – he changed his own name to Mobutu Sésé Seko Nkuku Ngbendu Wa Za Banga or 'the all-powerful warrior who goes from conquest to conquest, leaving fire in his wake'.

'All-powerful warriors' don't tend to have much time for democracy. Mobutu was officially elected three times during the 1970s and 1980s, but the polls were not what anyone would call free or fair. At the last election in 1984 voters were given the choice of picking a green card or a red card in front of government officials. Green meant a vote for prosperity and Mobutu; red was a vote for total destruction. At many polling stations red cards were not even available. Mobutu won more than 99 per cent of the vote.

Mobutu, rarely seen without his leopard-skin hat, became the archetypal African 'big man', ruling for thirty-two years and stealing billions of pounds from the state coffers. While many of his people starved, Mobutu built himself palaces across the country and bought mansions in Europe. His home village,

Gbadolite, was transformed – not only did Mobutu build one of his presidential palaces there, he also had a runway installed that was long enough to land Concorde.

The USA didn't seem to mind, though, and backed him until the end of the Cold War. They believed Mobutu was a strong anti-Communist, and that was good enough for them. Ronald Reagan praised Mobutu as a 'voice of good sense and goodwill'.

But with the demise of the Soviet Union and the subsequent end of the 'Soviet threat' in Africa, Mobutu lost his usefulness. Western aid dried up and the country began to slide towards bankruptcy. Mobutu and his generals had plundered the state's coffers, killing the golden goose. Mining production in Katanga, which had once produced 80 per cent of the country's GDP, was almost non-existent.

And then events next door in Rwanda pushed Mobutu's regime to the brink.

*

On 6 April 1994 a plane carrying Juvénal Habyarimana, Rwanda's president, was shot down over Kigali, killing everyone on board. Within hours a genocide had begun. Over the next hundred days an estimated 800,000 Tutsis and moderate Hutus were slaughtered by extremist Hutu militias.

The country had been racked with ethnic tension between Hutus and Tutsis for decades. Belgium had favoured the minority Tutsis for administrative roles, and some of the Hutu leaders who took power following independence in 1960 stoked fears of an 'enemy within' that wanted to win back control. Tutsi politicians were arrested, villages were attacked and thousands of civilians were forced to flee.

Habyarimana, who took power in a coup in 1973, upped the volume of the anti-Tutsi propaganda and dramatically increased the size of the armed forces.

But following the end of the Cold War, the West began to push for democratic reforms across Africa. Habyarimana found himself under pressure to introduce multi-party elections and negotiate with the Rwandan Patriotic Front (RPF), a rebel group made up of Tutsi refugees who had fled to Uganda, whose leader was a wiry yet steely intellectual called Paul Kagame.

Habyarimana began talking about peace deals and elections, talk which didn't please all his allies. Espousing a philosophy of 'Hutu power', influential people within the armed forces and the government began to discuss plans to wipe out the Tutsis once and for all as well as their Hutu 'collaborators'.

Radio stations were launched which broadcast virulent anti-Tutsi propaganda. Weapons, mainly machetes, were bought in vast numbers and stored across the country. A youth militia was established, called the Interahamwe. Lists of Tutsis were drawn up. All it needed was a spark, which Habyarimana's death conveniently provided.

A UN peacekeeping force had been sent to Rwanda earlier in the year to oversee the implementation of the peace accord which had been signed between Habyarimana and Kagame. The force, known as UNAMIR, had been hamstrung from the start, lacking the funding, troops and mandate it needed to do its job. After the catastrophe in Somalia few within the

UN had the stomach for an intervention in another African conflict.

UNAMIR's commander, a Canadian called Roméo Dallaire, watched in horror as the genocide unfolded, unable to do anything to prevent it. Even as it became clear that Rwanda's Tutsi population was being exterminated, the West did little. Dallaire's request for more troops and a stronger mandate were ignored.

The RPF, led by Kagame, entered Rwanda from the north and headed for Kigali. They managed to take control of the capital and force the Hutu extremists to flee, but by that stage the damage had been done. The quickest genocide in history was over.

The *genocidaires* headed west in search of a safe haven and crossed the border into Zaire. Mobutu had provided support for Habyarimana and now gave those responsible for the genocide a place to regroup. At the same time some 2 million Hutu refugees also crossed the border, creating one of the largest humanitarian catastrophes the world had ever seen.

Although the genocide had ended, the crisis for central Africa had just begun. Kagame's Rwandan forces invaded Zaire in 1996 with the aim of tracking down the Hutu extremists. For Kagame, Zaire's ailing dictator was part of the problem.

Rwanda and Uganda gave their backing to a Zairean rebel leader, Laurent Kabila, who had led a series of failed rebellions against Mobutu in the mid-1960s. A small, fat man with little military training, Kabila was not the archetypal rebel. Che Guevara had spent several months working alongside Kabila in the 1960s but became so disillusioned he had returned to South America.

This time though, Kabila would be successful. The combination of Rwanda and Uganda's superior forces and the failure of Mobutu to pay his troops allowed Kabila to march on Kinshasa. On 17 May 1997 Mobutu fled and his government collapsed. It would not be the last time that Kagame would send troops into Congo. Over the next twelve years his forces would carry out a series of operations across the border – some publicised, others secret. Meanwhile, Rwanda's new leader went about rebuilding his country.

*

Since the genocide ended, Kigali, Rwanda's hillside capital, has changed beyond recognition. Kagame's government is one of the few in this region that has seriously encouraged private investment. It is remarkably simple to set up a business, there is a zero tolerance attitude to corruption and the government has been prepared to spend millions on infrastructure such as roads and high-speed Internet.

The country has also benefited from former refugees returning home. One of those is Arthur Karuletwa, the owner of Bourbon Coffee. As we sat in one of his three Kigali outlets, Karuletwa told me how he decided to return because 'there was a calling to come back and play a role in reconciliation'.

He had spent eight years in Seattle, the home of Starbucks, which is where the idea of setting up a coffee company in Rwanda came to him. The country has some of the best coffee in Africa but until recently it was poorly marketed, even to fellow Rwandans. Karuletwa has helped to change that. He has grown his business from one shop to three and now has his sights set on opening stores in the United States and Europe. He is not the only ex-refugee to come home and make a difference.

'There are people returning from all over the world and they are full of all kinds of ideas,' he says. 'Someone has been in Germany and takes a great idea from there, someone else has been in Britain, someone else in America. What we used to see as a plight – being a refugee – has become a positive.'

The original Bourbon Coffee shop is in the UTC, a modern shopping centre in the heart of Kigali. But outside the UTC there is little of the hustle and bustle I was accustomed to seeing in African cities. The motorbike taxis waited patiently for business, rarely arguing over a customer. Hawkers selling newspapers or mobile phone scratchcards politely offered their wares without saying a word. There was a silence to the city that was slightly uneasy. It was as if something terrible had happened and no one wanted to talk about it. Which, in a sense, is exactly right.

Football crowds are rarely quiet though. One Saturday afternoon I went to Kigali's Amahoro Stadium to watch Rwanda's under-20 side play Ghana in the African Youth Championship.

During the genocide this had been one of the UN bases. Dallaire had allowed thousands of Tutsi refugees through the gates, offering them what little protection he could while the killing that he couldn't stop went on outside. As I stared at the pitch, wondering what it must have been like to sleep there underneath the stars, waiting for help to come, I watched a small band of supporters dressed in yellow and blue make their way to the centre of the stand opposite me. It was the official supporters' club, the people you find at almost every international match who are paid by the FA or a sponsor to rouse the rest of the crowd.

As the rest of the stadium began to fill, the supporters' club continued singing and dancing. But unlike in other countries I had been to, no one else joined in. At the very least the fans around a club tend to get carried away, but here I could tell exactly where the club members started and stopped.

As the match progressed I became more interested in watching the fans than the players. They would get behind the team when they were on the attack, but they never got too excited. Maybe if Rwanda had scored it would have been different. As it was, Ghana won 2–0, both goals scored by Ransford Osei, a striker who would go on to help his country win the Under-20 World Cup in Egypt later that year.

At the final whistle, the crowd politely applauded and made their way home, including the man in the VIP box, President Kagame.

★

Like everything in Rwanda, the country's football team had to be completely rebuilt following the 1994 genocide. The country didn't enter a team for the African Nations in 1996 or 1998, but the football association felt able to start again for the 2000 tournament. The campaign was over by half-time in the first match. After forty-five minutes they were 3–0 down to Uganda and went on to lose 5–0. The second leg in Kigali was irrelevant, and Rwanda were out.

They fared little better in the qualifying campaign for the 2002 tournament, going out in the preliminary round again, this time losing 6–2 on aggregate to Congo-Brazzaville.

But Rwanda's national football team had an important supporter. Kagame is a big football fan and he was prepared to spend money on the team, despite the pressures to spend elsewhere. The team also benefited from the relaxed view taken of nationality. It was perhaps a little strange in a country where nationality and ethnicity had been such a potent issue, but many of those who turned out for the Wasps, as the national team is known, hadn't been born in the country. It was part of a deliberate strategy by the football association to recruit talent. So many young men had either been killed or forced to flee in 1994 that they felt this was the only way to replenish the pool. Some of the players came from Uganda and Burundi – more came from Congo.

The borders between Rwanda and Congo have long been porous. For decades a steady stream of Rwandans – frustrated at the lack of arable land in their tiny, overcrowded country – have migrated west across the border into North and South Kivu, the mineral-rich, fertile regions which lie at Congo's easternmost tip. This migration has led to outbreaks of violence and has created a long history of distrust between the two countries, a distrust only further entrenched by Rwanda's military incursions into Congo following the genocide. But it has also created hundreds of thousands of people who see themselves as both Rwandan and Congolese.

The two countries are chalk and cheese. Congo is big, messy and rich in resources. Rwanda is tiny, well organised and resource-poor. The same is true for its football. Congo should be continental giants, while Rwanda should be minnows. But for Congolese footballers with Rwandan heritage it makes more sense to play for Kagame's team than Kabila's.

At the 2004 Africa Cup of Nations, Ramadhani Nkunzingoma, Rwanda's goalkeeper, summed up the emotions that many of his team-mates were experiencing. 'In my head I feel Congolese,' he admitted to the BBC. It was hardly a surprise. Nkunzingoma, like several of his team-mates, *was* Congolese.

It was the first time Rwanda had qualified for the Africa Cup of Nations. Congo were there, too. Since the end of Mobutu's reign Congo had enjoyed a modicum of success, reaching the quarter-finals of the African Nations five times in the 1990s and 2000s, and even making it to the semis in 1998.

But despite having footballers like Lomana LuaLua, who played in the English Premier League, the team had been undermined by grand incompetence and corruption. Players and coaches didn't get paid. Development programmes fell apart.

The country's golden era had occurred in the early years of Mobutu's reign. The national side won the Africa Cup of Nations in 1968, and a few months before their World Cup disaster in 1974 secured the Nations Cup again, beating Zambia 2–0 in a replayed final. TP Mazembe, a club side from Katanga Province, reached the final of the African Champions Cup in four consecutive years, from 1967 to 1970, winning the trophy twice. But like everything in Congo, football suffered the longer Mobutu's reign went on.

There were sixteen teams in the 2004 tournament, split into four groups of four. Somewhat inevitably, Rwanda and Congo ended up in the same group. As if that wasn't enough, they were scheduled to play each other last. By the time they met, qualification for the quarter-finals was almost beyond Rwanda. They had lost narrowly to the hosts, Tunisia, before gaining a respectable 1–1 draw against Guinea. Congo's campaign, on the other hand, had been a disaster. They had lost both their matches, meaning the final game against Rwanda would just be a matter of pride.

It was a match which Congo should have won comfortably. Several of their players were contracted to European clubs, while most of the Rwandan team played in their local league.

There was only one goal, late in the game, and it was scored by Said Makasi, who was born and raised in Bukavu on the Congolese side of Lake Kivu, which lies between the two countries. Makasi, though, was one of the Congolese players in the Rwandan team. His goal sparked wild celebrations in Kigali – and riots in his home town of Bukavu. Fans watching the match at bars in Bukavu, who had spent most of the match labelling him and his fellow Congolese Rwandans 'prostitutes', tracked down Makasi's parents' house and burned it to the ground.

*

Not many cities could take the beatings that Goma has had and survive. Not only has it been at the epicentre of most of Congo's conflicts, it also seems to have got on the wrong side of Mother Nature.

Mount Nyiragongo, a volcano, looms over the city. On 17 January 2002 lava burst through the sides of the volcano, raced down the hill and swept into the city, knocking over trees, buildings and cars. Around 400,000 people were evacuated across the border into Rwanda, but the volcano claimed forty-five lives. The lava eventually covered almost 20 per cent of the city, and it's still there today, swathes of inky black scars striping roads and fields. Once the lava had cooled, Goma's citizens simply built on top of it.

As if the volcano isn't enough of a problem for Goma's residents, there's also Lake Kivu. It looks beautiful, but the build-up of methane gas under the surface threatens to cause an even greater catastrophe next time the volcano erupts. Any major geological shifts could release the gas, creating a poisonous cloud which could asphyxiate Goma's 250,000 residents.

Congo's elections were supposed to signal a fresh start for the country. When Laurent Kabila ousted Mobutu he changed its name to the Democratic Republic of Congo. But like most countries with the word 'democratic' in their title (the Democratic People's Republic of Korea and the German Democratic Republic spring to mind), elections were never scheduled.

Instead, Congo suffered another devastating war. Rwanda and Uganda refused to leave the east, hoping to carve up the region's minerals. Kabila sought new allies – Angola and Zimbabwe – both of which were promised diamonds and gold in return for their military support. It turned into Africa's bloodiest war, a conflict that at one stage dragged in the majority of Congo's eight neighbours and still rumbles on in 2010. It is estimated to have cost the lives of some 5.4

million people – more than any other conflict since the Second World War.

Kabila was assassinated in 2001. His son, Jospeh, was just twenty-nine but was installed as his successor. Within a year a peace deal had been signed with the warring factions in the east and elections were planned. The world's largest UN force, known by its French acronym MONUC, stationed more than 17,000 peacekeepers across the country and the international community agreed to fund the election – Congo's first in more than forty years – to the tune of $500 million.

By the time the elections took place in July 2006, Joseph Kabila, the incumbent, was the overwhelming favourite. He wasn't popular in the capital, Kinshasa, where many people suspected he was not truly Congolese. But where I was, in the east, he was – and I don't think this is too strong a word – loved. Unlike the other presidential contenders, who were all former warlords, Kabila Jnr was seen as a peacemaker.

There was a sense of real excitement across the country. The elections had been sold to the population as a panacea for all ills. Roads would be built, schools and hospitals constructed, teachers and nurses hired and trained. Programmes to disarm former militiamen and provide them with capital were under way. Change was in the air.

*

The night before the election I wandered down to the border post about 200 yards from my hotel. The border was due to be closed on election day. A steady stream of people were crossing into Congo from

Rwanda to make sure they were able to vote. Some lived in Goma but worked in Rwanda, but most of those who were coming across now were part of that nebulous group of people who were both Rwandan and Congolese.

On election day the UN organised a trip for foreign journalists. We travelled by helicopter to three different polling stations across North Kivu. At the first two everything appeared to be going well. The queues were long but peaceful, and international and local observers thought that everything seemed to be working properly. We got back into the helicopter and headed for the third and final destination. After fifteen minutes in the air the helicopter banked sharply to the right and started to circle.

Below us there was a field and what looked like a polling station. We continued to circle for another ten minutes. 'Does the pilot know where he's going?' someone asked.

We landed and it quickly became clear that no, the pilot had no idea where he was going. He had seen the crowd and assumed this was our polling station.

It wasn't. More than a thousand people crowded around the helicopter and watched in silence as we disembarked. It soon became clear we had landed deep in the heart of territory belonging to the FDLR, a rebel group made up of former Rwandan Hutu militias who had taken part in the genocide. This was not a place where the UN was welcome. The crowd was friendly but bemused. Few aid workers ever came here either, which made our white skin something of a novelty.

As a slightly panicked UN official shepherded us back onto the helicopter, I noticed something strange about the crowd. There were five boys wearing identical yellow Arsenal away shirts with 'Henry 14' on the back. As I climbed the steps I looked back. In fact there were more Henry shirts. At least ten. No, twenty. Hang on, thirty!

It may have been a forgotten corner of Congo, so obscure that even the UN hadn't made it there, but Thierry Henry certainly had.

That night I sat in an old school classroom in Goma watching the votes being counted. By the dim light of a paraffin lamp and under the watchful eye of a dozen polling agents, a Congolese election official carefully scanned a ballot paper, as large as a small tablecloth, before holding it up for all to see. A cross had been scrawled next to Joseph Kabila's name.

The polling agents dutifully, if a little wearily, noted it down. They had started four hours earlier, when the sky above Goma was still light. A pile of ballot papers was yet to be counted, but they all knew that Kabila's name would be marked on most of them.

Congo-watchers had expected Kabila to do well, but not this well. In some polling stations, including this one in a run-down school near a mansion built by Mobutu, Kabila won more than 95 per cent of the vote. But in the days that followed it became clear that his support in the west was far lower and that the election would require a run-off between Kabila and the one-time warlord Jean-Pierre Bemba three months later.

Kabila won with 58 per cent of the vote. Despite the fears of the Congolese people I interviewed, the election appeared to have gone off without a major hitch. The international community looked forward to a peaceful and democratic Congo.

When I returned to Goma two years later, though, little had changed. The roads were as full of potholes as they had ever been. The promised new schools and hospitals had not materialised. And some of Congo's myriad rebel groups were threatening to return to war.

As ever, it was the children who had suffered the most. Child soldiers have been used in wars and conflicts across the world, but the problem is worse here. Around 8,000 children are believed to be used as soldiers and porters in Congo's numerous militia groups, while an estimated 31,000 were demobilised between 1999 and 2009.

Almost 200 former child soldiers were living at a reception centre called CAJED in Goma. I spent an afternoon there, watching them play football and conducting a few interviews. All but two were boys, most of them aged thirteen to seventeen, although there were a few who were as young as ten.

Earlier that morning forty children had been returned home to their families. There was an odd, tense atmosphere at the centre. Some of the children were angry that they hadn't been allowed to go home. Others had been at the centre for just a few days and were still adjusting to not being in a militia.

The football match, which took place on the muddy courtyard in front of a row of classrooms, was more aggressive than other kickabouts I'd watched. I was viewed with suspicion by a group of older boys who stood behind one of the goals.

The children had come from a range of different militia groups, including the army. Some had escaped, while others were brought here when their units voluntarily disarmed, as all were being encouraged to do. They were given a programme of counselling and some basic vocational training. Most were keen to 'become citizens', Fidele Rutabagisha, the centre's director, told me. 'There are those who want to rejoin, but it is only a few,' he said.

The boys shared rooms, sleeping in bunk beds. Nightmares were not uncommon. 'Most of them have killed,' Fidele said.

He introduced me to a boy called Patrick. He was twelve years old and wore a green T-shirt with a picture of an eagle on it. He had a cheeky grin and swung his legs as he sat on a wooden chair. His tale was not unusual. While some children had been kidnapped and forced to join militias, many actually chose to join. For some it was a way to protect their family; for others – like Patrick – it was for a wage. After his father died, Patrick's mother could no longer afford his school fees. Nor were there any jobs. So one day Patrick turned up at a camp for a militia group called PARECO, a Hutu group aligned to the FDLR, and asked to join.

I'd interviewed several former child soldiers in the past. They tended to appear more soldier than child, no matter how old they were. Patrick was different. He described his battles as if he was recounting pretend war games he'd played with his friends. As he was trying to explain what had happened in his last battle, he made the noise of gunfire – 'ka-ka-ka-ka!' – and suddenly jumped off the chair and got down on his stomach, pretending to fire a gun as he crawled through the bush.

The battle began at five in the morning and lasted all day. There were forty fighters on Patrick's side, most of them not much older than him. Over the course of the day ten people in Patrick's unit were killed, some of whom he had grown up with. 'I had a fear,' he said, still crouched on the floor as if hiding behind a tree. 'But it was not possible to go back. I had to revenge my friends who had been killed.'

He claimed he killed ten people that day. 'They were our enemies. I killed them,' he said, a touch defiantly.

For most of the year he spent with PARECO he was happy. Compared to life in the village, things weren't too bad. He was given a week of basic military training ('how to move when you are fighting, how to use a gun and how to escape when you are surrounded'), but initially he was used as a cook, making simple meals of beans, yams and cassava for the other soldiers.

After a while, though, he was pressed into front-line duty. His bravado gently faded away the longer we talked. 'In that moment, for me, it was power. To see someone get killed. Now I am regretting. Why did I do this?'

Along with three other boys he hatched a plan to escape. Two weeks ago they had sneaked out of the camp just after midnight, taking civilian clothes with them. They changed out of their military uniforms and hid out in a village a couple of miles from the camp. The next morning they headed for the nearest UN compound and knocked on the door.

*

Congo's militia groups do not operate in a vacuum. PARECO is just one of several operating in the east of the country. Like the FDLR they are made up of

Hutus, some of whom bore some responsibility for the Rwandan genocide. The FDLR has long threatened to re-invade Rwanda, a threat which Kagame has used to excuse his country's regular incursions across the border.

Although Rwandan forces eventually left Congo, they left in place militias which had their full support. One of those was led by a man called Laurent Nkunda. His rebel group, the CNDP, claimed to be fighting for the rights of Congolese Tutsis, but in reality it was little more than a front for Rwanda's political and commercial interests.

Nkunda is a complex character. Born in Congo to Rwandan parents, he studied psychology before joining the Tutsi rebellion in Rwanda which eventually ousted the Hutu regime. He fought alongside Rwandan forces when they first invaded Congo in 1996 and subsequently led Rwanda's proxies when they left. Under one of the many peace deals he became a brigadier-general and was supposed to join the Congolese army. He refused to sign up, however. Instead, he launched an attack on Bukavu, the capital of South Kivu. His men raped, pillaged and killed – just as they had when he carried out a similar attack on the city of Kisangani.

Nkunda insisted, though, that he was a man of peace. And a farmer too. He claimed to own hundreds of cows which produced milk and cheese that were sold in Goma's markets.

The first thing he asked me when I met him in 2006 was whether I took sugar with my milk. He picked up a flask and began to pour a big mug of milk. 'It's from my cows,' he said. 'Fresh.' It was surprisingly tasty. He also had a pet goat, called Betty.

Getting to meet Nkunda had not been easy. Like most rebels he was media-friendly, but the logistics of arranging an interview in his mountain hideaway were complicated. Two battalions of Nkunda's rebels had joined the national army yet still took orders from their former commander. I was put in touch with one of Nkunda's men, Lieutenant Blaise, who agreed to take me through the army checkpoints.

We drove out of Goma early one morning and headed towards Sake, a small town about twelve miles down the road. The first checkpoint was controlled by the Congolese armed forces, the FARDC. Lt Blaise waved and smiled as we approached, and the barrier was lifted. The next checkpoint, about 500 yards further down the road, was manned by the UN. An Indian soldier took our ID and asked where we were going. 'Masisi,' I said, which was half true. 'Okay,' he replied and nodded us through.

The third roadblock came ten minutes later, just after we entered Sake. The soldiers wore a mix of types of camouflage; some were in wellington boots, while others wore flip-flops. They greeted Blaise like an old friend and lifted up the wooden plank which had been laid on two crates in the middle of the road. We were entering rebel territory.

We drove higher into the mountains and deeper into the jungle. At last, some six hours after we had left Goma, the Land Cruiser pulled up at a gate. Blaise got out to talk to the guard, and we were waved through into Nkunda's camp.

His base was full of large *tukuls*, circular brick buildings with thatched roofs. This had once been a tourist spot, Blaise said. We were deep in the mountains, surrounded by lush green forest. If you ignored the men with guns, it was incredibly peaceful.

We were ushered into one of the *tukuls*, where a dozen or so of Nkunda's men stood around chatting. The atmosphere was relaxed. They smiled and nodded when we walked in.

Nkunda had two other guests waiting to see him: black South African men, both dressed in smart trousers and white shirts. 'Are you journalists?' I asked. The men looked at each other and smiled. There was a pause. 'Diplomats,' one of them finally replied. They were ushered in to see Nkunda and left fifteen minutes later, grinning broadly.

Blaise came back in. 'The general is ready,' he said.

Nkunda greeted me outside a smaller *tukul* overlooking fields of brilliant greens. A few cows wandered nearby, a reminder that Nkunda liked to see himself as a farmer. He was a tall, slender man, neatly turned out in green military fatigues and carrying a silver-tipped cane. He ushered me into his *tukul*. Nkunda sat on a wooden chair while six of his men stood around him, Kalashnikovs at the ready.

After he had offered me milk, we talked for more than an hour and a half about his background, the wars, the future.

He had studied psychology before joining Kagame's army when they invaded Congo to oust Mobutu. Rwanda was a friend, he said, but it did not provide him with any support. 'I am fighting for the people of Congo,' he insisted, 'not Rwanda.'

He was prepared to talk to Joseph Kabila.

'We do not want to fight,' he said, 'but we are also ready to fight.'

Two mugs of milk later, Nkunda showed me his cows. 'They are some of the best cows in Congo,' he said. 'You must try some of the cheese.' One of his men went off to find some cheese, returning with a large ball of what looked like Gouda.

Three years later, in 2009, Nkunda's forces threatened to take control of Goma. A UN report pointedly accused Rwanda of funding Nkunda and providing him with weapons. Within a month of the report being published, Kagame decided to drop Nkunda once and for all. He was arrested, taken to Kigali and held under house arrest. For Kagame, Laurent Nkunda had outlived his usefulness.

There were plenty of people to replace him, though. The mix of rebel groups in eastern Congo was still as volatile as ever. Although 2009 was technically a peaceful year, thousands were still killed in skirmishes across the region. If there was one bright spot to be found in Congo, it was in Lubumbashi, a few hundred miles further south.

*

The governor of Katanga, a province in Congo the size of France, isn't happy. Moise Katumbi's football team, TP Mazembe, are losing 2–0. Resplendent in his all-white suit, a TP Mazembe crest sewn onto his blazer, he rises from his straight-backed leather chair in the VIP box the moment the half-time whistle blows and makes his way quickly down towards the dressing room, a look of fury clouding his face.

It's the semi-final of the African Champions League. Mazembe won the first leg against Al-Hilal of Khartoum 5–2, so even if the score remains 2–0 in the second leg Mazembe will go through to the final for the first time since 1970.

Katumbi expects a good performance, though. Thirty-five thousand fans have crammed into the Kenya Stadium in Lubumbashi, and so far they've been disappointed. This doesn't look like the best team in Africa, which is what Katumbi is determined to turn them into.

Katumbi's philosophy appears to rely on money – if you spend enough then things will get better. It's a policy he has employed for his football club, where he has put aside £3 million to bankroll the Champions League campaign. But it's also the method he has used for his province, Katanga.

When he took over in 2007 the province had no ambulances, so Katumbi dipped into his own pocket and bought sixty. Nor were there any hearses, so he bought some of those too. Despite not having the power to do so, he brought in a minimum wage of $150 a month, which most companies tried to keep to. He sometimes turns up at the tax office at eight o'clock in the morning to go over the figures himself – and check that his civil servants have arrived on time.

He operates like a village chief writ large, his hand never far from a pocket full of $100 notes, which he distributes liberally to aides and those who ask for his help.

He proudly told me that he won his election with 98.8 per cent of the vote, and in the few days I spent following him around Lubumbashi he seemed pretty determined to win the remaining 1.2 per cent.

He made his money through mining in a series of quarries across Katanga, and he isn't afraid to spend it. The driveway at his residence is filled with expensive new Audis, BMWs and Mercedes, and a six-foot-tall pyramid of emerald-green malakite stands in the middle of his reception room. As he shows me around his residence, he keeps one eye on a giant plasma screen broadcasting the local news. Katumbi breaks off from his conversation whenever the anchor introduces an item about himself. As Katumbi owns the television station this happens quite a lot.

Katumbi plays tennis every morning on his private court. Six members of his staff operate as ball boys and umpire. A wall along two sides of the court is decorated with a mural depicting Katumbi's life. It shows him on a jet ski on the lake by his rural home, fighting off a crocodile by the river and hitting an ace on the tennis court.

His real passion, though, is football. In the late 1960s Mazembe had been African champions two years running. Katumbi's dream was to bring the glory days back to Lubumbashi and win the African Champions League. He lavished money on the team, providing wages similar to those at second-tier English clubs. Win bonuses for Champions League matches amounted to thousands of pounds for each player.

Although he has been able to bring in talent from other African countries, the majority of the squad are Congolese. The club's youth programme has around 2,000 players, one of whom he thinks could be a global star. 'He's called Pele Pele and he's better than Messi,' he exclaimed. 'I'm sure.'

Katumbi's coach is a Frenchman called Diego Garzitto, who has coached in Africa twice before. He doesn't have particularly happy memories of either experience. His stint as national coach of Togo ended after one match – a 3–0 defeat to Kenya in Nairobi. He didn't last much longer in Ethiopia. Brought in on a two-year contract, he was pushed out after less than two months.

'They still owe me money,' he says, when we meet at a hotel the night before an African Champions League match.

'How much?' I ask.

'All of it! They owe me £125,000! Big problem!'

With Katumbi in charge there are no money problems at Mazembe. More importantly, Garzitto feels he has been able to build a strong team.

'When we started playing in the Champions League, our objective was just to be one of the good teams. Now we realise we can win the cup.'

Some of his players will end up playing in Europe, but he has had to work hard to get them into shape. 'Congolese footballers lack discipline and preparation. They are very good compared to other countries, but it is still a problem.' To counter it, he has taken his team to tournaments in Sudan and Zambia to help prepare them for the Champions League. He seems to have got a grip on discipline too. All of the players drift off to their rooms at 8.30 after dinner.

One is allowed to stay up to talk to me: Trésor Mputu, the team's star player. He had trials with Arsenal in 2008, but Mazembe officials claim the London club's bid of £1.25 million wasn't high enough. Everyone expects him to leave for Europe after the Champions League, though.

Unlike most African footballers still playing in their home country, Trésor's desire to move to Europe has little to do with money. Thanks to Katumbi's largesse he earns a basic salary of £10,000 a month plus substantial win bonuses in Champions League matches.

Trésor is one of the most famous footballers in Congo. His face is plastered across billboards advertising Primus beer, and he has become a regular in the national team, keeping players based in Europe out of the side. For the past two years he has been Congo's Player of the Year.

As he lounges in an armchair, occasionally fiddling with the diamond stud in his left ear, he ticks off a familiar catalogue of administrative failings, from lack of budget to lack of respect for players, that he believes have held the national team back. 'It's a dream of every player to reach the World Cup, and we have a big chance because our players are very good,' he says. 'But the organisation is very bad.'

Congo's other problem is that two of the best players in Europe seem to find it impossible to play in the same team. If Shabani Nonda, who plays for the Turkish side Galatasaray, is called up, Lomana LuaLua isn't, and vice versa. 'These two men have a problem,' says Trésor. 'They don't like each other, and they both want to be captain. In the national team everyone should play for the flag, for the honour of the country.'

Trésor was part of the Congolese team that had recently won the inaugural African Nations Championship. It's a tournament that sounds a lot more important than it is. The majority of players in the Africa *Cup* of Nations ply their trade in European leagues. So the Championship, known as CHAN, was launched to provide an outlet for players who remained at home.

A lot of countries sent weak squads or didn't even bother entering, but for the Congolese, twelve of whom played for TP Mazembe, it was an opportunity

Kenya's prime minister, Raila Odinga, meets the national team's star player, Dennis Oliech. Following the post-election violence which ripped the country apart in 2008 Kenyan football fans chanted Odinga and Oliech's name together, alongside that of another famous Luo, Barack Obama. *Photo by Mohammed Amin.*

(PREVIOUS PAGE) A goal celebration copied in playgrounds and Sunday League matches across the world. Roger Milla's goals took Cameroon to the World Cup quarter-finals and forced the rest of the world to take African football seriously.

Photo by Henri Szwarc (Bongarts/Getty Images).

Few rivalries are as fierce as Egypt v Algeria. The two countries met in a play-off in Sudan to decide which team would qualify for the 2010 World Cup. Algeria won 1–0 but the political fallout led to riots in four cities. © Mohamed Messara/epa/Corbis.

A rare sign of normality in one of the world's most dangerous cities. Thousands of people are killed in Mogadishu every year, but the Somali Football Federation still manages to put a national team together. When there is a lull in the fighting the streets fill with young boys playing football. Photo by Jehad Nga.

I met Patrick at a child-soldier rehabilitation centre in Goma, eastern Congo. He was just twelve years old, and had the cheeky grin of a child, but had already taken part in several appalling battles.   *Photo by Sarah Elliott.*

Nigeria's greatest footballer and one of the country's most popular figures. Kanu led Nigeria to the Olympic title in 1996, beating Argentina 3–2 in the final with a last-minute winner. *Photo by Bob Thomas (Getty Images)*.

Didier Drogba is escorted off the pitch following Côte d'Ivoire's 5–0 victory over Madagascar in an Africa Cup of Nations qualifier in Bouaké. The game, which took place in the former capital of the rebel-held north, was widely seen as the moment Ivorians believed peace would hold. *Photo by Issouf Sanogo (AFP/Getty Images)*.

Liberian amputees, who lost limbs in the country's brutal civil war, train on a sandy pitch in Monrovia. The national team won the amputee version of the Africa Cup of Nations in 2008. *Photo by Glenna Gordon.*

Bafana Bafana line up for the South African national anthem. Matthew Booth, centre, has become one of the country's biggest stars. *Photo by Jasper Juinen (Getty Images).*

Me on the pitch at the end of the 2008 East and Central African Cup in Uganda talking to Bobby Williamson, the Scottish manager of the Ugandan national team. He is texting his family to tell them his team won. Moments later there was a power cut and the stadium was plunged into darkness. *Photo by Frederic Courbet.*

(OVERLEAF) South Africa's multiracial national football team celebrates winning the Africa Cup of Nations in Johannesburg in 1996. Nelson Mandela, wearing the Bafana Bafana shirt, is in his element; FW de Klerk, wearing a suit, less so.

Photo by Per-Anders Pettersson (Getty Images).

to make up for their dismal performances in the World Cup and Africa Cup of Nations qualifiers.

Victory over Ghana at the final in March 2009 sparked wild celebrations back home. Up to a million people lined the streets when the team returned to Kinshasa, and President Kabila gave each player a brand-new Toyota Prado and an envelope stuffed with US dollars.

'How much?' I asked Trésor. 'Not telling,' he laughed.

He was pleased the team had won, but victory in the Champions League would be far more important, he said. And probably more lucrative too. Most of Katumbi's £3 million budget has been spent on win bonuses. Each victory earns the players a share of £150,000 – around £8,500 for each member of the eighteen-man squad.

The team are in danger of losing their bonuses in the semi-final against Al-Hilal, though.

In the dressing room Garzitto begins the team talk. The players have been too confident, he says. They think they have reached the final already. The talk is subdued and the players don't react. Katumbi takes over. This isn't good enough, he insists, striding around the room. You're embarrassing me.

The players are listening now. The governor makes some changes, switching the two wide midfielders and telling the defence to play a bit deeper. Garzitto sits on a chair behind Katumbi and nods in agreement.

Before leaving the dressing room to take his seat for the second half, the governor gathers the players in a huddle and leads a prayer for victory. It seems to be just enough to pull them through. Although Mazembe play a lot better in the second half, they don't manage to break down Al-Hilal's defence. At least they don't concede another goal. The match finishes in a 2–0 defeat, which means Mazembe go through to the final on aggregate.

Whenever Mazembe wins, the governor throws a party at his residence. The local brewery, Brasimba, has a truck on standby filled with dozens of kegs of Simba beer plus a five-foot-tall bottle of champagne. There won't be a party tonight, though. In the grounds of the residence Katumbi is sitting with a face of thunder, ignoring the glass of champagne by his side. The players turn up in the team bus, but an aide is dispatched to tell them the party is off. Garzitto, the coach, shows up and is given the cold shoulder by Katumbi. Garzitto sits on his own in the corner, gulping down the champagne.

'This team is good enough to win the cup,' Katumbi had told me before the semi-final. 'Our ambition is to be the best team in Africa. Then . . .' he laughs. The winners of the African Champions League are invited to the World Club Championship, in which they have a chance of playing either the champions of South America or the champions of Europe. Katumbi's dream is a match between TP Mazembe and Barcelona.

*

Mazembe meet Heartland of Nigeria in the final, which is played over two legs – one in Owerri and one in Lubumbashi. Heartland win the first leg 2–1. Garzitto appears to be confident before the return match, telling reporters he's certain they will win. Behind the scenes things are a bit more tense. Katumbi whisks the team off to Zimbabwe to prepare away from the glare of the media.

A 1–0 win for Mazembe will give them victory by virtue of scoring more goals away from home. With seventeen minutes to go, the score is still 0–0. Then a Heartland defender heads the ball into his own goal, and the stadium erupts. Mazembe hold on for the win.

The party at the governor's residence is still going by the time the sun rises the next morning.

The success of TP Mazembe has helped boost Katumbi's profile across the country. Katumbi has been quick to promote Mazembe's success as Congo's success. 'We are doing this for Congo,' he says. 'The whole country can take pride in what we are achieving.' There's history here. When Mazembe won the African title in 1968 and 1969, President Mobutu refused to celebrate. Katanga was a troublesome province and not one he wished to promote.

Katumbi isn't the only Congolese leader with a passion for football. The commander of the Congolese army, General Gabriel Amisi, owns Maniema Union, while the governor of Kinshasa, André Kimbuta, used to run AS Vita Club.

A quick glance at Congo's budget for the first quarter of 2009 gives an idea of the importance which the Congolese government attaches to sport. The justice department was allocated a mere £1.25 million, while the sports ministry was given £3.5 million.

Mazembe's success and Katumbi's raised profile have caused tensions between him and President Kabila. The two men were close. It was Kabila who invited Katumbi back into the country after his father had forced him into exile. Katumbi's brother had fallen out with Kabila *père*, leading to a row which dragged in the rest of the family. Kabila Jnr asked Katumbi to stand for election in Katanga, and the pair were seen as allies.

But Katumbi has been spoken of as a potential presidential candidate in 2011, possibly challenging Kabila. Katumbi denies he's interested, and Kabila made a point of attending the final in Lubumbashi.

'I have no interest in politics,' Katumbi insists. 'If I had to choose between politics and my football club I would choose football.' Which is just the sort of thing a politician would say.

6
THE SUPER EAGLES
Nigeria

The home side are going to score. I know they are. Sometimes, watching a match, you can tell a goal is coming. They've had chance after chance, the pressure is relentless, eventually you know it will happen.

But this time it's different. This time I know the home team will score because I've been told that's what's going to happen.

We've had ninety minutes. All that's left is the time the referee wants to add on for injuries and stoppages. There haven't been any, but for some reason the fourth official signals five more minutes.

Warri Wolves, the home team, get a free kick just outside the box. It didn't look like a foul from where I'm sitting, but there are a dozen or so Kalashnikov-carrying police officers standing in front of me, half blocking my view.

Warri's two big centre backs run forward, and as the free kick is taken one of them rises unchallenged, heading the ball goalwards. The keeper dives late,

155

the defender on the line doesn't move and the ball bounces slowly into the top right-hand corner.

The players celebrate wildly. The Warri Wolves general manager, Mike Idoko, jumps off the bench and races down the touchline towards the players, his coaching staff and substitutes running after him, his hand on his head to stop his checked fedora flying off.

Despite conceding a last-minute equaliser, the Bayelsa United players don't seem too concerned. There are still three minutes of injury time left, but the referee has had enough and blows his whistle. Now everyone is celebrating. Warri Wolves have got a draw and kept their pride. Bayelsa United have got the point they need to claim the title.

It's all so perfect.

There's a pitch invasion. A thousand Bayelsa fans, most wearing yellow T-shirts, mob their players and raise the manager onto their shoulders. A guy on a motorbike rides up and down the touchline pulling wheelies, riding with no hands, zig-zagging crazily. The players fight their way through the crowd to collect the trophy, a distinctly plastic-looking, gold-coloured cup decorated with yellow ribbons. Abel Tador, the captain, lifts it above his head with a roar.

*

Sometimes a match has so much drama it's almost as if the players are following a script. This is the first time I've watched a match where they really are.

It's the last match of the Nigerian Premier League season. Warri, in their first season in the Premier League, are in fourth place. Regardless of the result today, that's where they will finish. Their opponents,

Bayelsa, need a draw to win their first ever league title.

Everyone I speak to in the run-up to the match is sure it will be a draw. 'You must consider the politics involved,' Mozez Priaz, a presenter for Supersport, the pan-African sports broadcaster, tells me.

Warri and Bayelsa both lie in the Niger Delta, an oil-rich, often violent region in the south of Nigeria. A group of militants, which claims it's fighting for a greater share of oil revenues for the Delta, has crippled the industry, launching a wave of attacks on oil installations across the region.

The army hit back a few weeks ago, bombarding the militants' camps from the air and the sea. The militants' leader, the wonderfully named Government Tompolo, is now on the run.

A league title for Bayelsa could take the sting out of things, says Mozez. 'They're thinking: let these boys celebrate a title rather than become militants.'

Or it could just be about money. Bayelsa want to win the league and Warri can help them. Corruption is rife in Nigerian football. Referees are paid extra by clubs to give decisions their way. Deals are made between clubs to throw a match one way or another.

Warri can't just throw the game, though; partly because they have their own pride to think of. No team has come to this tiny, run-down stadium in the Delta and beaten them. But mainly it's because of the cameras. This is the biggest match in the Nigerian season, so Supersport is broadcasting it live across Africa. TV coverage makes it a little harder to fix matches. If the two teams have agreed to draw, they can't just play out a dull 0–0 with no chances. So the acting needs to be as good as the script. Goals cannot be conceded too easily. There must be drama. Perhaps a last-minute equaliser.

No one tries to deny what's happening. No one doubts it will be a draw. Not the players, not the fans, not the other journalists who wander with me across the pitch an hour or so before kick-off.

'Nil–nil or one–one?' asks Tony, a radio journalist from Lagos. His colleague George, a studious, quiet young man who writes for the *Daily Independent* newspaper, plumps for 1–1. 'They have to make it look exciting,' he says.

They do. Actually they make it more exciting than we anticipated. At half-time it's 2–1 to Bayelsa. Warri's goal looked suspiciously soft, but maybe I'm just looking for conspiracies now. 'No,' says George, 'it was soft.'

Before the second half starts I ask Mike, Warri's general manager, what he thinks the final score will be. 'Two–two,' he says, grinning. 'Really? Bayelsa look pretty strong.' 'It'll be 2–2, I'm telling you.' He's laughing now. We're both laughing.

Sure enough, Bayelsa look a different side in the second half. They rarely break out of their own half despite being put under little pressure by Warri. A goal would be inevitable, as Mike suggested, if only Warri were able to get a shot on target.

The result may be preordained, but it still requires someone to put the ball in the net. With five minutes to go, it looks like they've finally done it. The ball breaks for a Warri striker inside the penalty area. With no defenders anywhere near him, he has time to slide it past the goalkeeper and into the net.

The celebrations start, but no one seems to have noticed the flag. The linesman on the near side has ruled the goal out for offside. It seems not everyone got the memo. The Warri players are furious, but Mike doesn't seem too flustered. He pulls his players away from the official, telling them to calm down.

A few minutes later the inevitable equaliser arrives. The linesman doesn't raise his flag this time.

After the final whistle, after the trophy is lifted, I try to get to Abel Tador, the Bayelsa captain. I don't expect him to give a particularly illuminating interview straight after winning the league, but hopefully I can get his number and we can arrange to meet later in the week. Reaching him isn't easy. Hundreds of fans surround the players, all trying to get close enough to touch the trophy.

Then I get distracted. Standing on the pitch is a man in a Villa shirt. In the three years I've been criss-crossing the continent I've met just three people wearing the claret and blue of the Midlands' finest. Two of them were in Kibera, the vast slum in Nairobi. They weren't Villa fans, though – they had just picked up their shirts at a market and had no idea what they were. The third person was a ten-year-old English boy, so he doesn't really count either.

Winston counts. He's surprised to find another Villa fan. 'No one supports them here,' he admits. His reason for committing himself to a life of misery is Gabriel Agbonlahor, a Birmingham-born striker whose father is Nigerian. There's some talk in Nigeria of him switching nationality and representing his paternal homeland. Even if Agbonlahor sticks with England, Winston is sticking with Villa. 'They play good football,' he says as I nod vigorously.

Winston's shirt looks almost genuine. It's the current season's shirt, complete with the name

'Acorns' emblazoned across the front. (Unlike every other club, Villa don't have a commercial sponsor; we have chosen to give the space for free to Acorns, a Birmingham children's hospice.) But it's definitely a fake, which, strangely, makes me even more excited. Someone, somewhere, obviously thinks it's worth his while making fake Villa shirts. There must be a market for them.

I excitedly give Winston a potted history of the club – our club – although it's not until later that I realise his eyes glazed over shortly after I mentioned we were one of the founding members of the Football League in 1888. 'In fact,' I burble, 'the league would never have happened if it hadn't been for William McGregor, Villa's founder, who first gathered together a group of clubs and suggested they set up a proper competition.'

Azuka Chiemeka, Warri's media officer and the man who promised me a lift back into town, is tugging at my shirt. 'We need to go before it gets dark,' he says. 'The roads aren't safe at night.' I swap numbers with Winston and agree to take him one day to Villa Park.

As we wander towards the car we see the Bayelsa team pile into their bus, trophy on board. Azuka promises to find me a number for Tador. I ask him what he thought of the match. 'Abracadabra,' he laughs. 'What can you say? This is Nigerian football.'

At least our match wasn't the worst fix. Another team playing today, Zamfara United, needed to win by at least six goals to avoid relegation. They won 9–0. The fans know exactly what's going on. Entrance was free, but there are only about 2,000 people at the biggest game of the season. Few football supporters in Nigeria seem to care about their own league. If the English Premier League season was still on, there would be even fewer fans here. They'd be in the bar watching Bolton v. Tottenham on satellite TV. 'Some of the players would want to be in the bar too,' admits Azuka.

There were more Manchester United, Arsenal and Chelsea shirts in the crowd than Bayelsa or Warri. Who can blame them? 'It's not football,' I say. 'It's politics.' Azuka just nods and keeps on driving.

*

Unlike in Europe, lots of clubs in Nigeria are owned by politicians. Warri Wolves used to be the company team of the Nigerian Ports Authority before it was bought by the governor of Delta State and renamed. During his 2007 election, Emmanuel Uduaghan promised that Warri Wolves, then in the first division, would gain promotion to the Premier League. He delivered on his pledge.

This season he promised continental football. Again, somehow, he has kept his vow. The fourth place that Warri have secured gets them a place in the West Africa Football Union Cup.

Warri and the governor haven't had it all their own way, though. They had a chance of coming third – until the away match against Enugu Rangers a couple of weeks ago. As the teams came off the pitch after the pre-match warm-up, one of Warri's backroom staff noticed a group of Rangers fans had surrounded the referee and his assistants. The fans were trying to influence the officials, threatening to beat them up unless they ensured Rangers won the match. A couple of Warri staff, including Azuka, went over to try and stop them. A fight broke out between dozens of Rangers fans and the Warri squad.

'I got the beating of my life,' says Azuka.

Warri's goalkeeping coach was stabbed in the arm, while their reserve goalkeeper, Orobosa Adun, was struck violently in the chest. The match was abandoned. A few days later Adun collapsed and died.

In any other country it would have been Enugu Rangers, the side whose fans started the fight, that would have been hauled in front of the disciplinary committee. Not here. Rangers tried to rearrange the match, but Warri, not unreasonably, refused to go until they had received assurances of police protection. They didn't get any. The FA decided to blame Warri and dock them three points – three points which have now cost them a place in the African Confederations Cup.

*

As we're driving back to town, speeding down single-lane highways with no streetlights or road markings, Azuka catches sight of the personalised number plate of the car in front of us, a shiny silver jeep. It belongs to a friend of his, the son of a Nigerian 'big man' who works in the oil industry. The son didn't bother with school and hasn't done a day's work in his life, Azuka says. His father gives him as much money as he wants. Azuka flashes his headlights to get his attention, but the big man's son speeds off. 'He probably thought I was an armed robber,' Azuka laughs.

The next morning I wake to find a text message from Azuka. There won't be any interview with Tador. The Bayelsa captain was driving down that same road last night, a couple of hours after us, when he was stopped at a roadblock. In the darkness he could just make out that the men stopping the traffic were not police. As he tried to reverse one of the men shot him in the head.

*

The Delta has a reputation for being a dangerous place. Oil was first found here some fifty years ago, but the 'black gold' has been more of a curse than a blessing. Billions of pounds have been pumped out of the land with nothing in return. The jobs that the oil industry promised to provide have gone elsewhere, to well-paid foreigners and Nigerians from less marginalised parts of the country. To make matters worse, many of the industries that people in the Delta used to survive on before have now gone. Those who used to fish, winding their way along the countless tributaries and rivers in small wooden boats, find little these days. Oil spills have polluted rivers and land, making fishing and farming impossible.

The Delta's swamps have become chaotic, a place of armed gangs, kidnappings, daily violence. In the past few years shadowy militant groups like the Movement for the Emancipation of the Niger Delta (MEND) and the Niger Delta People's Volunteer Force have taken advantage of rising local anger towards the oil industry. They have started kidnapping foreign oil workers and attacking oil installations. Almost all of those kidnapped are returned unharmed once a hefty ransom has been paid. The oil companies and the Nigerian government always insist that no money changes hands – but no one believes them.

For the oil firms a seven-figure ransom is a small price to pay in order to keep on producing. At five cents a barrel, getting oil out of the ground is ten times cheaper in Nigeria than in Saudi Arabia.

MEND, meanwhile, claim they are fighting for a fair share of oil revenues to be spent on the Delta. But nothing is straightforward. The militant groups may like to portray themselves as rebels fighting on behalf of the people, but many of them are little more than guns-for-hire taking advantage of the chaos. Sometimes they work for gang bosses, sometimes politicians, but the result is always the same. The ransom ends up in some overseas bank account and those living in the Delta get poorer.

Those same accounts are also regularly feathered with money made from a practice known as 'bunkering' – stealing oil direct from the pipeline and selling it on the black market.

But for all the problems in the Delta, the state's largest city, Warri, doesn't look like it's part of a war zone. Around half a million people live here. There are street hawkers and shoeshine boys, but there are also clothes shops selling the latest Ralph Lauren and Yves Saint Laurent fashions shipped in from Europe.

Justin Rewane takes me on a tour of the city. He's a big man in Warri, part of one of the major political families and well connected to the state governor. We go to the city's main stadium, which is currently being rebuilt. (Warri Wolves' home matches have been moved to Oleh, an hour's drive away.)

Nigeria is due to host the Under-17 World Cup later in the year, and Warri has been shortlisted as a probable venue. But the stadium is in such a bad state that it has needed some serious renovation. A FIFA delegation was due to visit the stadium but cancelled the trip after the Nigerian military launched its attack.

As we approach the stadium it becomes clear that Warri had a lucky escape. If FIFA had seen it looking like this, they would have struck the city off the list of venues immediately. The stadium still looks like a building site. The gates are broken, the walls are crumbling and the practice pitch looks like a bog.

Justin is furious. 'Fire brigade!' he shouts, reacting to the emergency of the situation. He bangs his hand against the steering wheel. 'These guys are fire brigade! These guys aren't ready!'

He parks the car at the entrance to the stadium. Inside, three men are painting a wall, while another is pouring diesel into a dirty, rusting generator. 'Fire brigade,' Justin whispers to himself.

The pitch is even worse. A South Korean company was supposed to be laying a new artificial surface, but they haven't got very far. Although strips of green plastic turf have been laid, it's nowhere near ready to play on. The running track alongside the pitch has been ripped up, and bags of cement and gravel are lying about.

Justin introduces me to Amaju Pinnick, Delta State's sports commissioner and the man responsible for getting the stadium ready in time. Amaju, a gold watch on his wrist, sparkling mobile phones in both hands, is yelling at one of his labourers. He's shouting in pidgin English so I can't understand much of it, but I get the gist. It ends, bizarrely, with the labourer on his knees begging forgiveness. Amaju turns away with a dismissive sucking of his teeth.

Despite all the problems, Amaju is convinced the tournament will come to Warri. 'What does FIFA stand for?' he asks, as he takes us on a tour. 'Peace and unity. FIFA shouldn't be running from war, they should be running *to* war.' I struggle to imagine Sepp Blatter agreeing.

Amaju's team has at least managed to get the VIP lounge ready in time. It's all powder-blue leather sofas and lemon-yellow armchairs at strange angles. The press lounge looks pretty good too – forty brand-new computers and a hundred-seat suite for press conferences.

We wander out onto the pitch while the PA system is tested. A voice sings: 'Feel refreshed in God's presence / Take me to where you are / I just want to be with you / Make it your prayer tonight,' at high volume. Amaju nods. 'It works.' The electronic scoreboard is also trialled. A DVD of American WWE wrestling is put on. The picture – a large, muscly bloke slamming a chair against the head of another large, muscly bloke – seems sharp enough.

Justin wants to build a shopping centre in the stadium, underneath the stands. 'It's a great opportunity,' he says. Amaju isn't so sure yet. The two disappear into the VIP lounge to talk about it.

As I leave the stadium, Justin urges me to return to Warri for the tournament. I don't get the chance.

A few months later FIFA announces the venues for the Under-17 World Cup. Warri isn't on the list. Pointing out that FIFA had made 'special efforts' to help Warri, the organisation's vice-president, Jack Warner, says: 'FIFA cannot approve a venue in which one of the most critical elements, the main pitch in the stadium, is in an extremely poor state at the time of the final inspection." I can just imagine what Amaju is yelling at his Korean contractors.

*

Getting the stadiums ready in time is just one of the problems Nigeria faces ahead of the tournament. The biggest concerns the team.

Although Nigeria have sometimes struggled to perform at the biggest tournaments (their best World Cup performance is reaching the second round in 1994), their youth teams have an excellent record. The Under-17s won the last World Cup in 2007, while their Under-20s have twice finished runners-up in the World Youth Championship.

The difference between Nigeria's dominant performances at youth level and their less than stellar record at senior level appears strange on the face of it, but it can be explained.

International youth football has a problem in the developing world. 'Age cheating' – picking players who are over age – is endemic. The coaches and the federations often turn a blind eye or actively encourage it because they want to win. The players will do it because it will help them prolong their careers and maybe get a lucrative move to Europe.

When I've asked young footballers across Africa their age they've given me two numbers, their real age and their football age. The difference is often at least five years.

Nigeria is especially sensitive about it. The Everton manager, David Moyes, was criticised by some here when he talked about the age of his striker, Yakubu Ayegbeni. 'He's only twenty-five, albeit a Nigerian twenty-five, and so if that is his age he's still got a good few years ahead of him,' Moyes said. The Nigerian Football Federation wrote to the English FA, calling for Moyes to be disciplined. 'His statement is insulting to the Nigerian nation and unbecoming of a Premier League manager,' said its spokesman, Ademola Olajire. Moyes swiftly apologised.

Privately, though, most Nigerians connected with football acknowledged he was on to something. During my time here I have been reliably informed of the real ages of several of Nigeria's stars. It's impossible to prove, though. In countries where many people don't have birth certificates, how does anyone know for sure? The first time many top players get any form of official identification is when they are picked for an international match and they have to apply for a passport. In Nigeria they simply have to swear an affadavit, saying, 'yes, Your Honour, I really am seventeen', and that's that.

The Nigerian federation is keen to put on a good show at the Under-17 World Cup, but the fear of being accused of age cheating has caused them to be more stringent than in the past. The team's coach isn't so worried. He has been trying to take twenty-five- and twenty-six-year-olds from the national league and pass them off as teenagers. No one outside of Nigeria will have heard of the players, so he thinks he can get away with it.

The federation isn't very happy, though. One of the federation's officials tells me how he tried to reason with the coach. 'I told him, if you must cheat, cheat gently,' he says. 'Take twenty-year-olds instead.'

That would still be against the rules, I point out. The official waves away my protest. 'Everyone cheats, not just the Africans. Some of these South American players are older than they say too.'

The coach doesn't listen and is sacked. But the problems don't end there. FIFA has tried to introduce MRI scans that can give a fairly accurate prediction of a player's age, but the technology hasn't been used properly yet. The mere suggestion that it might work, though, has already made a difference. After the federation informs the new squad that the scans will take place, sixteen of them – more than half the squad – decide to quit the training camp.

The controversy continues into the tournament itself. Nigeria reach the final before losing to Switzerland 1–0. But after the first match the team's captain, Fortune Chukwudi, is accused of being twenty-five – nine years older than he claims to be.

'It's still a huge problem,' Emeka Enyadike tells me. 'You can tell it still happens. Not enough of our youth players go on to play for the national team.'

Emeka is a bit of a wheeler-dealer in Nigerian football. Amongst other things he organises commercial endorsement for players and arranges sponsorship deals between companies, clubs and tournaments.

He's passionate about his football and convinced that if any African team can win the World Cup it's Nigeria. In fact, he claims, Nigeria are unlucky not to have won it already.

*

At the 1994 tournament in the USA, Nigeria had its strongest side ever. Daniel Amokachi, Rashidi Yekini and Emmanuel Amuneke led the line, with Sunday Oliseh and Finidi George influential in midfield. It was the first time Nigeria had reached the finals, but the squad showed no signs of being overawed by the occasion.

In the first round they topped their group, beating Greece and Bulgaria while losing narrowly to Argentina. They came up against Italy in the second round and took the lead after twenty-five minutes through Amuneke. The Italy side was one of the strongest in the tournament, boasting seven stars from AC Milan's European Cup-winning side and led from the front by one of the world's greatest-ever players, Roberto Baggio.

The longer the game wore on, with Nigeria holding on to their lead, the more desperate the Italians became. Then, in the final minute, just as it looked as if Nigeria might snatch a famous victory, the ball was pulled back to Roberto Baggio on the edge of the penalty area. His low shot went through a defender's legs, hit the inside of the post and went in. Baggio would later credit that goal to his Buddhist spiritual master. 'Many people called it lucky,' he said, 'but then again . . . maybe there was something special in that moment. Maybe, that time my Master gave me a bit more help than usual.'

Ten minutes into extra time Italy won a penalty, which Baggio converted, and Nigeria were out.

'If we had beaten Italy, we would have won the tournament,' Emeka says with conviction. Certainly the teams which Nigeria would have played to reach the final (Spain in the quarters, Bulgaria in the semis) were not as strong as Italy. But even if they had managed to reach the final – and that's rather a large 'if' – they still would have had to beat Brazil to win the trophy. It wasn't the greatest Brazilian side, but I think Emeka is being a bit unrealistic. 'We could have beaten that Brazilian side,' he insists. 'We really were that good.'

★

The 1994 World Cup not only proved the power of Nigerian football on the world stage, it also showed how influential it is on the rest of Nigerian society.

A year earlier Nigeria had suffered its greatest crisis. In 1993 the military regime of Ibrahim Babangida was preparing to hold elections and hand over power. The elections were the cleanest in Nigeria's history, with little of the ballot box stuffing and violence that had overshadowed previous polls. But when it became clear that the opposition leader Chief Moshood Abiola was going to win, Babangida suddenly annulled the election.

One year on, protests were planned for 12 June – the day the election had taken place. Pro-democracy activists prepared for a national strike, with millions expected out on the streets. But there was a problem. The World Cup was about to start. So the strike was postponed.

'The day after we lost to Italy,' said Emeka, 'there was a strike.'

Nigerian football transcends the political and religious issues that bedevil Nigeria, Emeka believes. The most populous country in Africa, Nigeria is relatively evenly split between Christians (mainly in the south) and Muslims (predominant in the north). Religious clashes, killing hundreds, are not unusual, and no government can survive unless it's seen to be balanced between north and south, Muslim and Christian. The current president, Umaru Yar'Adua is Muslim and northern; his vice-president, Goodluck Jonathan, is Christian and southern. Under the previous regime of Olusegun Obasanjo it was the other way round.

'All this talk of balancing between north and south, Christians and Muslims. In football, nobody cares,' says Emeka. 'The team could be eleven Christians or eleven Muslims. The only religion that unites Nigerians is football.'

*

One footballer who unites Nigeria more than most is Nwankwo Kanu. On billboards towering above the bridges and highways of Lagos, Nigeria's largest city, Kanu is omnipresent: looking solemn as he persuades passing motorists to bank with Fidelity; smiling broadly as he juggles a football with a young boy in an effort to sell milk.

Kanu's finest hour came in the 1996 Olympic Games. Nigeria were playing Brazil in the semi-final. Almost 80,000 fans were packed into the Sanford Stadium in Athens, Georgia. Although the Olympics were restricted to players under the age of twenty-three (plus three over-age players), this Brazil side featured some of the best in the world, including Ronaldo, Rivaldo and Bebeto. They had raced into a 3–1 lead by half-time and in the second half had wasted numerous chances to make it four.

Nigeria, captained by Kanu, refused to give up. They missed a second-half penalty but kept pressing, eventually pulling the deficit back to one in the seventy-eighth minute when Ikpeba scored from the edge of the area.

Then came Kanu's last-minute magic. Standing two yards out with his back to the goal, he nonchalantly flicked the ball up in the air, turned and lobbed it over the goalkeeper. The match went to extra time. Under the golden goal rule the next goal would win. Kanu scored it, capping a brilliant Nigerian comeback.

The final against Argentina was almost as exciting. The South Americans went ahead twice, but on each occasion Nigeria pegged them back. With the ninety minutes almost up, Nigeria scored a winner, Joseph Dosu grabbing the goal that made them champions. It was the first time an African side had won a major international tournament.

Kanu's crucial role in the Olympic victory – Nigeria's greatest-ever sporting triumph – turned him into a huge celebrity. He had already won the European Champions League with Ajax in 1995 and had made a big-money move to Italy's Inter Milan. But within a few weeks of the Olympic triumph, Kanu was in hospital. During a routine test doctors had discovered a serious heart condition which threatened to end his life, let alone his career. He recovered and soon moved to Arsenal, where he played some of the best football of his career under the management of Arsene Wenger.

Kanu's age has long been the subject of rumours. After he won the FA Cup with Portsmouth in 2008, his manager, Harry Redknapp, joked that he was 'about forty-seven'. By 2009 he was officially thirty-three but was playing with the speed of someone several years older. His legs had gone, but he was still coming on as a substitute for Portsmouth in the English Premier League as well as starting games for Nigeria during their World Cup qualifying campaign.

His career is clearly winding down, but his celebrity in Nigeria is still going strong. In a public vote to choose Nigeria's greatest living legend, the only person who beat Kanu was the country's leading Pentecostal leader, Pastor Enoch Adeboye. Football may be more important than religion, but church leaders are clearly a lot better at organising their followers than footballers are.

*

Lagos has its poverty – vast shanty towns of breeze-block huts and sheet-iron shacks – but it also has unbelievable wealth. One evening I head out for a tour of Lagos's more upmarket nightspots with my friend, Matt, who has lived here for the last two years.

The roads turn to rivers when it rains, and tonight it's really raining. Traffic grinds to a halt. Outside Jade Palace parking attendants hustle for business, squeezing cars into small spaces, offering customers umbrellas to shelter them from the downpour. Women in stylish dresses and men in sharp suits race into clubs, splashing their way through puddles.

'We have a saying in Lagos,' says Matt. 'You can wear Gucci but you still have to step in shit.' There's a lot of Gucci around and, judging by the smell coming from the gutter, a lot of shit.

Inside Jade Palace young executives and wannabe business tycoons drink cocktails and work the room, lounging on red leather sofas. Bottles of Moët champagne are lined up along the bar. I meet a twenty-three-year-old in private equity, two women who work for a technology company and a couple of bankers.

We move on to Number 10, which belongs to Jay Jay Okocha, one of Nigeria's most famous players. Okocha was one of the stars of the 1998 World Cup, a tournament in which Nigeria once again reached the second round but failed to go any further. They beat Spain 3–2 in the group stages but were humiliated by Denmark in the next round, losing 4–1.

Okocha was a creative midfielder with fantastic close control and a powerful shot. Despite his obvious talents, he never played for a major European club. His longest spell was at unfashionable Bolton Wanderers in the English Premier League, where he spent five years. He retired from international football in 2006, but when I was last in Nigeria in 2009 there were still regular demands for him to be recalled.

Okocha had been brought into the training camp as a mentor for the players, but he saw himself as more of a businessman. His club, Number 10, doesn't look like much from the outside. It appears to be in an industrial area, with warehouses along both sides of the deserted street. To get in, we have to pass one by one through airtight security doors. Inside, hip-hop videos play on a big screen and there's a whiff of cigar smoke. A few women dance in the roped-off VIP area – black leather sofas, red carpet – while men sit and talk, drinking Heinekens that cost twice as much as the ones you get elsewhere in the bar.

Number 10 has nothing on Auto Lounge, though. We are ushered upstairs to the champagne and spirits bar. Everything has to be bought by the bottle, and the most expensive costs 150,000 Naira – about £600. It doesn't seem to put too many people off, though. Every table is taken. We decide to go downstairs, where they serve beer. When the national team players, known as the Super Eagles, are in town, this is one of the places where they hang out. They don't struggle to get a table. They are the country's biggest celebrities.

Tonight, though, the players are on their way to Abuja, the bizarre Potemkin capital city in the centre of the country, where they are due to play Kenya.

*

Abuja is the polar opposite of Lagos. The main roads are smooth and lined with trees. Modern buildings, some made from granite and marble, rise above the pavements. Expensive new houses line the streets climbing out of the city, giving their owners expansive views of the gleaming capital. Slums appear to be non-existent.

Three decades ago none of it existed. As the chaotic sprawl of Lagos and the ethnic and religious battles of the whole country grew ever larger, Nigeria's then military rulers sought to create a new capital for Africa's most populous country. They chose a spot in the geographical centre, a piece of land inhabited by a sprinkling of farmers.

But as impressive as it looks, Abuja is really little more than a show city. There is poverty – it's just very well hidden. Most of the government employees who work in Abuja can't afford housing there. Instead, they live in satellite towns as far as twenty miles away.

There are some slums, but they lie back from the main highway between the airport and the city.

Abuja styles itself as the 'centre of unity', a city where everyone in Nigeria is welcome. The grand white gate at the end of the airport road marks the entrance to Abuja with the words 'You Are Welcome'. But it's clear not everyone is welcome. For a start, only the president, vice-president and visiting dignitaries are deemed welcome enough to drive through the gate – everyone else has to drive around it.

Beyond the gate, the national stadium rises into view. It's an impressive-looking 60,000-seater venue that the government built in the hope that Abuja would get the 2014 Commonwealth Games. They went to Glasgow instead. There are whispers that it was also part of an elaborate money-laundering scheme. In fact, much of the city appears to be built with dodgy money.

The Super Eagles like playing here, though, because the crowd tends to be supportive. At previous matches in Lagos the fans have turned on the team if they feel they're not playing well enough and started cheering for their opponents. Having drawn their last match, away in Mozambique, Nigeria desperately need to beat Kenya if they want to stay in contention for the World Cup. They are coming into the game in good form after two friendly matches in Europe. They drew 1–1 with a decent Republic of Ireland team before going to St Etienne and beating a full-strength French side 1–0. What makes the result even more impressive is that a handful of Nigeria's top European-based players weren't involved. Everton's Joseph Yobo, Chelsea's Jon Mikel Obi and Newcastle's Obafemi Martins all failed to turn up.

No one in the Nigerian camp had been able to track them down. Another player claimed he couldn't get a visa – an excuse that members of the technical team found hard to believe.

Unsurprisingly, they've all managed to get themselves to Nigeria for the World Cup qualifier against Kenya, but after the unexpected victory against France the coach, Shaibu Amodu, is threatening to keep them out of the team.

The night before the match against Kenya, pundits on a football show called *Argument Proper* are discussing whether the stars should be brought back. The pundits appear to be in rare agreement: the team that played in France deserve the chance to play again.

★

On the morning of the match I buy a ticket at the side of the road near the stadium. It costs 300 Naira – about £1.20. On the walkway up towards the stadium young men are selling food and drink, T-shirts, hats and flags. A man with dozens of sun hats perched on his head blocks my path. 'Patronise me,' he says. 'We support your teams, now you support mine.' I can't really argue with that. The sun hats, green and white, are emblazoned with the slogan 'Up Super Eagles!' As I hand over the money (250 Naira, negotiated down from 300), another man tries to hand me a small book of psalms from the New Testament. 'It's free,' he says, shoving it into my hand.

'It's a way of spreading the gospel,' says Shola. He doesn't need one – he has just come from church and is still clutching his Bible.

Shola is a vet by training, although at the moment he's teaching physics at secondary school. His class is 'quite small', he says, 'just forty'. A lot of other classes are often twice as large. In a few months' time he will start National Youth Service, a one-year secondment to a government department. 'If you ever want to work for government, you have to do it. You need the certificate.'

Shola hasn't been to a live match before. 'Every Nigerian has to experience this once,' he says.

But first we need to get in. Thousands of fans are strolling towards the stadium. Dozens of black-clad policemen are marching back the other way. They carry branches ripped off nearby trees, waving them menacingly above their heads. Anyone without a ticket gets a beating. We wave ours frantically. One fan struggles to get his out of his wallet as three police officers take aim at his legs and back.

When we finally reach the stadium we find the gates are locked. At first, people queue in a good-natured fashion in front of a dozen or so turnstiles, waiting for stadium officials to unfasten the chains around the gates. One of the officials has a large key ring with what look like more than fifty keys on it. The crowds get bigger, the queues a little more tense. A police horse to our left can't move, pressed in against bodies on all sides.

This is turning into a crush. Knees and elbows are digging into my body. Through the crowd I can see the man with the key ring. He looks panicked. None of the keys appear to be working. A police officer on the stadium side of the gates picks up a rock. He starts smashing it against one of the chains. He smashes it and smashes it. The crush gets tighter. Shola glances back at me with half a smile. I try to smile back. It has become just a little bit harder to breathe.

Finally, the chain breaks and the gate opens. The policeman moves on to the next chain and starts hammering away at that one too. Everyone surges towards the open gate. We stagger through, one by one, grinning and laughing when we make it to the other side.

As the stadium fills up, a small, bustling, informal market takes shape on the walkways behind the stands. Two men are doing a brisk trade in pirated Nollywood DVDs with titles like *Hard War 2* and *African Soldier 3*. Next to them is a man selling football posters – Chelsea, Arsenal and Manchester United. Further along, someone is selling prints of English country watercolours. Then a man selling rice, scooping it from a vat into plastic containers.

In a corner, slightly shaded and away from the commotion, a dozen or so Muslim men are praying. Three other men nearby are taking off their shoes and washing their hands and feet.

It's still two hours before the match kicks off as Shola and I take our seats in the lower tier. There's a sound of booing from the other side of the ground. 'Is it Kenya supporters?' asks Shola. We peer across. There's a group of people waving blue posters and scarves. 'I think they're Chelsea fans,' I say. A group of Manchester United fans retaliate with a poster of Ronaldo.

The official supporters club arrives, led by a man called Dr Utoh. Hundreds of trumpeters, drummers and dancers, all dressed in their sponsored green and white tops, run around the track to huge cheers from the crowd. The ball boys juggle footballs in front of the main stand. When one of them balances the ball on the back of his neck, the crowd erupts.

Dr Utoh leads his band of merry men into our section of the crowd. He bounds over to me, grinning and sweating in equal measures. 'Did you see us?' he asks, somewhat unnecessarily. His followers try to find seats, but there's no space. Some stand in the gangways, playing their trumpets and banging their drums. After a few minutes even the gangways are full.

Over the public address system the stadium announcer implores people to move to other areas where there's seating. No one moves. From where I am, there doesn't seem to be any spare seating. Away to the right there was a gap where I could make out the walkway from the stadium to the road, but now it's packed. So is every other entrance. Access between the stands and the pitch is blocked by a large wire mesh fence, similar to the ones found in England before the 1989 Hillsborough disaster. If anything went wrong, there wouldn't seem to be a way out.

A police officer in the gangway nearest to me is shouting at people to move. There's a cracking sound. He has pulled out a cattle prod and is waving it in the direction of the fans. It makes no difference – there's nowhere for them to go. When the match starts, supporters and police alike focus on the game. The coach has taken a risk and kept the same team which beat France. Although the majority of commentators agreed with the decision before the match, they will still blame him if it proves to be the wrong decision.

Nigeria start the match brightly. They are on a high after the victory in St Etienne. Ike Uche, who plays for Getafe in Spain, is already causing problems for the Kenyan back line. In the third minute he bursts past two defenders and slips the ball past the advancing keeper. The noise from the crowd is deafening. 'Three–nil,' says Shola. 'Five–nil,' says Dr Utoh. Kenya look shell-shocked as they try to deal with the noise of 70,000 Nigerians as much as with the swift passing of the Super Eagles midfield.

But Nigeria start to sit back, seemingly confident they will be able to score again if need be. Kenya begin to settle. They have a couple of shots from distance and Dennis Oliech, their star striker, takes the ball past two players but can't get a shot in. Then, a real chance. Oliech plays a one-two with McDonald Mariga. His shot from the edge of the box clips the bar and goes over. A few minutes later he gets another chance, turning his defender well but screwing the shot wide of the post.

The fans are still getting behind Nigeria. To the tune of *Give Peace a Chance* they sing, 'All we are saying is give us a goal.'

A fan near me screams: 'Another goal, another goal.'

As the first half draws to a close, Nigeria create a couple of chances, both falling to Peter Odemwingie, a lively forward who plays in Russia for Lokomotiv Moscow. His first shot is beaten away at the near post, the second is inches wide. The crowd is becoming restless. Seyi Olofinjana, who plays his football for Stoke, is bearing the brunt of the fans' frustrations. He has misplaced a couple of passes, missed a few tackles. Mikel Obi normally starts in his position and most fans seem to think Mikel should replace him.

The half-time entertainment on the pitch is dancing girls and backflipping boys. In the stands near me, a man is spinning metal plates. The crowd roars as he manages to spin one on his chin.

Kenya start the second half brightly. A scuffed shot is cleared off the line, then Oliech takes the ball past the keeper but is forced too wide to get a shot in. Nigeria are living dangerously, but they break on the counter and Odemwingie is brought down inside the area. Nsofor Obinna, a youngster at Inter Milan, slams the penalty home and the match is as good as over. Obinna puts it beyond doubt five minutes later, switching the ball from left foot to right and smashing it into the top right-hand corner of the goal.

The crowd is chaotic. Away to my right two police officers wade in to beat up a fan throwing bottles. Other fans turn on the police. 'Please, please, please: stop throwing bottles,' the PA pleads.

The police come to the front of our stand, waving their hands to urge people to calm down. Next to them is Dr Utoh, encouraging supporters to make more noise. Shola and I nervously eye the exit, trying to working out an escape route if it's needed. It's not. The match finishes 3–0 – as Shola predicted – and the stands quickly empty.

Walking back towards the main road, we find the atmosphere is celebratory. Vendors sell rice and yams as people wait for buses. The road is a sea of cars not moving in either direction, but no one seems to mind too much. Away to our right a small crowd has developed. We wander over to take a look. The black-clad policemen who had beaten people with sticks a few hours earlier are now dancing and singing. A hundred or so fans watch, laughing and clapping. Shola's bus finally arrives and we head off in different directions.

7

LES ÉLÉPHANTS

Côte D'Ivoire

On a patch of ochre-coloured dirt and gravel in the village of Monogaga, twelve miles north of the coastal town of San Pedro, twelve-year-old Olivier Kwasi is practising his headers. He juggles the ball on his head, then he and an older boy from the village start heading it back and forth between them. They manage seven or eight before the older boy heads it too high or too low. Every time it happens Olivier throws him a look. After a few minutes, Olivier gives up head tennis and juggles the ball by himself, keeping it in the air with ease, despite playing barefoot.

This is Côte d'Ivoire's cocoa region. Every spare scrap of fertile land in the hills and valleys which surround Monogaga has been covered with cocoa plants. This valley was once a dense forest, but some trees have been chopped down to make way for cocoa. Those trees that remain bear no leaves on their branches. Villagers have lit fires at their bases to kill their roots so that all the goodness in the soil can be used by their cocoa plants. The result is a macabre forest of dead trees the colour of ash.

Olivier, like most of the boys in Monogaga, works in the cocoa fields with his family. It's hard work and gives him blisters on his hands, which he occasionally picks at as we sit on wooden benches overlooking the makeshift dirt football pitch. The benches are in one of three sheds used as classrooms. We talk about school. When his friend Samba, who wears an old Liverpool shirt with the faint outline of the Carlsberg logo on the front, lists the subjects he likes ('Maths, geography and science'), Olivier just shrugs and says, 'I like football.'

When Samba says he'd like to be a footballer or a policeman, Olivier says, 'I will play football'. It's a fact, not a wish. 'That's what I want to do and that's what I will do,' he adds.

His route is mapped out. Once he has finished school, he will enrol in a local football school in San Pedro, one of hundreds of academies across Côte d'Ivoire. Then he will be scouted, move to Europe and play for a big club, only coming back to West Africa to play for Côte d'Ivoire's national team, Les Éléphants. 'Just like Didier Drogba,' Olivier says, then turns his head to look out at the pitch where half a dozen of his classmates are chasing a ball.

*

A few hundred miles to the west, Didier Drogba and the rest of Les Éléphants are gathered in Abidjan's luxury Golf Hotel, preparing for a World Cup qualifier against Burkina Faso. Victory will take them to the brink of qualification. Over the course of a morning most of the players wander through the hotel lobby, flip-flops flapping on their feet.

Bakari Kone, a forward for Marseilles, sits in the corner with a couple of friends, all three of them constantly taking calls on their mobile phones. Emmanuel Eboue and Didier Zokora sprint through the lobby trying to playfully wrestle each other to the floor. Kolo Toure, fresh from his move from Arsenal to Manchester City, is followed everywhere by his agent, a bulky man wearing a replica City shirt with '28 Toure' on the back. Similarly, two men constantly trail Chelsea's Salomon Kalou, both of them in Chelsea shirts marked '21 Kalou'.

For Kalou this World Cup campaign means a bit more. Before Germany 2006 he played in the Netherlands for several years and toyed with the idea of switching citizenship. Marco van Basten, the then Dutch coach, was keen to fast-track his application, but it didn't come through in time for the World Cup. Despite entreaties from numerous Ivorians, including his brother, Bonaventure, who played for the national team at the time, Kalou refused to play for his homeland.

'You learn from your mistakes,' he told me. 'I have no regrets. It has made me an even stronger person. I can't regret what makes me strong.'

Since pledging himself to the country of his birth, Kalou has become an integral part of the Côte d'Ivoire team and secured a move to Chelsea.

'The Chelsea fans sing, "He comes from Ivory Coast", but I don't think they even know where Ivory Coast is,' he said. 'People love you for what you do on the pitch, but they don't know what's going on here.'

For much of the past decade what has been going on here is war. That it has now ended owes much to the players, who mingle freely with fans in the lobby, posing for endless pictures.

One of the hotel's doormen attempts to stop too many people coming in. Young boys, their entrance blocked, peer through the windows trying to glance a passing Elephant. Most national teams are worshipped by their fans, but in Côte d'Ivoire the bond is that little bit deeper. Les Éléphants are not just a football team. To many, they are the men who ended the war.

★

From independence in 1960 until the early 1990s, Côte d'Ivoire was an island of stability in an increasingly volatile part of the world. As civil wars broke out and coups took place across West Africa, Côte d'Ivoire's president, Felix Houphouet-Boigny, kept a tight grip on power from 1960 until the day he died in December 1993. With some of the largest cocoa and coffee crops in the world, Côte d'Ivoire also became a regional economic powerhouse, attracting migrant workers from neighbouring countries.

By the time Houphouët-Boigny died, around a quarter of the population were migrants. The political fight that followed became increasingly ethnic. The phrase *Ivoirité* ('Ivorian-ness') was introduced to separate 'pure' and 'mixed' Ivorians. Many of those now viewed as 'mixed' lived in the north. As if the ethnic division wasn't enough to create sparks, there was a religious one too, with the south being dominated by Christians and the north by Muslims.

Six years of political unrest culminated in a bloodless coup, followed a few months later by an election marred by rigging, boycotts and violence. The coup leader, General Robert Guëi, who like all coup leaders had selflessly put himself forward as a candidate, dissolved the electoral commission while the votes were being counted and claimed victory. Supporters of his main opponent, Laurent Gbagbo, took to the streets. Within days Guëi had fled, and Gbagbo was declared the true winner.

The violence didn't stop, though. It got worse, and increasingly religious and ethnic in its nature. Churches and mosques were burned to the ground, while hundreds of northern opposition supporters were arrested, tortured and killed by Gbagbo's security forces.

For the next two years the situation remained tense but, on the whole, peaceful. Gbagbo's government was still not accepted by many in the north and issues of nationality went unresolved.

On 19 September 2002 rebellious soldiers attempted a coup in Abidjan. The resulting fighting left at least 400 people dead, but the rebels failed to take the city. They retreated to Bouaké, 150 miles to the north, and set up their headquarters there. Within a month a ceasefire had been agreed, and French troops were sent to monitor the line that now existed between north and south.

Côte d'Ivoire was split in two. It would be another five years before the country was united again.

For the most part it was a cold war, with little fighting between north and south. The worst violence occurred in the west of the country, where Liberian rebel groups were used on both sides.

With the country in crisis, the football team became one of the few things that all Ivorians – north and south, Muslim and Christian – could support unreservedly. The team was becoming one of the strongest in Africa, with most of the squad playing in Europe. With Drogba as captain, the team qualified in October 2005 for the country's first ever World Cup finals.

The atmosphere in Abidjan following qualification was 'fantastic', Kolo Toure tells me when we meet a couple of days before the Burkina Faso match. 'We were having a lot of problems, but it gave people something exciting to celebrate.'

Kolo and his brother Yaya, who plays for Barcelona, both hail from the north. Both men were playing in Europe when the war started.

'It was difficult being abroad,' he says. 'You hear on the news that people are dying and you don't know if it's one of your parents. You're really scared. I was one of the lucky ones. My family was okay, but there were plenty of people here who had problems.'

Qualifying for the World Cup helped to take some of the heat out of the political situation, Kolo argues. 'In our national team you have players coming from all the different parts of the country. We played together and qualified for the World Cup. That showed all the people in the country how important it is to work together. We would not have qualified if we had players just from one part of the country. We showed how important it is to be united.'

There were several abortive attempts at peace deals before Gbagbo and Guillaume Soro, the leader of the main rebel group, the Forces Nouvelles (FN), signed an agreement in neighbouring Ouagadougou in early

2007. The deal would see the country reunified and the line between north and south dismantled. Doubts remained, though, and in the first few weeks after the deal was signed little progress was made. Then Didier Drogba came to Bouaké. He had been named BBC African Player of the Year and wanted to bring his trophy to the north. Drogba was a southerner and hadn't set foot in the north since the war had started. If he had any doubts that he was worshipped as much on this side of the 'green line' as he was on the southern side, they were erased the moment he stepped off the plane.

Tens of thousands of fans had come out to greet him. The award, Drogba said, was not just for him but for the whole of Côte d'Ivoire. To show he meant it, he told the crowd he wanted Les Éléphants to play their next match, a World Cup qualifier against Madagascar, in Bouaké.

'It will be a memorable day', he said. 'It will be the victory for Ivory Coast football, the victory of the Ivory Coast people and, quite simply, there will be peace.'

*

Our car slows to a halt on the outskirts of Abidjan. This is 'le corridor', the final security checkpoint on the edge of the city before the road runs north out of the country's biggest city and towards Bouaké. Hawkers crowd around the cars and lorries heading north, selling bags of apples and boxes of tissues. A gendarme checks our papers – driving licence and passports – then smiles and nods us on our way: *'Bonne chance.'*

The checkpoint is closed down at night, preventing people leaving or entering the city. We speed away out of Abidjan, five-foot-high grass and shrubs pressing into the road on both sides. We pass rubber plantations and palm trees, and after an hour the dual carriageway becomes a single-lane, pothole-ridden track. Upturned lorries, overloaded with goods, lie on either side. A few other lorries have simply broken down and stand marooned in the middle of the road. Young men are up on the roof of one of them, frantically waving branches to direct traffic around the obstacle.

The road suddenly widens again as we reach the outskirts of Yamoussoukro, Côte d'Ivoire's bizarre capital city. It was the hometown of Houphouët-Boigny, and in 1983 he decided he would turn it into the capital. Swamps and fields would be turned into a presidential palace and a parliament. Every ministry would be moved. A parliament would be built with space for more than 500 MPs, even though there were then only 225. A senate house would also be built, even though the country didn't actually have a senate.

Houphouët-Boigny didn't live long enough to see the city completed. But he was still alive by the time the Basilica was finished.

The Basilica's vast dome rises out of the jungle as we approach the city. It cost an estimated £125 million, contains more than 75,000 square feet of Italian-made stained glass and rises to a height of over 500 feet. My guide proudly points out that it's fifty-five feet taller than St Peter's in the Vatican.

By the entrance to the Basilica we stop to eat coconuts bought from Ali. He has a prime spot, but business is slow, he tells me, as I slurp coconut juice.

Apart from Sundays, when hundreds turn up for Mass, he reckons the Basilica attracts twenty or thirty visitors on a good day. When I go inside the Basilica I hand over my passport so they can write my name in the visitors' book. It's about 2 p.m., and I'm the ninth person to enter.

The Basilica can hold 7,000 people, but it has been full only twice. The first was for the consecration in 1990, the second was for Houphouët-Boigny's funeral three years later.

Houphouët-Boigny asked Pope John Paul II to come to the consecration. The Pope was wary about giving his blessing to a £125-million church built in a country with serious poverty problems. I'll come, he said, if you also build a new hospital. Houphouët-Boigny agreed, and on the day the Pope consecrated the Basilica he also lay the foundation stone for a vast new hospital that would be built in the Basilica's shadow.

Some nineteen years later the foundation stone is still the only part of the hospital that has been built. A computer-generated image of a rather impressive-looking hospital has been erected nearby, but no one appears to know when, or if, construction will ever begin. 'Soon,' says Ali, more in hope than expectation.

We drive on towards Bouaké, passing through what used to be the 'Zone of Confidence', the green line between north and south. Under the terms of the Ouagadougou peace deal, government forces (FDS) and rebels (FN) will soon be working together. The first 'mixed brigade' has already been established and is supposed to oversee security during the elections, which are scheduled to take place two months later. (They don't. The electoral commission postpones them for a fifth time and reschedules the vote for March 2010. One month before the new polling day, they are postponed again.)

We stop at a base for the new mixed brigade. Three officers are sitting in the shade of the mango, avocado and grapefruit trees in the dusty courtyard. Lieutenant Bamba, a member of the government forces, gives me a tour of their bare offices. He points to the computer and printer which he usually writes his reports on. 'It's broken,' he grins, gesturing towards the printer. An old typewriter has been hauled out and placed on a nearby table.

One of Lt Bamba's junior officers, a man name Yeo, comes over to chat. Yeo used to be a rebel, but the two men, once enemies, have an easy demeanour with each other. 'We eat together, we drink together, we play football together,' Yeo tells me. 'We even chase women together,' he adds as the two men collapse in laughter.

We continue on to Bouaké. On the outskirts of the city half a dozen men in military fatigues flag us down. Government troops and officials have come back to the city, but the Forces Nouvelles are still the ones in charge. The FN rebels who have pulled us over check our papers, but it's not quite enough. Fatiga, our driver, hands over 1,000CFA and we move on. Not very far, though. No more than twenty yards down the road is another checkpoint. A young man in shorts and football shirt stands in front of a row of metal spikes, angrily berating us for not giving him any money. 'I'm standing here in the rain,' he shouts, before sullenly beckoning to his accomplice to move the spikes.

'These are the thieves who took Bouaké,' Fatiga mutters as we pass. Under the terms of the peace deal, several thousand of the FN troops will be assimilated into the main army. Most of them, though, lack basic training. The original rebellion was about 500-strong. The rest of the rebel forces were young men recruited after the initial split in the country. Incorporating thousands of untrained militiamen into a relatively professional army isn't going to be an easy task.

One of those who will be a key figure in the assimilation programme is Commander Famoussa. He's one of the most senior rebel officers in Bouaké, but he spent most of the war trying to end it.

Famoussa was a reluctant rebel. He had joined the military academy after leaving school and trained as an officer. His first position was in the north, controlling a main road, looking out for bandits. When the rebellion began his family was split between north and south.

'I was just a civil servant deployed in the north. When the rebels took control of the town they were asking, "Are you going to stay with the south or join us in the north?" I didn't have much of a choice.'

Famoussa was given the task of organising security for the Africa Cup of Nations qualifier in Bouaké. Government soldiers came up from the south in what became the first joint operation between government and rebel forces since the war began. Soldiers from both sides had mixed on occasion, though. Famoussa had helped to organise a football match in 2002 with the international forces from France and West Africa on one team and FDS and FN soldiers on the other. 'It was very emotional,' Famoussa says, 'meeting up with former colleagues. I didn't know who was still alive.'

The man who trained Famoussa as an officer and a handful of men who qualified in the same year as him were at the match. 'We've got to put an end to what we're doing here,' he recalls saying to his old friends.

After the match Famoussa said a few words on camera. 'I apologised for any suffering. I said, "We're all Ivorian."' His parents saw the television broadcast. It was the first time they had seen their son since the start of the war.

★

In the run-up to the 2007 Côte d'Ivoire v. Madagascar match, Bouaké's stadium, a simple concrete bowl that seats around 25,000 people, was given a new lick of paint, a roof for the main stand and a fresh pitch.

The match was sold out. 'Everyone was dressed in orange [the colour of the national team]. The atmosphere was incredible. Like a carnival,' Famoussa recalls. About 700 FN soldiers were on duty that day, but there was little for them to do. 'We forgot about our jobs and watched the match.'

At their best, Madagascar would struggle to even come close to beating Côte d'Ivoire. On an occasion like this they didn't have a chance. With ten minutes left on the clock, Les Éléphants were winning 4–0. The only thing that was missing was a goal from Drogba. He duly obliged.

'The key moment was Drogba's goal,' says Famoussa. 'There were goals before, but that was the most important. It felt like a goal rescuing us from a sticky patch.

'War is something that divides a country. Two camps, two sides. But in football it's not about ethnic groups. We are working together. The peace accord had been signed, but there was still a lot of mistrust. In football everyone is together, praying for the same thing. When you watch it you watch it as an Ivorian. You are there for the whole team.'

Later that evening, when Famoussa got home to his wife and children, he replayed the match on his video. 'From the first moment of the match I hoped peace was possible. It made me realise how thirsty people were for peace. But when I rewound the film and reflected on what happened, that's when I knew peace was possible.'

The stadium was given a new name: the Stade de la Paix.

The carnival atmosphere inside the ground was replicated that night throughout Bouaké. Thousands of people in Abidjan had used the match as an opportunity to venture north to find family and friends they hadn't seen in years. 'People were walking around taking photos of the city,' Famoussa recalls. 'A lot of myths were broken that day. People thought there were weapons everywhere, that the city would be destroyed. They saw the reality on the ground.'

Bouaké had been completely cut off from the economic heart of the country in the south, although the infrastructure had suffered little damage during the war. A handful of buildings had been destroyed when the Ivorian air force carried out two days of bombings in 2004, but for the most part this was a cold war.

Everywhere I went I came across stories of people who had tried their best to make life go on as normal. The French owner of a local bookshop had refused to leave when other foreigners fled. Instead, she became a one-woman postal service. Letters and parcels were no longer delivered across the green line, so she established a PO Box in Yamoussoukro which people could use if they wanted to send something to Bouaké. Every now and then she would sneak across the green line to Yamoussoukro to deliver letters and pick up the post. She would bring it back to her bookshop, where customers would come to collect their letters.

Moïse Koné tried to establish an air of normality through radio. Communications were cut after the war began, but Kone, then a twenty-two-year-old journalism student, was asked to set up a rebel radio station. He called it Ivoir' FM and tried to keep politics to a minimum. While the rebel television station became little more than a propaganda machine, Moïse insisted that guests refrained from criticising the government in Abidjan. Although his presenters read out press releases and communiqués from FN leaders, they 'never did propaganda', Moïse insists.

After fiddling around with the transmitter, he was able to reconnect Radio France Internationale, which had been one of the main sources of news and information in the region. 'People needed information,' Moïse said. When the feed was cut, people were forced to 'use megaphones in the street to tell people about attacks'.

Ivoir' FM had little in the way of funding. Moïse had to beg, steal and borrow equipment from friends and family in France and the USA while a local NGO offered him a computer.

But with what little he had, Moïse managed to turn Ivoir' FM into a proper radio station. 'It's about music, phone-ins, social stuff,' he said. 'We do shout-outs about people who went missing in the war, then there's jokes and games. It's everything and nothing.'

Since the war ended, Moïse has had more competition. The BBC relaunched here, as did four commercial radio stations. 'We're still number one, though,' he points out.

*

Just as the nation's reconciliation attempts have been reflected and amplified through the national football team, so have the divisions. Aruna Dindane, who moved to Portsmouth FC in 2009, was once dismissed as a Burkinabé by none other than Laurent Gbagbo, the country's president. Drogba and Dindane, meanwhile, have reportedly had a testy relationship, as have Drogba and Kader Keita, another northerner.

More dramatically, the rise of Yaya Touré, also from the north, laid bare the ethnic tensions splitting the country in two. Yaya was Barcelona's defensive midfield linchpin in their European Cup-winning side of 2009. Yaya and Drogba lined up against each other in a semi-final clash between Chelsea and Barcelona. In the days leading up to the first leg, RFI had described it as 'Côte d'Ivoire v. Cameroon', a reference to Barcelona's Cameroonian striker, Samuel Eto'o. Yaya was furious.

'I spoke with my father and I said, "I want to stop playing for the national team",' Yaya told me. It was more than six months later but he was still shaking with anger as he retold the story. 'When I go to other countries people say, "Where do you come from?" and I say, "I come from Ivory Coast." Then these stupid people say I come from Guinea or Mali. It's unbelievable. My grandfather comes from Ivory

Coast, my father comes from Ivory Coast, I come from Ivory Coast.'

Afer talking it over with his father and his wife, Yaya decided he would carry on playing. 'But not for the stupid people,' he emphasised, waving his finger.

When Yaya returned to Abidjan with the European Champions League trophy, President Gbagbo, perhaps in a spirit of reconciliation, made a point of apologising to him on behalf of the nation.

*

The 2009 match in Abidjan between Côte d'Ivoire and Burkina Faso took on added significance in view of the fact that the presence of Burkinabé refugees in Côte d'Ivoire had been one of the catalysts for the conflict.

Many of the immigrants who had come into northern Côte d'Ivoire in the 1980s and 1990s were Burkinabé. A conflict over land in late 1999 forced 10,000 Burkinabé to flee. It was one of the first anti-immigrant clashes. During the 1990s and at the start of the next decade one of the leading opposition figures, Alassane Ouattara, was accused of being Burkinabé in an attempt to bar him from presidential elections. Burkina Faso's president, Blaise Compaoré, was accused of helping a failed coup attempt in Abidjan in 2000. Compaoré was also believed to have backed the coup attempt in 2002 which led to the split in the country. After the north separated, Compaoré supplied weapons to the rebels.

By 2007 Compaoré had turned peacemaker. He was the key figure in peace talks between Gbagbo and Soro, bringing both men to Burkina Faso's capital,

Ouagadougou, to broker a deal. In the long run, the war had done little to help Compaoré. The divide had become a racket. FN commanders could demand high 'taxes' from traders from landlocked Mali, Niger and Burkina Faso heading south to the port in Abidjan. There was a similar charge for all goods going back the other way. The impasse was adversely affecting Burkina's economy.

There were still hundreds of thousands of Burkinabé living in northern Côte d'Ivoire and similar numbers of Ivorians across the border in Burkina. As Emerse Fae, an Ivorian midfielder who plays for Nice, pointed out to me, those blurred nationalities exist on the football pitch too. 'Some players from Burkina were born in Ivory Coast. The same is true of some of the Ivory Coast players – they were born in Burkina.

'So we are brothers,' he said. 'Maybe after the game we can go to the party together, but on Saturday at five o'clock we will not be brothers.'

Around 2,000 fans from Burkina Faso were due to make the trip, and there could have been more local Burkinabé in the ground if it had been full. The capacity had been limited, though, after a tragedy at Les Éléphants' previous qualifier, against Malawi. Too many tickets were sold. Unlike in Abuja, there were no lucky escapes. In the chaos of a crush and stampede nineteen people lost their lives.

The authorities tried to pin the blame on the fans – a tactic practised by football associations and police the world over. A ticketing scandal soon emerged. The head of the Ivorian federation's match-organising committee had printed extra tickets in order to make more money. When too many people surged into the stadium, riot police fired tear gas into the crowd, creating panic and sparking the stampede. The official was jailed for six months.

FIFA reduced the capacity for the Burkina Faso match from 35,000 to 20,000, but the local football federation still managed to make as much money. Top-priced tickets were doubled from 10,000CFA to 20,000, while the cheapest rose from 500 to 1,000CFA.

After the tragedy at the last match, security is understandably tight around the stadium. Police block off the main roads for about a mile all around, and anyone with a ticket is allowed through only after they've been thoroughly frisked.

The stadium stands on the banks of the lagoon, in the shadow of the city's impressive skyscrapers. It's a simple stadium by continental standards, lacking the grandeur of the Chinese-built grounds in Dar es Salaam and Abuja.

Inside the stadium the crowd is entertained before the match by a who's who of Ivorian music. Ismael Isaac, a reggae star who had polio as a child and still needs to use a walking stick, may have to hobble around the perimeter track, but he still manages to do it with a certain amount of swagger.

Towards the end of the track *Magno Mako* ('Pity') he stops singing and listens to the crowd singing his lyrics back to him. He stands there, one hand on his walking stick, the other waving his microphone above his head, as the fans unite in one voice.

Ismael is followed by Espoir 2000, a popular Zouglou group, who sing *Abidjan Farot*, popularly known as 'Abidjan est Doux' ('Abidjan is Sweet'): 'Even people in Paris know Abidjan is where it's at / It's true that we don't have anything / But we will party until morning.'

The final act is DJ Arafat, dressed all in black, who comes out to perform with a sidekick dressed all in white. When Cameroon played here recently, Samuel Eto'o and Didier Drogba hung out with Arafat after the match. Eto'o reportedly gave Arafat a £60,000 diamond watch.

Arafat's performance comes to an end as the players emerge for their pre-match warm-up. Several of the players, including Drogba, exchange high-fives with Arafat on their way out of the tunnel.

There's one more appearance to come before the match can start. A convoy of black Audi saloons and Mitsubishi jeeps enters the stadium at the far end, lights flashing. They keep coming, twenty-two in all, before one of the saloons in the middle comes to a stop just in front of where I'm sitting.

Out steps President Gbagbo, wearing a white shirt hanging loose over black trousers. The crowd has cheered every Zouglou and reggae star. When Les Éléphants came onto the pitch, the roar was even louder. But the reception for the president is muted. Gbagbo smiles, kisses his fingertips and raises his arms. The applause is polite, nothing more.

*

Côte d'Ivoire line up in a 4–3–3 formation, with Drogba at centre forward and Kalou and Kader Keita on either side, playing more as wingers.

A win will almost certainly seal qualification for Les Éléphants, but Burkina are a strong side. The first match between the two, in Ouagadougou, ended 3–2 to Côte d'Ivoire. The fans are confident, though, that the return match won't be as close. Les Éléphants have won their four previous home matches, scoring thirteen and conceding none.

Despite the smaller attendance, the crowd are noisy, with pockets of fans from official supporters clubs singing and chanting throughout the match. Even the VIP area to my right, which appears to be almost entirely filled with Lebanese Ivorians, is lively.

If Côte d'Ivoire have a weakness it's in defence. Kolo Toure may be superb, but his partner at centre half, Souleymane Bamba, is less assured. Behind them, the goalkeeper, Boubacar Barry, looks even weaker. He plays for a small Belgian side, Beveren, and, despite the national side's impressive defensive record, has never looked entirely convincing.

He gets a chance to prove his worth early on. A mistake by Bamba allows Burkina's big centre forward Moumouni Dagano to race through unchallenged. The fan club to my left momentarily stop beating their drums. Barry saves, and the drums start up again.

Despite the early scare, Côte d'Ivoire quickly establish a rhythm. Yaya Touré is at the centre of every attack, playing a far more creative role than the one he plays for Barcelona. In the ninth minute he combines nicely with Eboue to set up Les Éléphants' first goal, with Kader Keita's shot turned into his own net by a Burkina defender.

Les Éléphants relax a bit until half-time, and Burkina nearly find their way back with a couple of half-chances. Within ten minutes of the restart, though, the match is over. Drogba scores from a direct free kick, then Yaya picks up the ball in the centre circle and sprints towards the goal, holding off two defenders, before slotting the ball past the onrushing keeper. As Yaya falls to his knees in celebration Drogba rushes over to him, waving his arms to the rest of the team, beckoning them to join in the celebration. Soon Yaya is at the bottom of a ten-player pile-on.

Burkina throw on two extra forwards, but it makes no difference. With more gaps in their defence, they can do little to prevent Drogba scoring the fourth and Kader Keita a fifth.

When the final whistle blows, Les Éléphants have all but qualified for the World Cup. They would need to lose both of their remaining two matches – one of which is against bottom-of-the-group Malawi – and Burkina Faso would have to win both of theirs for Côte d'Ivoire to stand any chance of blowing it.

Drogba leads the players in a dance in the corner in front of their fans.

*

That night John James, the local BBC correspondent, and his wife Therese take me out for dinner to the Allocodrome. It's a large outdoor eating area with wooden tables and plastic chairs. At a series of counters the women cook fish, chicken and pork dishes. They hustle for business, talking up the quality of their food, while the men try to move us towards a table.

Over the loudspeakers a DJ is playing a series of Zouglou hits. The atmosphere is lively. A young boy, no more than twelve, stands on a small plinth dancing to the music. He's brilliant. Diners watch and applaud. An hour or so later the boy comes to each table, a posse of other kids in tow, dancing for money. A man, possibly his older brother, rallies support and holds out a plate for donations.

We're here to see off one of John and Therese's friends, Wise, who is heading to China the next morning to study international relations at Jilin university in the country's northeast. Wise has been offered a full scholarship. He's excited but worried.

'Do they have liquor?' he asks.

'Yes,' I say. 'I'm sure they do.'

'What about the women?'

'Of course they have women!'

'No! What are they like? Are they fat like here?'

'Um, no, probably not.'

He looks disappointed.

Wise had been studying English in Abidjan, and, while it's certainly better than my French, he might struggle to follow a graduate course on international relations taught in English. 'I know I have to improve,' he says. He seems confident that he can.

The food arrives and it's communal. We break open the plastic bags of *attiéké*, which looks and tastes a bit like couscous, and dig into the fried fish, chicken legs in sauce and pork chops. We order beers. John tries to order Drogbas, litre-sized bottles of beer named after Didier, but they don't have any, so we settle for Castel.

Beer isn't the only thing to take the Drogba name – a way of life is even named after him. In Bouaké I spotted an old billboard poster for a mobile network. Drogba is pointing to the camera in a 'your country needs you' pose. Above him is the word *Drogbacite* ('Drogba-ness').

He was already a star after taking Côte d'Ivoire to the World Cup and the final of the African Nations in 2006, but the events in Bouaké transformed him into something far bigger. He became an icon. Guys wanted to be him and girls wanted to be with him.

Drogba has also inspired a new generation of would-be footballers, from young Olivier in San Pedro through to the players in the local league and beyond. It's not unusual for young footballers to dream of becoming strikers. But it seems to be more common here. And there's only one striker they try to compare themselves to. Even Commander Famoussa told me he plays like Drogba.

Mustapha Baba Diaby is the same. '*Neuf*,' he says, '*à la Drogba*,' when I ask him what position he plays. Mustapha thought he would be playing in Europe by now, but when we meet a few days after the Burkina Faso game it's in a small room that belongs to his friend Ahmed.

Mustapha's father had always told him to study hard. Football was no career, he said. Mustapha didn't believe him. He played football every moment he wasn't in school. Soon he was playing when he should have been at school. By the time he was supposed to sit his exams, he had left altogether and joined a local football academy.

He was playing in a competition organised in his neighbourhood when a football agent approached him. 'He said, "I can help you fulfil your dreams",' Mustapha recalls.

The agent told Mustapha he was good enough to play in Europe. He could take him to Greece, he said, where he would play for one of the top clubs in Athens. Mustapha was keen, but wanted the agent to talk it through with his parents first. The agent provided reams of papers detailing dozens of other players he had found clubs for. The only thing the agent needed was money. If Mustapha could provide 1.5 million CFA, the equivalent of £2,000, the agent could take him to Greece.

'I thought it would work for me,' Mustapha says. His parents weren't convinced. They refused to pay. Mustapha's father told him he should go back to school. Undeterred, Mustapha went to see his big brother, Ali, who works for the forestry department. He gave Mustapha the money, plus an extra 500,000CFA just in case he had any problems.

The big day came. The agent told Mustapha the flight would go via Morocco. After they landed in Casablanca, they would have to wait an hour before the flight to Athens. Mustapha was nervous but excited.

'My dream was to become a famous footballer like Zidane. I was at the door of success.'

That was as far as he got. Moments after they disembarked in Casablanca, the agent disappeared. 'The sky fell on my head,' Mustapha says.

Dejected, Mustapha used the extra money his brother had given him to buy a one-way ticket back to Abidjan. When he got home, his mother and brother were supportive. His father, though, still hasn't forgiven him.

Mustapha earns a bit of money as a trader, selling clothes and shoes in the street. He still dreams of becoming a footballer, though. 'I'm still a very good player,' he insists.

There are countless Mustaphas in Côte d'Ivoire. Save the Children conducted a small study and found scores of unregistered football academies in just one district in Abidjan. Families pay fees for their children to attend in the hope that their son will be the one who makes it. Some get into serious debt, selling land or the lease on their home in order to give their son a chance of playing football in Europe.

Mark Canavera at Save the Children told me about one mother he had interviewed, whose son had gone to an academy. 'She said: "I'll never forget the day my son sold his school books for a football." And that was a good thing.'

*

Watching Drogba lead Côte d'Ivoire to the brink of the World Cup, I found it easy to see why so many young Ivorians dreamed of following in their footsteps. This group of footballers, and one in particular, would always be treated as legends. In the country's darkest hour, Drogba and Les Éléphants had provided the sense of national unity that the politicians had so conspicuously failed to deliver.

Getting hold of Didier Drogba for an interview proved to be difficult, though. While most of the squad happily wandered through the Golf Hotel, posing for pictures with fans and chatting with waiting journalists, Didier was nowhere to be seen. Official requests for an interview were met with requests to write a letter. It didn't seem to matter that I'd written several letters already.

His agent in London was similarly unhelpful. He had recently got rid of his traditional sports agent and employed the services of the woman who used to do PR for Posh Spice. Drogba's reputation in the

UK bore no relation to his reputation here in Côte d'Ivoire. While Ivorians saw him as a hero who had almost single-handedly brought a once-divided country together, football fans in the UK had a very different view. Drogba was a cheat and a maniac, someone who dives in an attempt to win penalties and free kicks, and who rages at referees when decisions go against him.

After one particularly intense match, the Champions League semi-final between Chelsea and Barcelona, which the Spanish side won in controversial circumstances, Drogba had stormed up to a television camera and screamed, 'It's a fucking disgrace!'

I had hoped that his PR woman would see the benefit of organising an interview that would inevitably show her client in a far more positive light. I was wrong. It looked like the only way I was going to get to meet him was by finding him and shoving my recorder under his nose.

*

After the final whistle, after the celebrations and the dancing, I find my way to the depths of the stadium, where Drogba is giving a press conference to Ivorian journalists. Outside the room a phalanx of paramilitary police is lined up, providing a cordon to shepherd Drogba to the safety of the team bus. Dressed in Robocop-style black body armour and armed with cattle prods and rifles, they are clearly not to be messed with.

While Kolo Toure and Salomon Kalou have been happy to talk to me about the importance of football in ending Côte d'Ivoire's civil war, Drogba is the one who had the biggest impact. I want to know whether he really thought he could make a difference, what he felt when he went to Bouaké with his trophy and whether he really believes football has helped to bring the country together.

There's a commotion at the door. Drogba is coming out and the Robocops close in around him. Somehow I manage to squeeze myself in between two officers and stick my Dictaphone under Drogba's nose. He talks as we walk. I introduce myself and start with a couple of questions about the match. He mutters a few 'it was tough', 'pleased to win', 'nice to score' platitudes. I ask about the importance of football in Côte d'Ivoire. He mentions the war. 'Football united people,' he says.

'Yes, now on that point ...' I feel the police close in. We're walking up the stairs.

'I can't talk about this now,' Drogba says.

Out through a door.

'Perhaps we could talk about this later.'

The team bus is waiting.

'Maybe,' he says.

Two police officers block my path.

'When?' I ask.

One of the police officers raises his cattle prod.

I decide it's time to leave.

'Thanks, Didier.'

8

THE LEONE STARS
v. THE LONE STARS

Sierra Leone v. Liberia

Moussa Manseray would prefer it if I call him Messi. He's just like the Argentine forward, he claims. He's fast, he's got fantastic close control and he's lethal in front of goal. There's one big difference between them, though. Moussa has only one leg.

Sierra Leone's civil war left tens of thousands dead and a third of the 6 million population displaced. It also created thousands of amputees. Many of them had their arms or legs amputated by rebels.

The first football team for amputees was launched shortly after the war. The idea quickly spread, and before long there was a league of six teams and a national team.

'I thought there would be no hope for me,' says eighteen-year-old Moussa, who lost his left leg at the age of nine. His village came under attack by rebels. As he tried to run away he was shot in the leg.

'I became very isolated in the community. When you become a disabled person they abandon you like that. Being part of this team I feel more encouraged.'

One morning in Freetown, Sierra Leone's ramshackle seaside capital, I go down to Lumley Beach to watch Moussa train with the Single Leg Amputee Sports Club.

The heat and humidity on Lumley Beach is almost unbearable. It has just turned nine o'clock in the morning, but I'm already scrambling for a patch of shade underneath a battered and abandoned lifeguard hut. The amputees aren't the only footballers playing on the beach. In both directions along the strip of sand there are training sessions, kickabouts and impromptu matches. The air is filled with yells to pass and goal celebrations, mixed with the sound of Atlantic waves crashing against the shore.

The biggest crowd of onlookers is for the amputee team. The head coach, Moses Mambo (who prefers the nickname 'Ferguson'), puts out cones for the players to dribble around. All of them are impressive, but it's not hard to see why Moussa's team-mates gave him his nickname. There's something rhythmic about his movements as he swings from side to side on his crutches, tapping the ball with the inside of his foot, then with the outside. He dribbles faster on one leg than I do on two.

After training we sit at the side of the road eating bread rolls filled with condensed milk – a surprisingly tasty combination. It's no overstatement to say that football has changed Moussa's life. The self-confidence he regained from football has been put to good use. He's about to finish school, something he wasn't able to do during the war. He has read all the books in the school's meagre library and says his favourites are *Last Duty* by the Nigerian writer

Isidore Okpewho, Nikolai Gogol's *The Government Inspector* and *Hamlet*.

'I like *Hamlet* the most. The play captivates me. I've watched it in the movie.'

Ultimately, though, his dream is to go to university and become a lawyer. 'I want to bring justice to my people,' he says solemnly.

*

His people need it. Two decades of dictatorship preceded the civil war, which began in 1991. Previous leaders had made themselves rich on Sierra Leone's diamond mines but left the country desperately poor. The Revolutionary United Front (RUF), which started the war, was backed by a Liberian, Charles Taylor.

Taylor had spent the previous two years trying to overthrow the Liberian government. By 1991 he had gained control of large swathes of the country, but the diamond mines of Sierra Leone, which began just fifty miles across the border, were a far more alluring prize. The RUF leader in Sierra Leone, Foday Sankoh, soon took control of the diamond mines. Meanwhile, Sierra Leone's president, Joseph Momoh, struggled to stave off the rebellion and within a year had been ousted by a twenty-seven-year-old captain, Valentine Strasser.

The civil war continued, despite elections held in 1996. Foreign mercenaries, both South African and British, came and went. Taylor launched a new attack in 1998 – code-named 'Operation No Living Thing' – which led to widescale massacres of men, women and children. A UN peacekeeping mission was sent, but it wasn't until Britain intervened in May 2000 that the violence was finally brought under control. A peace deal was signed, and by the start of 2002 the war was officially over. It had cost the lives of at least 50,000 people, and around three-quarters of the population had been displaced.

Charles Taylor's rebel forces had a similarly catastrophic effect on Liberia. The country had been ruled by one of the world's more bizarre dictators, Samuel Doe, who had come to power in a coup at the age of twenty-eight. Despite banning political parties, closing down the free press and stealing tens of millions from the state, Doe received full backing from the USA, who saw him as sufficiently anti-Communist to deserve their support. The fear of another 'red' state in Africa prompted the USA to back some of the continent's most brutal dictators, Doe included.

Taylor's National Patriotic Front of Liberia (NPFL) launched its rebellion at the end of 1989, and within six months they were laying siege to the capital, Monrovia. Civil war racked the country for the next seven years. More than a dozen peace accords were signed and ignored until elections were held in 1997. Taylor threatened to go back to war if he didn't win. His slogan – 'He killed my Ma, he killed my Pa, but I'll vote for him' – summed up the fear he had spread throughout the country.

Taylor's interference in Sierra Leone and his sponsorship of rebel forces in other West African countries eventually led to his downfall. Guinea's president, Lansana Conté, backed a new Liberian rebel group, the Liberians United for Reconciliation and Democracy (LURD), and by 2003 another group had helped LURD surround Monrovia. Taylor left the country for exile in Nigeria before being arrested in 2006 and sent to The Hague, where he's currently on trial for war crimes committed in Sierra Leone.

Both Sierra Leone and Liberia are now democracies, although the path out of poverty is long and arduous. Roughly four in five Liberians live on less than sixty pence a day, while Sierra Leone can be found at the foot of just about every global table of development indicators. The only time either country has enjoyed a good press in the past decade has been through football.

*

Not that either country has a particularly good record. Both have qualified for the Africa Cup of Nations on just two occasions, while the World Cup has remained a distant dream. But both countries have been blessed with a superstar striker. And both strikers have happened to play their best football in Milan.

Liberia's George Weah is arguably the greatest-ever African footballer. He was the first African to be named World Player of the Year, when he was playing for AC Milan. Sierra Leone's Mohamed Kallon never reached quite the same level, but he still played for nine years in Italy, including a spell at Milan's city rivals, Inter.

Both men captained their national team and both men dreamed of playing at the World Cup – a dream neither managed to achieve.

Weah remains immensely popular in Liberia, so much so that he stood for president in 2005. It was Liberia's first election since the end of fourteen years of civil war. Weah, resplendent in an all-white suit, toured the country, promising to bring schools, hospitals and jobs to Liberia's poor. His campaign was unashamedly populist. 'The other candidates criticise me for having no education,' he told a crowd of more than 2,000 in Zwedru, a small town in the east of the country. 'Yes, I'm only a footballer, but I have used my success and my professionalism to help you. They are covered in degrees, but they have destroyed your lives. What have they done with our country's money? There are no roads, no schools, no hospitals, no electricity and no running water . . .

'I am like you. I know what it's like to be hungry, or to go to school barefoot. Things must change, take your destiny in your own hands!'

Weah also spoke convincingly of the need for a 'non-violent revolution' and urged Liberia's many different tribes to 'make peace' with each other.

Weah may have painted himself as the anti-elite candidate who had never been to school, but, as his speeches made clear, he fully understood the importance of education. So too did his main rival, a candidate who could not have been more different. For a start, Ellen Johnson Sirleaf was a woman. She was also nearly twice Weah's age. More importantly, she was a Harvard-educated former World Bank employee, who claimed she would turn around Liberia's failing economy.

In a crowded field of twenty-one candidates, no one was going to get the 50 per cent plus one needed to win on the first round. Weah came first, with 28 per cent of the vote, while Johnson Sirleaf was in second place with 22 per cent. It was then that the veteran's superior political nous made the difference. Johnson Sirleaf skilfully struck deals with her former opponents, building a coalition that eventually won convincingly.

Johnson Sirleaf became Africa's first female head of state, while Weah moved back to Florida and began studying for his high school diploma.

*

I missed Weah by a week. He had come back to Monrovia for a few days to play in a testimonial match for Kelvin Sebwe, one of his former Lone Star team-mates. Thousands of fans had turned out to see him, and many of them implored him to stay in the country and run against Johnson Sirleaf in the next presidential elections, which were due in two years.

President Johnson Sirleaf may have been fêted abroad, but many people in Liberia had become increasingly sceptical. Allegations of corruption were common, and ordinary citizens pointed to the lack of basics like electricity and water.

Just before Weah arrived, Johnson Sirleaf had been accused of providing support to rebel groups in a report by the country's Truth and Reconciliation Commission. Several politicians faced similar accusations, and Johnson Sirleaf admitted giving money to Charles Taylor in the 1980s and to LURD in the 1990s. Few leading figures – Weah aside – seemed to have clean hands.

The report recommended that Johnson Sirleaf be banned from politics for thirty years, although the chances of parliament enforcing this were extremely small.

Weah, having successfully completed his high school diploma, was now studying at university. He kept quiet about his political aspirations when he was in the country for the testimonial match, but he made another visit a few months later to support his party's candidate in a senate election. Thousands turned out for his rallies.

Not all of Weah's former team-mates supported his political ambitions, though. 'I don't think it was a wise decision,' Musa Shannon told me. We were sitting in a restaurant and bar called La Noche, an upmarket slice of Western life on a grotty, potholed Monrovia street. There's a piano in the corner and artwork on the walls. The furniture – sofas and armchairs – is a mixture of browns, dark greens and burnt orange.

'He could have been more effective as a private citizen than as a politician.'

Shannon was Weah's room-mate during the early 2000s, when the Lone Stars came within a point of qualifying for the World Cup. He had worshipped Weah as a child, 'practising all his moves', so jumped at the chance to share a room with him on international duty.

'At first I thought, this is great. Then I realised why no one wanted to room with George. You get no privacy. Journalists, people, coming and going.'

Shannon's family left Liberia and moved to the USA when the civil war started. He played football at university and became a professional when the US Major Soccer League was launched in 1997. He played for the Tampa Bay Rowdies alongside the Colombian Carlos Valderrama and made his debut for Liberia in 2000 in a qualifier for the 2002 World Cup.

After beating Chad over two legs, the Lone Stars were drawn in a five-team group which included

Nigeria and Ghana. With only one team qualifying for the tournament in South Korea and Japan, Liberia were the clear underdogs.

After a terrible start, losing 2–0 away to Sudan, Liberia got their campaign back on track with a 2–1 win at home to Nigeria. They followed it up with an even better result, beating Ghana 3–1 in Accra. Shannon scored the final goal. 'That was the most important goal I ever scored.'

Two further home wins against Sierra Leone and Sudan, followed by a defeat away to Nigeria, left the Lone Stars needing to win their last two matches – at home to Ghana and away to Sierra Leone – to qualify for their first-ever World Cup.

At a time when the country was still at war, it would have been an astonishing achievement. 'Football was all the country had to look up to. It was the one thing that kept our name out there in a positive light. It was a salvation for the people. We felt the energy of the people.

'That's why the loss to Ghana was so devastating.'

At half-time the score was 1–1. Ghana scored fifteen minutes into the second half, and Liberia were unable to come back.

'There were accusations that we took bribes, that we were out partying, that FIFA didn't want us in the World Cup because of Charles Taylor. The truth is we had a lot of injuries and a lot of yellow cards. We were missing maybe six or seven guys. We just weren't good enough.'

Since Weah's retirement in 2002, the Lone Stars have failed to come even close to qualifying for the African Nations, let alone the World Cup. It's unlikely they will anytime in the near future. The most recent campaign ended in three draws and three defeats.

*

While Weah moved swiftly into a political career, Mohamed Kallon has been more wary. He's several years younger than Weah and has only just ended his international career. The sign on the door of his Freetown office reads: 'Please be brief. Others are waiting.' At the end of the darkened corridor, framed shirts of Kallon's previous football clubs lining the walls, at least twenty people are crammed into Kallon's waiting room. They're an assortment of local businessmen looking for favours, women asking for help with school fees and young men hoping for a leg-up. A smartly dressed entourage hangs around in the corridors, occasionally ushering the next visitor towards Kallon's office.

He may not have any aspirations to become a political figure, but this is the sort of scene you expect to see when visiting a head of state, not a footballer. He's more interested in turning himself into the country's biggest mogul. He owns a newspaper and a radio station, a sports shop and a nightclub, a tea company and a hotel. Not to mention a Premier League football club, which he has named after himself.

Sitting behind a large oak desk, two mobile phones constantly flashing, Kallon appears comfortable in his new role as a would-be tycoon. He has been spending his days talking to business partners, going over accounts and overseeing construction of his new beach-front hotel.

'It's very different from playing football,' he says, 'but I like it.'

Kallon made more than 200 appearances for a host of European sides. He joined Swiss side Lugano in 1995 and scored more than fifty Serie A goals for half a dozen Italian clubs, including Inter. But few other players in Sierra Leone came close to matching his success. The Leone Stars reached the Africa Cup of Nations in 1996 soon after Kallon made his debut, but they failed to qualify again.

'I was always expecting to go back to the Nations Cup. With the talent we have we can make it. After 1996 the current squad was the best – we were very close.' Not close enough, though. The Leone Stars took four points off South Africa during the recent qualifying campaign, knocking out Bafana Bafana (as the South African team is known) in the process, but a 4–1 defeat to Nigeria in the last match meant they missed out on the final qualifying round.

Kallon's football career appears to be over. He has recently been playing his football in the Emirates – a place that's little more than a very well-paid retirement home for former internationals.

Officially he's twenty-nine, which would suggest he still has a few years left in him. Unofficially – well, it depends who you ask. Kallon smiles when I ask him his real age. 'I'm twenty-nine – thirty in October. Everyone knows that.'

He was dubbed 'Wonder Boy' after appearing in the 1996 Africa Cup of Nations, when he was supposedly just sixteen. Either way, he thinks he has probably played his last game for the Leone Stars, having resigned as captain after the Nigeria match.

Kallon had a running battle with the Sierra Leone Football Association (SLFA), mainly conducted through the press. When he quit the national team in 2008, he blamed the Leone Stars' exit from the World Cup qualifiers on poor management by the football association. Several times, he claimed, he had bailed out the team, paying tens of thousands of pounds for players to travel to matches.

'We didn't have the right people to take care of football. They don't have the right mentality. They haven't lived the football life,' he says.

His coach, Ahmed Kanu, echoed some of the complaints, arguing that the government and the association had failed to provide money for even a 'single bottle of water' for the players.

Kallon's biggest regret is that so few of his countrymen got the chance to see him play. Freetown's bars and video shacks are packed when top European matches are on television, but Kallon played most of his football during the civil war, when Sierra Leone had little electricity, let alone satellite television. 'It would have been nice, you know?'

*

Not everyone in Sierra Leone thinks Kallon is a hero. Alimu Bah, the SLFA's secretary general, laughs when I tell him I've just met Kallon. 'That man! What did he say about me?'

Bah and Kallon fell out over the management of the Leone Stars. 'He didn't understand that we didn't have any money,' Bah says when we meet at the football academy. It looks like quite a run-down building, but Bah assures me it has only recently been completed. The artificial pitch was supposed to have been laid by now, but piles of black plastic shreds sit by the side of the half-finished pitch.

Bah boasts that he's one of the longest-serving football administrators in West Africa, having joined the SLFA in 1994. Two of his brothers played for the national team, although Bah himself wasn't good enough. 'Definitely not,' he laughs.

Like most African countries, Sierra Leone suffers from the popularity of the English Premier League, which is broadcast here on satellite television. It's cheaper to go to a video shack and watch the English league than to go to a stadium and watch a Sierra Leone Premier League match. So Bah has started arranging league matches at different times to ensure there are no clashes.

'We cannot compete with the English Premier League. The quality of their game is so much better. So we play at night, or on weekdays in the provinces where there are no floodlights.'

The shift has made a big difference. It's not uncommon for the local league to attract crowds of 10,000 or more. It used to be just a few hundred.

Bah hopes a more professional league will help the national team. He has also drawn up a list of players in Europe who have Sierra Leonean parents. He hopes to persuade them to play for the Leone Stars.

Two Villa players are on Alimu's list of targets: Nigel Reo-Coker and Curtis Davies. Reo-Coker, who spent his first six years in Sierra Leone, suggested in an interview in 2006 that he might one day consider playing for the country of his birth. Davies, whose father was born here, has been picked for the England

Under-21 squad but, so far, hasn't been capped for the full national team.

'Those two players would make a big difference to us,' Alimu says. 'Do you know them?'

I confess I don't know anyone at Villa, not even a cleaning lady.

'Oh.' He seems surprised at my lack of access. 'But you could ask them, couldn't you?'

'If I ever meet them,' I promise.

'Good.'

✱

If Reo-Coker or Davies were to make the switch – and it's pretty unlikely – they would be following in the footsteps of Leroy Rosenior, who was born in London to Sierra Leonean parents and spent most of his life in England. Towards the end of his career he agreed to play for Sierra Leone and made two appearances. A few years later he came back, briefly, as head coach.

Rosenior's first match in charge was at home to Togo in June 2007. His side fought hard but lost 1–0 to a side that would ultimately qualify for the World Cup. The match was irrelevant, though, compared to its aftermath. The Togolese delegation – twenty-one officials and politicians – were killed when the helicopter ferrying them from Freetown across the bay to the airport at Lungi fell out of the sky.

His next match was two weeks later, away to Mali, a fast-improving side that had reached the semi-finals of the Africa Cup of Nations in 2002 and 2004. Rosenior arrived in Mali on a flight from Paris, expecting to meet his players. The squad had been due to meet up in Freetown, before travelling on together to Bamako, the capital of Mali. But all the European-based players failed to turn up. They hadn't been able to get flights to Sierra Leone in time.

Rosenior's threadbare squad of local players, none of them good enough to get contracts abroad, collapsed to a 6–0 defeat. 'I decided it wasn't for me,' Rosenior said. He quit on the spot and flew back to the UK.

Sierra Leone is trying to market itself as a holiday destination. The famous Bounty 'Taste of Paradise' adverts in the 1980s were filmed on the country's pristine white sand beaches. But that journey between Lungi airport and Freetown was never one for the faint-hearted. The first time I went to Freetown, just a few months before the Togo crash, I took the same helicopter. It was an old, creaking Russian-made machine flown by an old, creaking Russian-made pilot. There were maybe thirty of us crammed onto the two benches at either side of the helicopter, with all our luggage squeezed into the middle. The relief that greeted the safe landing in Freetown was quickly overtaken by the realisation that I would have to take the same helicopter back to Lungi a week later.

*

A new president, Ernest Koroma, was elected in 2007, and, as the helicopter ride indicates, things are slowly, very slowly, beginning to improve. The previous government had faced serious corruption allegations, but unlike in Kenya and Nigeria the elections here were free and fair. The ruling party accepted the results grudgingly, but at least they accepted them.

One of the first things Koroma did after his election was to establish an anti-corruption commission.

The man he chose to head it, Abdul Tejan-Cole, has approached the job with gusto. When I meet him midway through 2009, he has already had sixteen convictions that year. 'They are not small fry,' he says of those he has put away. The former government ombudsman and the head of the post office have both been convicted, while he currently has trials pending against a judge and a magistrate.

'It's not just about prosecutions. It's about prevention too,' he says, pointing to the work he's doing with the ministry of health to streamline their procurement process. At the moment, he argues, it's almost impossible to track where the money is spent, making it far easier for corrupt officials to avoid detection.

Football is also a priority, he says. He's investigating the FA, but can't go into too many details while the probe is ongoing. 'Football is so important here for people. From a public education point of view, if we target football it sends a message that corruption can be tackled.'

Abdul likes to describe himself as the 'only Ipswich Town fan south of the Sahara'. A couple from Suffolk, Graham and Elizabeth White, had run a printing company based in Freetown in the 1970s. The Whites were friends with Abdul's parents and offered to take him to Suffolk on holiday. He had already watched Ipswich play on television – there was a weekly programme in Sierra Leone called *Big League Soccer* – but seeing Portman Road for the first time sealed the deal.

'Ipswich were doing very well then,' he reminds me. 'John Wark, Alan Brazil, Bobby Robson.' He's right. Under Bobby Robson, Ipswich enjoyed their most successful period in history, winning the FA

Cup and the UEFA Cup. They also narrowly missed out on the title in 1981. Villa pipped them to the post. 'You were lucky,' he says. I politely disagree.

He has high hopes that Ipswich, currently languishing in the Championship, will become a big club again. When we meet, Roy Keane has just taken over as manager. 'I'm excited about Keane. I think he'll do great things.' Abdul has just joined the Ipswich Town Supporters Club on Facebook.

Being responsible for ending corruption in a country racked by graft is a demanding job. It has also turned out to be rather a lonely job too. Abdul is invited to functions on most nights but turns most of them down. 'My social life is terrible!' he laughs, but his reasoning his sound. 'If they don't have access to me, it reduces the chance for them to try and influence me. People don't say categorically "lay off". You get subtle approaches. "Why don't you . . ."'

He's targeted less than his junior officers – mainly, he suspects, because people know the president is on his side.

'That might not last forever,' I say. 'Do you know John Githongo?'

'I've just read the book,' he says excitedly, referring to Michela Wrong's *It's Our Turn to Eat*, which brilliantly chronicled Githongo's attempts to blow the whistle on corruption in Kenya. 'There are a lot of parallels. It has put me on my guard.'

One of the first indicators Githongo had that his influence with President Kibaki might be waning was when his direct access began to diminish.

'I was at the president's office the other day,' says Abdul, 'thinking, do I still have the same level of access? It's something I need to look at.'

Corruption is a security issue, he argues. 'It was one of the reasons for the war. The threat of violence has not passed. Those issues are still there. As long as you have young boys in their prime without means of living ...' He leaves the thought hanging.

There are two television screens in Abdul's office. One is tuned to CNN; the other, right opposite his desk, is a CCTV feed of the corridor outside.

'Is that for security?' I ask.

He nods. His office is as far away from the front entrance as it can be – up three flights of stairs and at the end of a long corridor.

'You never know if someone might try something. We have had mysterious fires in Sierra Leone before.' He smiles and shrugs his shoulders and we go back to talking about Ipswich Town.

A few weeks later Tejan-Cole sends me an email. 'This story may be of interest to you,' it reads, with a link to an article in a local newspaper. The headline, 'Two Bankers in ACC dragnet', details the arrest of two employees at Standard Chartered. It's the final paragraph which Tejan-Cole thinks I'll be interested in: 'Meanwhile the Commission has charged Alimu Bah, General Secretary of the Sierra Leone Football Association, with the offence of misappropriating donor funds contrary to section 13 of the Anti-Corruption Act 2000 as amended. The Commission alleged that he dishonestly appropriated donor funds to the Sierra Leone Football Association by the Confederation of African Football.'

*

One of the biggest legacies of the wars in Sierra Leone and Liberia affected children. Boys and girls as young as eight were forced into rebel groups, often fighting and killing on the front line. It has left an entire generation of children with little or no education and some serious psychological scars. It has also created a strange sense of respect for authority. Children became used to taking orders, often from teenagers not much older than themselves. The consequences of such an upbringing can be slightly surreal, as I experience one Saturday afternoon.

AC Milan are preparing to play Manchester United at Newport Elementary School. The two teams, six boys on each side, all of them wearing their respective replica kits, go into a pre-match huddle and say a silent prayer. They break off and start jumping up and down, shaking out their arms and legs, preparing for the kick-off.

On the sidelines American and Liberian hip-hop blasts out of a stereo attached to a car battery. Six or seven teenage boys sit around, moodily nodding their heads in time to the music.

In the middle of a crowd of twelve- and thirteen-year-old boys, Suleiman is trying to keep order. Sixteen years old and serious, very serious, he writes out the schedule of matches on his notepad. Real Madrid will play Arsenal in the second match, while Lyon and Benfica will contest the third.

Satisfied, he walks towards the middle of the pitch, a small, bumpy, muddy, sandy, puddle-filled space sandwiched between two old school buildings. The two teams come together and shake hands. Suleiman reminds them that he won't tolerate bad behaviour. They nod in agreement. Suleiman checks both goalkeepers are ready (they raise a thumb to indicate they are), walks to the side of the pitch, leans back on the old classroom wall behind him and blows the whistle.

With one eye on the game, Suleiman tells me why he organises his Saturday league. 'When the school is closed the children are doing nothing. They are learning nothing.'

He doesn't just coach his footballers in how to pass and shoot. 'I teach them how to be respectful, how to be yourself, how to prevent yourself from Aids.'

The Man Utd player with 'Rooney' on his back gets shoved off the ball. Suleiman gives his whistle a short, sharp blast and strides over. 'You kick him again, a card for you,' he tells the Milan player, who nods solemnly. At the slightest hint of aggression Suleiman is bounding off his step, making sure it doesn't develop. After being upbraided for one foul, a United player – 'Evra' – half salutes Suleiman as he's beckoned forward for admonishment.

United score a controversial goal. 'Carrick' and 'Evra' combine well on the right and 'Ronaldo' forces it in. The Milan players don't think it crossed the line, though. 'Ball crossed,' says Suleiman, ending the argument.

The boys do not question Suleiman and listen to everything he tells them. 'Yes, they respect me,' he says when I tell him this wouldn't happen in the UK. Teenagers like Suleiman have had to step in where older men would be in a country that hadn't been ravaged by war. Around 250,000 people were killed out of a population of 3 million, and many of those killed in battle were young men – the sort of people who might now be organising matches and training sessions for boys.

Instead, boys like Suleiman take control. He's not the only one organising tournaments here. On a smaller patch of dirt behind another school building I find three thirteen-year-olds coaching a group of nine- and ten-year-olds. Around the corner a group of girls are playing 'football baseball' – one of them 'pitches' or rolls the ball to another, who thumps it as hard as she can before running round a baseball diamond.

Ibrahim Gassama, their male coach, has found it a useful way to introduce them to football. The girls had been hanging around watching the boys play for several weeks, so he decided to get them involved. 'Once they are used to kicking the ball, I will start teaching them passing,' he says.

Ibrahim would prefer to be playing football himself, but he has struggled to find a club. 'You have to do some bribing to get into a team.'

The biggest clubs in Liberia train at the old airfield. There may have once been grass there, but now the pitch is made of sand. It rained all day yesterday, so this morning large pools of water dot the training field. A river runs through the penalty area at one end of the pitch.

Watching the Invincible Eleven train is Dennis Toe, a local businessman who describes himself as one of the 'concerned few' who help fund the club. The players haven't been paid in ten months. 'We can't even come up with fifty dollars each,' he says. He points at the sand beneath our feet. 'It's a beach. We don't have the facilities.'

The team's captain, Kelee Hina, played abroad in Cameroon and Guinea, hoping to get a move from there to Europe, but it didn't happen. 'My dream is to go again. I've put my whole mind to it. I'm not going to sit and wait. I've got to be 175 per cent every game, every practice.'

As in so many countries in Africa, the English Premier League takes precedence over the local game. Monrovia has a daily sports paper, the *Champions Sports*. It carries eight colour pages of tightly packed news about the English Premier League, Barcelona and Real Madrid, cut and pasted from the BBC and the newswires, and only one story about Liberian football.

'If I know there's a big game in England, I don't even watch my own team,' says Toe.

Invincible Eleven was the club where Weah started his career, but it has seen far better days. 'Before the war our league was one of the best in the region,' says Sam Bedford, general secretary of the Liberia Football Association. Not any longer.

But there's one Liberian side that has had international success. The amputees.

*

Before they play, they pray. A dozen men, all missing a limb, lean on crutches and bow their heads. Shouts from a nearby football match and the sound of cars passing on the road beside us fill the air. The coach mutters an 'amen', and the men lift their heads and begin warming up. They move on their crutches with ease, dribbling around cones at pace, using the inside and outside of the foot.

They train on the same sandy wasteland used by the Invincible Eleven, but the handful of passers-by who stop and watch are more interested in the men on crutches than the Premier League team. After all, they are the champions of Africa.

Early in 2009 Liberia hosted the Africa Cup of Nations for Amputees. Sierra Leone sent a team, as did Nigeria and Angola. Liberia reached the final, where they beat Sierra Leone 3–0. 'It was a great day,' says Eric Myers, the vice-president of Liberia's Amputee Football Federation.

Victory helped to change attitudes among the wider public. After the war Liberia's amputees tended to be shunned. With no public transport system in Monrovia, people rely on a small number of battered yellow taxis to get around. Taxi drivers used to ignore amputees, leaving them with long, painful journeys on crutches.

'They think that we are the men who destroyed the country,' says Myers.

Some of those in the Liberian national amputee team are indeed veterans of the country's civil wars. Myers himself fought for Taylor's NPFL. He lost his leg in 'an active battle', as he describes it with a smile. 'We were not many, maybe fifteen,' he says. His group was caught in an ambush, and Myers was on the wrong side. At least ten bullets hit his leg, from the thigh down to the ankle. It was several days before he was able to find a doctor, by which time many of the bullet wounds had become infected.

Playing amputee football had been 'like psychological counselling', he says. 'Before we played most of us never accepted our condition. Now we accept it.'

Some of those in the team were, conversely, victims of the war. Samuel Eastman, the secretary general of the federation, lost his right leg in 1992. His school was in the town of Gbarnga, which at the time was Charles Taylor's base.

Eastman heard the rumbling of a plane overhead. Seconds later it bombed the nearby water plant. His cousin, who worked there, ran over to survey the damage. Eastman went with him. They were placing the wounded in a Red Cross jeep when another explosion went off. It shredded his right leg with shrapnel. Doctors at the hospital amputated it.

'You have to accept it and move on,' he says with a shrug.

Eastman has no problem playing in the same team as former rebels. The past is the past, he argues. 'If we can come together,' he says of his team-mates who fought, 'then the whole country can come together.'

Life is still a struggle for most of the amputees, though. Few of them can find work, and many are forced to beg. Outside every shopping centre in Monrovia there are amputees begging for change. One of them is Prince Chea. Like the players in Sierra Leone, the amputees here have named each other after stars in Europe. Prince's name is Eto'o, after the Cameroonian striker at Inter Milan. 'I play almost like him,' he says with a touch of modesty.

Like so many Liberian teenagers, 'Eto'o' had dreamed of becoming a professional footballer, but he lost his right leg when he was hit by a mortar in 2001. He has no job and little chance of ever finding one, but playing for the amputee team has at least changed one thing. 'People know me now,' he says.

With the warm-up over, the coaches split the amputees into two teams and prepare for a training match. 'Eto'o' lines up on one side, while two other global stars are in the opposition team. Everyone calls Festus Harrison 'Kaka'. Unlike his team-mates, 'Kaka' has been playing on one leg for most of his life. He lost his left leg when he was two and grew up playing football with two-legged boys.

He won the player of the tournament award at the Africa Cup of Nations, and it's not hard to see why. His movements are far more graceful than those of his team-mates.

Running at pace towards the corner, he suddenly plants one crutch in the sand and swings through 270 degrees, taking the ball with him. The defender trips over his own crutches and 'Kaka' steams towards goal.

And then there's 'Drogba'. Moses Koli, as his mother called him, was one of Taylor's child soldiers. He signed up when he was fourteen after 'the enemy', as he describes them, destroyed his village. 'Drogba' is short, no more than five feet, but he puffs out his chest when he talks about the war.

'I was a soldier. I used to go to the front line.' He killed 'plenty of people', he says. 'It was not good, but you have to.' As with Myers, his leg was injured in battle. A doctor could have patched him up, but it would have been several weeks before he could have got to one.

He doesn't have any regrets, though. He just says: 'It's what happened.'

His team-mates call him Drogba because he scores goals. 'I will score two today,' he says just before the match starts. Five minutes later he taps one in from a yard out. A few minutes after that he pokes home a cross.

'Drogba' swings on his crutches in an elaborate celebration, then looks over at me with a 'told-you-so' grin on his face as his team-mates – both former rebels and former victims – hop over to embrace him.

9
THE WARRIORS
Zimbabwe

She was sitting in a cot in the corner, a blanket wrapped loosely around her stick-thin body. Two years old, eyes bulging out of her emaciated head. Her parents were already dead, and within a few days she would be too. Doctors at the Mpilo Hospital in Bulawayo couldn't do anything to save her because they didn't have any medicine. They had nothing.

I had lied my way into the hospital, posing as a priest from a European church. Doctors and nurses sat on chairs in the corridors, chatting. With no medicine to administer there was hardly anything for them to do. Most of their colleagues had left for better-paying jobs in South Africa, Botswana or the UK.

As I left, I glanced at the clipboard propped up at the end of the little girl's cot. It said her name was Perseverance.

Zimbabwe was a country in crisis. The economy was in meltdown, with inflation rising daily. Supermarket shelves were empty. People were forced to queue for hours to buy just one loaf of bread. It was the same for sugar, salt, fuel. There were even queues at ATMs for the worthless currency.

Teachers hadn't been paid for months. Nor had nurses. Unemployment was around 90 per cent. Many of those that did have jobs didn't get paid enough to cover the bus fare into work the next morning.

For the past week I had been travelling across the country, driving from the capital, Harare, south to Bulawayo, the second city and the opposition stronghold. Myself and Frederic Courbet, a Belgian photographer with whom I was travelling, had been trying to get a feel for the political landscape in the country ahead of the 2008 elections.

We had met white farmers and the black settlers who had been given their land, interviewed fervent Mugabe supporters and nervous opposition backers, stood in queues with those waiting for bread and fuel.

At first glance Harare had not appeared to be the capital of a failed state. Harare International Airport is clean and modern, built by the Chinese in the 1990s. The only indication of any problems is the silence. There are hardly any other travellers.

The roads leading into the city are smooth, the buildings are shiny and tall, and expensive Prados, BMWs and even the occasional Hummer can be seen on the highway.

At the fancy Meikles Hotel, where we stayed, a tuxedo-clad pianist plays in the restaurant, where patrons have to wear a shirt and a jacket.

It didn't take long to see through the cracks, though. The porter who carried my bags up to the room explained that his bus fare to work cost more than his wages. This was a common tale. Waiters, shop staff, mechanics – no one seemed to be able to earn enough to get to work, let alone make enough to feed their families once they got home. So people hustled. They bought and sold, borrowed and stole.

Nothing was straightforward. There were two ways of getting hold of Zimbabwean dollars. The official way was to exchange money at the bank, but the rate there was 30,000 Zim dollars to one US equivalent. Alternatively, we could do it on the black market, where the rate was 2 million Zim dollars to one US – sixty-six times better.

I was introduced to a money-changer called Clever. He used to be a maths teacher, but as inflation grew and his wages shrank he decided to use his arithmetic skills in a different way. 'If you can make good money, why not?' he asked. He had picked me up outside the hotel and was now driving us to the outskirts of the city in his brand-new Audi. He found a quiet spot, pulled over and went to the boot. Underneath the spare tyre were several plastic bags packed full of Zim dollars. I handed over US$200 and he gave me two plastic bags containing 400 million Zim dollars.

As we drove back towards the Meikles, we discussed the roots of Zimbabwe's economic crisis. 'We can't get money from the World Bank, from the IMF. Our banks can't get credit. If these rich countries lifted the sanctions, things would improve.'

Mugabe's land reforms, which forced white landowners off their farms, often violently, were essential, Clever said. 'Those whites had all those acres. Is that fair? They were just farming for one individual. Those whites did not share.'

This was not an analysis that everyone agreed with. Most economists believed that the economic downturn began when Mugabe encouraged the first invasions of white-owned farms in 2000.

An opposition group, the Movement for Democratic Change (MDC), had been established a year earlier, led by a trade union leader, Morgan Tsvangirai. In 2000 Mugabe had proposed a new constitution, which would have granted him more powers. The MDC led the successful 'no' campaign at the referendum – Mugabe's first political defeat since he had come to power twenty years earlier.

In the immediate aftermath of that defeat, hundreds of so-called 'war veterans', men who had fought in the war of liberation against Ian Smith's Rhodesian forces, began to occupy land owned by whites.

Mugabe argued that whites shouldn't own thousands of acres while poor blacks had nothing. A scheme was in place to compensate white farmers who gave up their land, but arguments between Britain and Zimbabwe over who should be paying the compensation had stalled the programme.

Regardless of the politics involved, the white farmers had been effective in turning Zimbabwe into the 'breadbasket of southern Africa'. The farm invasions seriously damaged Zimbabwe's agricultural output. Not only did the country lose some of its best farmers, but those who took over often had no interest in running the farms. Most of them were cronies of the ruling ZANU-PF party.

In Bulawayo I met Thys de Vries, a white farmer who can trace his ancestry back to the Dutch settlers who arrived in southern Africa in the 1600s. He lost his 20,000-hectare property in Hwange National Park to the brother-in-law of the trade minister and the local governor. The family was given just six hours to pack up and leave.

De Vries ran a successful game park, employing 200 people and bringing in £1.25 million a year. Now it lay in ruins. All the equipment, from the tractors to the irrigation pumps, had been sold off. 'They got a full jug of milk when they took it over,' de Vries said. 'They drank all the milk without producing any to replace it. Now there's none left.'

De Vries and his family had moved to a 150-acre plot in Bulawayo to rear chickens. The business had been going well, producing a million chickens a year at its highest point in 2006. But the year after, de Vries was hit by Mugabe's latest economic disaster.

As inflation spiralled out of control, prices rose dramatically. It had got to the stage where the price of a loaf of bread would rise between morning and afternoon. In a desperate attempt to stop the constant rises, Mugabe announced that all prices had to be halved with immediate effect. The policy had a devastating effect on businesses, including de Vries's.

'We were forced to sell everything at a loss,' he said. Once everything had been sold, there wasn't enough money to buy new stock. Shops remained empty, unable to fill their shelves.

The armed forces enforced the policy, going from shop to shop, often followed by senior officials from ZANU-PF, who greedily bought up all the bargains. It was a fire sale. Shops were emptied within hours.

*

The image of the empty supermarket shelf was the one which summed up Zimbabwe's economic collapse better than any other. Frederic was determined to get that shot. Working as a journalist in Zimbabwe was difficult, though. Mugabe had banned foreign journalists, so we had entered the country as tourists, occasionally changing our back story when we sought to gain access to places like hospitals.

It wasn't just the normal police we had to avoid. Mugabe's notorious secret police, the Central Intelligence Organisation (CIO), were everywhere. More money was spent on the CIO, sometimes called 'Charlie 10s', than the health department.

One afternoon we had gone into a supermarket to look at the empty shelves. As Frederic was surreptitiously taking his shot, a Charlie 10 was watching. He was a young guy, twenty-four or twenty-five, and clearly a bit nervous about arresting anyone. Frederic quickly deleted the pictures on his memory card as he was taken outside.

'You must come with me,' the Charlie 10 said. 'Both of you.' Then he seemed to change his mind, perhaps wondering what he could charge me with. Let off the hook, I raced back to our hotel to hide a couple of memory cards. We had spent the morning interviewing an opposition leader. If the police decided to come back to the hotel and rifle through the rooms – which they later did – we would have been in serious trouble. As would the opposition politician.

I hid the cards at the bottom of Frederic's washbag and checked that my notes, which I had surreptitiously scribbled in a barely legible scrawl on the side of a newspaper, couldn't be deciphered, then made my way to the police station.

An officer led me along a dank corridor. A door to the right opened on to a small ragged lawn covered with half a dozen wooden coffins. The officer saw me pause to look at the coffins. 'Keep walking,' he instructed. We went down a flight of stairs into the basement and past a series of gloomy cells. 'We will put your friend in here,' smiled the officer.

I found Frederic in an office, looking bored. Two police officers were pressing buttons on his camera, trying to find pictures that were no longer there. At a wooden desk another officer was writing up his report on an old typewriter.

The officer on the typewriter appeared to be in charge. He introduced himself as the deputy of the Criminal Investigations Division. The law had been broken, he insisted, so it had to be investigated. Knowing Frederic was safe and not wanting our driver, Staff, to get into trouble too, Staff and I left the police station. The officer promised he would call when his investigation was complete, and he and Staff exchanged numbers.

An hour later we got a call from the officer. There was another way to sort it out, he explained.

That evening I sat in Staff's car outside Harare Central Police Station. The officer sat in the back.

'$200 is okay,' he said.

'$100,' I replied.

'Your friend has committed a very serious crime.'

'Taking a photo isn't a crime.'

'This is Zimbabwe.'

'Okay, $120.'

'Very serious. $150.'

'Okay. In Zim dollars, yeah?'

He laughed, and I handed over 150 US dollars. The transaction done, he opened the door to go and get Frederic. Before he got out he paused. 'My friend, leave Harare early tomorrow morning. These men will try and arrest you again.' The secret police, he said, didn't care about Zimbabwe's reputation. Life was hard and getting harder. The country needed foreign journalists to tell the world what was happening.

I tried to interrupt, repeating the line about being a tourist.

'I know,' he said. 'Don't use my name in your newspaper, okay?'

I smiled and he went to get Frederic. The next morning we left the hotel at six, heading for Bulawayo. Staff kept a close eye on the rear-view mirror, checking for cars which might be following us. There was nothing. We were in the clear.

*

Like everything else in Zimbabwe, the country's football had suffered. The best players – even the half-decent players – had moved abroad, most of them to South Africa. While the regime of Robert Mugabe had damaged the country's economy, the rule of another Mugabe was blamed by many for the failures of Zimbabwean football.

Leo Mugabe, the president's nephew, was chairman of the Zimbabwe Football Association (ZIFA) from 1993 to 2003. He claimed he had been elected because of his record and his vision. Others thought it had more to do with his surname. Leo was a confident man, eager to point to his successes. He was made his school's sports prefect when he was in form two, ordering about children two years older than he was. 'So there must be something in me,' he said, opening his hands, inviting agreement.

We met at the offices of one of the many businesses he owns, a water irrigation system manufacturer. He was also involved in mobile telecoms, the defence industry and farming, and was just about to launch Zimbabwe's first commodities exchange. 'I just take advantages of the opportunities,' he said. 'No one can complain; it's all public.'

People did complain, though, pointing out that he got many of his opportunities because of his family connections. The USA and the EU had their concerns too, putting him on the sanctions list, which prohibited him from travelling to the West or doing business with anyone there.

This criticism didn't seem to bother him. He leant back in his chair, gave his salt-and-pepper goatee a little stroke, then started to list his successes at ZIFA: starting the country's first junior leagues, introducing women's football and, most importantly, qualifying for the Africa Cup of Nations for the first time. By the time he was ousted in 2003 – the result of corruption allegations, which he was ultimately cleared of – Zimbabwe was ranked fortieth in the world and eighth in Africa, its highest-ever ranking.

'I got us there,' he said.

He appeared keen to get his old job back. 'For us to come out of this will be very difficult unless we have a visionary. I am the most experienced football administrator this country has, but they won't involve me. Nobody talks to me. It's very funny.'

He didn't go to matches any more, he said, because 'people will be saying, "Why don't you come back?" It's not fair on those in charge now.'

One man who certainly didn't want to see Leo Mugabe back in charge of football was the man who actually deserved the credit for qualification for the 2004 Africa Cup of Nations.

'He was terrible,' said Sunday Chidzambwa when I met him the following morning. 'I cannot describe how much I hate him.' I was a bit taken aback. For the past hour Sunday had been smiling and joking as we talked about his career and the state of Zimbabwean football. He had been reappointed as coach of the national team seven months ago, and he had even managed to raise a chuckle when he told me he hadn't received his first pay cheque yet.

'That man knows nothing about football,' Sunday spat. 'Nothing.'

Sunday was Zimbabwe's first national team captain following independence in 1980. Prior to independence, Rhodesia, as the country was then known, was banned from international football. The only teams Sunday and his colleagues could play against were those from apartheid South Africa.

Sunday had dreamed of playing in England, but by the time Zimbabwe was born he was twenty-eight. 'In my twenties I could have played in the top division for sure. I feel I was a lot better than some of the defenders I see in the Premier League now.'

Together with two other senior players, Sunday went to England in 1982 to train with top-division clubs. The players were seen as potential coaches, and the trip would give them some experience of European coaching. Sunday was sent to Birmingham to train with Aston Villa.

He was there during Villa's most recent glory days. We won the league in 1981 – the first time since 1910 – and then went on to lift the European Cup a year later.

'I was training with the first-team guys. Peter . . .'

'Withe?'

'Yes, Peter Withe and Gary Shaw were the strikers. They were very difficult to mark. Very strong. If I had gone there in my early twenties . . .'

'So you're a Villa fan now?' I asked, half knowing I wouldn't get a positive answer. Sunday laughed. 'Manchester United. But I sympathise with Aston Villa.'

'Oh, thanks.'

'I want Villa to beat everyone except Manchester United.'

Sunday's experience in England helped him move into coaching once he retired. He won the league with Dynamos, Zimbabwe's biggest club, and also took them to the final of the African Champions League in 1998, a performance yet to be matched by any other Zimbabwean team.

The 1990s was a decade of near misses for Zimbabwean football. The Warriors had come close to qualifying for the 1994 Africa Cup of Nations under the German coach Reinhard Fabisch, but conceded a late goal in their final qualifier against Zambia. The same year they came the closest they have ever come to reaching the World Cup finals, losing to Cameroon in the final match, when victory would have taken the Warriors to the USA.

By the time Sunday was appointed Warriors' coach in 2002, Zimbabwe's economic and political problems had deepened. As a result of the land grabs, the West had cut aid to Zimbabwe. Food shortages had become severe. Drought hadn't helped, but food analysts believed the biggest factor was the disruption to agriculture caused by the farm seizures.

Mugabe won re-election, but the poll was marred by allegations of vote-rigging. The Commonwealth voted to suspend Zimbabwe's membership.

Sunday hoped that his team might be able to bring a touch of hope back to the country. His first task was qualification for the 2004 Africa Cup of Nations in Tunisia. Money was almost non-existent, making travel to away matches difficult. Peter Ndlovu, the team's star player, who had spent more than a decade playing in England, often had to dip into his own pocket to buy food or training kit for the rest of the squad.

On the eve of a crucial African Nations qualifying tie against Mali, the team were stranded at Johannesburg Airport, unable to get the connecting flight to Bamako because ZIFA couldn't pay the airfares. Sensing an embarrassing international incident, the Zimbabwean government stepped in, rustling up enough money to charter a plane to Mali.

Despite the less than ideal preparations, perhaps even because of them, the Warriors held on for a draw against Mali. That point turned out to be crucial. A 2–0 victory at home to Eritrea a fortnight later secured Zimbabwe's qualification for their first-ever Africa Cup of Nations.

Sunday quit after a row with the new ZIFA management in 2004, but the Warriors managed to qualify again two years later. The next two campaigns weren't so successful, and Sunday had been brought back as national team coach almost a year ago, following the short-lived and unsuccessful reign of a Brazilian, Valinhos, who had been in charge for the 2010 World Cup qualifiers.

The Warriors made a decent start to this World Cup campaign, drawing 0–0 away against group favourites Guinea before beating Namibia at home 2–0. Their matches with Kenya would be crucial. In front of a packed crowd at Nairobi's Nyayo Stadium, Zimbabwe lost 2–0. The return match a week later ended 0–0. Zimbabwe would need to win their last two matches – home to Guinea and away to Namibia – to stand any chance of going through to the final round. They drew with Guinea and lost to Namibia.

Valinhos was sacked, and Sunday was asked to take over. He agreed, but by the time I met him a few months later he seemed to be regretting it. ZIFA had organised a series of friendlies with Asian countries that were more about money than football. In the past nine months Zimbabwe had travelled to Bahrain, Oman, Jordan, Yemen, China and Vietnam. Each trip was fully paid for by the host country and ZIFA was also paid a fee – usually around £6,000. But Zimbabwe hadn't won a single match, and as a result the team had slipped to 120th in the FIFA rankings.

Whatever money ZIFA was making wasn't trickling through to Sunday, though. He hadn't been paid in seven months. Valinhos had suffered a similar fate. He was still owed six months' wages when he was sacked.

Part of the reason Zimbabwe had lost the matches in Asia was because Sunday had been unable to assemble his strongest squad. ZIFA told him they couldn't afford to fly in the players based in South Africa, let alone those playing in Europe like Benjani Mwaruwari, who was playing in the English Premier League for Manchester City. Sunday had to make do with local players, but even then it was a struggle. If an international match was organised at the same time as league matches, the local clubs would refuse to release their best players.

He was thinking of giving up. He ran a little sports shop in town, although that was also suffering because of the economy. 'Sometimes we struggle to pay the rent.' Two jobs and no income – he had had enough.

'There's no point,' Sunday said. 'These matches are a waste of time.'

*

Sunday's boss, Henrietta Rushwaya, disagreed. 'That is what has kept us going. If we don't have those friendlies, we won't be able to buy toilet paper or printer toner.'

She wasn't concerned about the defeats. Using young players, often amateurs, wasn't a problem, she insisted. Anyway, she said, it was good to use the local players because those based abroad lacked commitment. 'When you look at our players, the Benjanis, they don't care. They've become so rich and comfortable.'

Henrietta was ZIFA's chief executive. Her appointment in 2007 seemed to make little sense when she explained it. She studied physical education, then spent several years as a lecturer at a government college before taking a master's in sports science.

Then she was appointed to the most powerful position in Zimbabwean football.

She had no background in football and no background in management. But as others pointed out, she had been very close to the late vice-president, Joseph Msika.

'ZIFA has been far too closely aligned to ZANU,' David Coltart, the new sports minister told me. Coltart, a member of the MDC, was part of the new unity government which had been formed following the violent and rigged 2008 elections. Tsvangirai had clearly won the first round, but the Zimbabwe Election Commission had refused to announce the winner for weeks, eventually claiming that neither Tsvangirai or Mugabe had won enough first-round votes.

Before the run-off could take place, ZANU-PF launched a campaign of violence. Thousands of opposition supporters were beaten and scores were killed. Tendai Biti, the MDC's secretary general, was arrested on charges of treason and thrown in jail. Tsvangirai, fearing for his life, sought sanctuary in the Dutch embassy and pulled out of the election.

In previous years Western leaders and ordinary Africans had loudly voiced their disapproval of such tactics while African leaders had looked the other way. Not this time. Kenya's prime minister, Raila Odinga, who knew a thing or two about stolen elections, publicly criticised Mugabe, as did Ian Khama, the new president of neighbouring Botswana.

Mugabe eventually relented, agreeing to a power-sharing deal with Tsvangirai and Arthur Mutambara, who led the breakaway faction of the MDC.

Since the establishment of the unity government a few months earlier, Henrietta had been trying to portray herself as neutral. 'You have to be apolitical,' she said when we met. That had rarely happened in Zimbabwe, though, where football and politics have always been closely linked.

The biggest club side, Dynamos, was launched in 1963, the same year as ZANU. The club was established as a 'blacks only' club at a time when many of the other football clubs in Rhodesia were 'whites only'.

Football was one of the few activities where thousands of blacks could gather together. Public meetings were banned, but Dynamos matches provided an opportunity for ZANU to mobilise support.

The links between football and politics continued after independence. Zimbabwe has an unusually large number of high-profile matches connected to government celebrations. Big games are organised to celebrate Africa Day, Defence Forces Day and Independence Day. For twenty years one of the biggest cup competitions was the Unity Cup, established to celebrate – if that's the right word – Zimbabwe's rebirth as a one-party state in 1987, when ZANU swallowed ZAPU and became ZANU-PF.

Rufaro Stadium, where Dynamos play their home matches, was the site of Mugabe's independence declaration in 1980. It was also where Morgan Tsvangirai addressed a rally in 2000, ahead of the parliamentary elections that almost gave the MDC a majority.

Tsvangirai's speech at Rufaro was filled with football metaphors. 'The people of Zimbabwe say to Robert Mugabe, "We showed you the yellow card at the time of the referendum, and now today, Robert Mugabe, we are showing you the red card! Get off the field, Robert Mugabe! Your time is over!"'

The crowd waved red cards, a theme that ran throughout the MDC's campaign. At MDC rallies supporters were handed red cards bearing the slogan 'Send Mugabe and ZANU-PF off!'

In defiance of Mugabe's pumped fist, the MDC's symbol was the outstretched palm. At rallies across the country – on the occasions the MDC was actually allowed to hold rallies – vast crowds would raise their open hands and cheer, much like footballers do when they salute the crowd. 'It became very difficult to celebrate during that time,' said Sweeney Mushonga, a Harare football official. 'These guys on the pitch had the fear of being labelled an MDC supporter.'

*

I met Sweeney at a Harare restaurant called The Pot that serves traditional African fare: meat, beans, greens and the ubiquitous maize-based white lump that sits on your stomach for several hours after you've finished eating. In Kenya it's called *ugali*; here it's known as *sadza*.

Most of the decision-makers in Zimbabwean football appeared to be having lunch there. Sweeney and I were joined by Tawanda Murerekwa, former secretary general of Dynamos, while at the next table Henrietta was holding court to two club owners and three ZIFA executives.

Regardless of who was at the next table, Sweeney criticised Henrietta's rule. Administration was poor, he said, and the failure to get sponsorship for the league couldn't be pinned on the economic crisis alone. 'They have failed to separate football and politics,' he said. Players had been selected for the national team not on merit but on which part of the country they were from. Sweeney sat on the finance committee, but he had never been shown the accounts. 'All we get is a budget. You don't get to see the accounts for the previous years.'

What little money there was in the game wasn't getting through to the clubs, claimed Tawanda. Primarily a businessman, supplying water purification chemicals to Harare City Council, Tawanda was a big Dynamos fan and for a short time joined the club's administration. He was secretary general when the club reached the semi-finals of the African Champions League in 2008, only the second time a Zimbabwean side had got that far.

Flourishing in the African Champions League isn't quite as lucrative as success in its European equivalent. Tawanda estimated that of the £300,000 Dynamos won in prize money the vast majority was spent on airfares and other administrative costs. Financially, Dynamos were doing far better this year, when they were not playing in any pan-African tournament, than during the successful Champions League season.

Monomotapa, champions last year and African Champions League participants this year, experienced similar problems. At one point they were on the brink of dropping out of the tournament because they couldn't afford to travel to Tunisia for a group stage match.

Few people seem to make money from football in Zimbabwe. The average annual costs of a Premier League team are around £150,000. There's no sponsorship and little income, even on match days. None of the clubs owns a ground. Instead, they have to rent one off the city council, paying them 20 per cent of all gate receipts.

Few of the clubs, Dynamos and Highlanders aside, have much connection to a local community. The successful clubs in the 1970s and 1980s were linked to mining companies, but as those mining industries began to collapse the clubs folded.

In their place came a series of clubs founded and owned by individuals or small groups. One of those clubs, Gunners, had been set up in 2005 by a handful of Arsenal fans. In just four years they had got promoted to the Premier League and were now battling with Dynamos for the title.

★

The Gunners coach was Moses Chunga, a former Dynamos hero who had been the first Zimbabwean footballer to play in Europe. He spent seven years playing in Belgium during the 1980s, until knee injuries brought his career to an abrupt end.

We sat together on wooden chairs at the side of a school playing field, as Moses watched Gunners train ahead of a cup match against his old team. One of his strikers missed a good chance and laughed with his team-mates as he jogged back to the centre circle. 'Why's he laughing?' Moses wondered aloud. 'He's not taking this seriously.'

Moses certainly is. He spent a lot of his time as a player analysing the way different managers approached the game, and he claims to be the first coach to introduce proper pre-season training.

Like Sunday and Sweeney, he bemoaned the lack of investment in Zimbabwean football. The success of Dynamos and Monomotapa in the Champions League had meant Zimbabwe would have an extra place next year, all but guaranteeing Gunners a place. 'We will struggle to compete with the best in Africa,' Moses said. 'Some of them have got everything – the fields, equipment, money.' He looked around at the school playing field Gunners were training on and opened his arms. 'And this is what we have.'

That weekend I went to the Rufaro Stadium to watch Moses's Gunners take on Dynamos. As the players warmed up, I chatted to the Dynamos assistant coach, Tonderai Ndiraya. Although the team was second in the table, the pressure was on Tonderai and the head coach, Elvis Chiweshe.

'If you lose three games in a row, you get fired. It's as simple as that. There's a lot of pressure from the supporters. It's the people's team.'

Dynamos had lost the week before. 'If we win the next two games, then the pressure will become less. So we better win,' he laughed.

The stadium was perhaps two-thirds full, with at least 10,000 fans inside. 'Football here is on the up. The crowds keep coming, despite the hardship,' said Tonderai.

Most of them were backing Dynamos. The stands were full of people wearing blue. Dynamos – like the vast majority of African clubs – didn't produce replica kits for their fans to buy. Many of those wore the blue of Chelsea instead.

At the front of one of the stands the Dynamos mascot sprinted back and forth, ringing a cow bell. He looked a little like Robert Mugabe, with big glasses and a slightly crazed glint in his eye. His T-shirt had a curiously defensive slogan: 'If God Had Hated Dynamos Why Did He Make the Sky Blue?'

Before the match began, both teams prayed. The Gunners team formed a huddle in the middle of the pitch, while Dynamos all knelt along the goal line. It's not uncommon to see African teams pray before a match, but the image of eleven men with their eyes closed and on their knees on the goal-line was rather striking.

If God was watching, he probably wouldn't have been impressed by the level of violence that followed. Benjamin Marere, the Dynamos centre forward, was knocked unconscious shortly after scoring the first goal. It was not the first injury and it wouldn't be the last.

Just before half-time, with Dynamos leading 2–1, I got a taste of what Chiweshe had been talking about when he had mentioned the volatile nature of the Dynamos crowd. Over on the far side the crowd got angry when the ball appeared to go out for a throw-in but it wasn't given. A couple of minutes later there was another contentious line call and they started throwing bottles at the linesman. I've seen crowds get angry at officials before, but I've never seen missiles thrown at a linesman over a disputed throw-in.

Dynamos made it 3–1 early in the second half, catching Gunners on the break. They were all over them and should have made the game safe, but they couldn't get a fourth and the fans voiced their disapproval, whistling when passes were played backwards or crosses were over-hit.

Gunners were also lucky to keep all eleven men on the pitch after their left back scythed down the Dynamos winger. The referee checked the defender's number on the back of his shirt, realised he had booked him already and decided to let him off.

With just a few minutes left, Gunners pulled one back to make it 3–2. And then, in the final seconds, they won a free kick on the edge of the area. With the last kick of the match, Ali Sadiki swung his left boot at it. The ball curled over the defensive wall. The keeper was caught on the wrong side and could only watch as the ball sailed inches wide of the far post. The final whistle blew, and Dynamos were through to the semi-finals.

Their fans didn't seem too happy, though, and head coach Chiweshe disappeared down the tunnel. He would be sacked two months later.

The fans cheered only when Moses Chunga took a bow. He may have been the Gunners coach, but he was still a Dynamos man.

*

By the time the new unity government came to power in early 2009, inflation had risen to a scarcely believable 500 billion per cent. The $200,000 note I had kept as a souvenir of my previous trip had become utterly worthless. If you saw one lying in the gutter, you wouldn't bother picking it up. The highest denomination note was now $100 trillion, which was worth about £5.

The man responsible for rescuing the world's worst economy was Tendai Biti. He was the MDC's secretary general, and under the terms of the deal struck between Tsvangirai and Mugabe the MDC would get the finance portfolio. To say it was a poisoned chalice would be a gross understatement. Still, at least he couldn't do any worse than his predecessor.

Like many in the MDC, Biti had had a fraught relationship with Mugabe. The president had thrown Biti in jail during the election crisis, accusing him of treason. Biti had pointed out that it wasn't necessarily treasonous to call for the president to go during an election. That was what some people called 'democracy'.

Once Biti was Mugabe's finance minister, though, they got on surprisingly well. 'I'm fixing his mess,' Biti told me. 'He's open to persuasion.'

One of Biti's first acts was to scrap the Zim dollar and replace it with hard currency like the US dollar and the South African rand. Few tears were shed. All public servants were now paid in US dollars, and salaries – even for ministers – were capped at $150 a month.

Biti's office was on the sixth floor of a nondescript government office block in downtown Harare. A portrait of Mugabe hung on the wall just behind Biti's head. His team was about to start work on their first budget, but it was not an easy process. The economic crisis had decimated the country's finances and led to a massive brain drain, which had also affected the finance ministry. Biti was seventy economists short, and many of those he did have had only just graduated from university. 'They are little girls and little boys,' he said.

The morning we met, Biti was far happier talking about the financial situation at his favourite club, Arsenal. 'If there are injuries to Gallas and Vermaelen, we're in trouble,' he said, lamenting the lack of cover at centre back. 'Silvestre is crap.'

It was the same up front, he said. 'If van Persie gets injured, we're in trouble. So it's three players for me – one defender, a striker and a midfield anchor. I don't know if Song is good enough.'

The night before, Villa had beaten Liverpool at Anfield. I was, understandably, in a good mood, but Biti didn't seem to think I had much to crow about. 'Liverpool are crap,' he said with a dismissive wave of the hand. 'They're crap.

'Your team was very organised. Your midfield was excellent. But you could only score from mistakes. You went there for damage limitation. It was one crappy side against a crappier side. With respect to you.'

His passion for Arsenal had grown over the previous decade as Zimbabwean football sank deeper into the mire. He used to support a local team, Black Rhinos. 'I used to go to every game. It didn't matter if it was in Harare or 400 miles from here.'

Not any more, though. Rhinos is owned by the army. When Biti helped form the MDC in 1999, he cut his ties with his football club. 'I felt I would be compromising my friends,' he said. His old friends at Rhinos 'didn't know how to relate to me, so I stopped. It was too awkward.'

It wasn't just the politics that turned him off, though. The standard, he argued, had fallen dramatically. 'We've got a bunch of little boys playing football, whereas in the past we had great players. In the 1980s and 1990s you had teams that could compete with anyone. We had real superstars: Moses Chunga, the late and great Stanley Ndunduma, the late and great Joel Shambo, the late and great Shackman Tauro. Players who could have played in any league in the world. Benjani Mwaruwari can't tie the shoes of Peter Ndlovu.'

The problem, he says, is poor administration and a lack of sponsorship. 'Football in this country has never been well run. There's no vision. With all the money they get from FIFA they should have a very thriving academy. The private sector will always support something that is bankable. Six years ago we were at the African Nations. Now we are not. We could have gone to the World Cup. We were this close. Now we are not even going to Angola. We are losing to Kenya of all teams.'

Zimbabwean football was in a bad state, but it could have been so much worse. Yes, the football association hadn't bothered to pay a national coach for the last eighteen months, and yes, there was clearly no money and little hope of sponsorship to fund the leagues and cup. But during the worst years of Mugabe's rule, at a time when every other part of Zimbabwean life was falling apart, the country's footballers had managed to compete with some of Africa's finest. The Warriors had managed to qualify for the Africa Cup of Nations, and Dynamos had reached the semi-finals of the African Champions League. Given the circumstances, they were remarkable achievements. Against a backdrop of hunger, violence and uncertainty, these teams had brought a slice of normality and success to a country starved of both.

10
BAFANA BAFANA
South Africa

Mark Williams is reminiscing about the day in February 1996 when South Africa became champions of Africa. It's a story he has told dozens of times before, and he clearly knows how to keep his listeners engrossed, whether it's the hundred-strong crowd he addressed in a pub last night or just me the next day.

Williams describes his conversation with Nelson Mandela, who had become South Africa's first democratic president two years earlier. 'He hugged me,' Williams says, 'then looked me in the eye and said: "Today we are going to war. Whatever happens, remember, the whole nation is behind you." I knew then. I knew.'

Later that evening South Africa's football team took on Tunisia in the final of the Africa Cup of Nations. It was the first time South Africa had taken part in the event – they had been banned since 1957 for refusing to field a multiracial team. CAF, the Confederation of African Football, had made South Africa the hosts, and the players had made up for lost time by beating some of the best on the continent – including Ghana in a thrilling 3–0 victory in the semi-final – to reach the final.

Soccer City, the vast stadium in Soweto, was full several hours before kick-off. Williams, though, hadn't been picked for the team. At half-time it was still goalless. 'I was thinking, I've got to find a way to attract the coach's attention. I knew I would score if I got on.'

As the second half progressed it remained o–o.

'I was sat right at the end of the bench, so I turn to look round at the fans and they started cheering,' he remembers, smiling. 'So I thought, I'll warm up.' He stands up and starts exaggeratedly jogging up and down on the spot. 'The crowd start cheering again. I think, I've got his attention, he'll bring me on.'

At first Clive Barker, the coach, ignored Williams. He decided to make a substitution, bringing on the midfielder Helman Mkhalele, but when that didn't make any difference he finally turned to Williams.

'I knew I was going to score. I knew.'

He did. Twice. The goals gave South Africa victory in their first-ever Africa Cup of Nations. Mandela, wearing the gold, white and green Bafana Bafana jersey, handed over the trophy to the captain, Neil Tovey.

A year earlier Mandela had been handing over a different trophy on the other side of town. In front of a mainly white crowd at Ellis Park, Mandela, wearing the green Springbok jersey, presented the Rugby World Cup to South Africa's captain, François Pienaar, after they had beaten New Zealand in the final.

It became an iconic image: Mandela, the man who had led the African National Congress in the fight against apartheid, wearing the shirt which had come to symbolise white rule. It was the moment the world believed that South Africa had become the Rainbow Nation.

And yet in many ways the football victory was far more important than the rugby victory. Williams's goals earned him the nickname 'Nation Builder'.

All but one of the fifteen players in the rugby final was white. Chester Williams, a winger, was 'coloured' – as people of mixed race were, and still are, called in South Africa. The football team, on the other hand, was more representative of the real South Africa. Tovey, the captain, was white; Williams, the hero, was mixed race; while some of the best players, like John 'Shoes' Moshoeu, were black.

'I don't like talking about colour,' Shoes tells me when we meet at the training ground of Bidvest Wits, a local Premier League side. 'But it was an important issue. The white team had won the year before. As the predominantly black team, we felt under a lot of pressure to show that we could win too.'

Bafana Bafana (it means 'the boys' in isiZulu) were not considered favourites, but thanks in large part to Moshoeu's creative scheming in midfield they fought their way to the final. He scored two goals in the semi-final victory over Ghana, a match still considered one of South Africa's greatest performances.

'To assemble a team that could beat the continent, within such a short space of time, was amazing,' Shoes recalls. In two short years South Africa had come a long way.

*

About seven miles off the coast of Cape Town lies Robben Island. This rocky outpost was home to South Africa's political prisoners, including the most famous of them all, Nelson Mandela. The complex is a series of single-storey grey buildings, but in between two of the prison blocks is a football pitch. It's little more than a rock-strewn patch of dirt with two small, rusting goal frames, but for the men who played here it meant the world.

The prisoners established a football association, Makana FA, in 1965. It was one of the few things that enabled them to retain a semblance of normality. A league was set up which was played every Saturday. Jacob Zuma, who became South Africa's third democratically elected president in 2009, was a somewhat uncompromising centre half.

Mandela, who had been jailed for life, wasn't allowed to play, but the guards let him watch. Initially, at least. When they realised how much he enjoyed watching the matches, they built a wall to block the view between his window and the pitch.

Football during apartheid was a release, Shoes explained. Born and raised in Soweto at the height of the battles against apartheid, Shoes has been playing football since he was a small boy. 'We could forget about everything else and just play,' he said, whether they were kicking a plastic ball around the township's dusty streets or watching the two giants of South African football, Orlando Pirates and Kaizer Chiefs, play at Soccer City.

'You can play anywhere, anytime. You don't need specific equipment. You can get something round to kick about. For me, football is a poor man's sport. It has given a lot of people from underprivileged societies a lease of life. It was something that would make us happy. Something where black people would be in a position to win, to conquer. Unlike other things.' He's old enough to remember 'the fumes of the tear gas' during the Soweto uprising in 1976, and was playing professional football in the township for Kaizer Chiefs during the last violent days of apartheid.

As in every other field of South African life, races were kept apart. An anti-apartheid football association, the South Africa Soccer Federation, was established in 1951, which organised leagues and cups. None of the players and clubs were allowed to join the South African Football Association (SAFA). Despite the racial ban, FIFA had no problem accepting the all-white SAFA into its ranks in 1952.

It would be more than a decade before international sporting bodies saw fit to boycott South Africa. CAF, the African football association, wasn't quite so understanding. South Africa was one of four countries scheduled to take part in the inaugural Africa Cup of Nations in 1957, alongside Egypt, Ethiopia and Sudan. But the country's refusal to send a multiracial team caused CAF to throw South Africa out. After it tried to send an all-white team to the 1959 tournament too, CAF suspended its membership.

FIFA followed suit in 1961, although South Africa looked like they had won a reprieve after suggesting they could include non-white players. The suspension was lifted, but SAFA then announced it would send an all-white team to the 1966 World Cup and an all-black team to the 1970 tournament. FIFA renewed its suspension.

In the latter years of apartheid, football was one of the few activities where South Africa's different races were able to mix. White footballers started playing in 'black' teams from the late 1970s and early 1980s. Tens of thousands would turn out to watch every week – the only large-scale gatherings of blacks that the apartheid government allowed.

*

As the ball comes to the only white man in the South African team, the overwhelmingly black crowd greet him with a chorus of boos. They last as long as he's on the ball, stopping abruptly as soon as he passes to a black player. This isn't the Rainbow Nation I'd been told about. Nick Said, a South African football journalist sitting next to me, sees the look on my face. 'Don't worry, they're not booing him, they're just saying his name.'

Matthew Booth is one of the most popular players in the South African team – a shaven-headed, six-foot-five-inch central defender with a broken nose and an uncompromising attitude. Whenever he gets the ball fans yell 'Boooooth!', just like they once cheered another centre half, Mark Fish, by yelling 'Fiiiiiiish!' or the magic feet of John 'Shoes' Moshoeu by chanting 'Shooooooes!'

Since performing well against Spain and Brazil in the Confederations Cup, Booth has become a star. His face peers down from billboards across the country, advertising a mobile phone network. On the day we meet he has been asked to lend his name to a global campaign to get children into school. He's filming his message about the importance of education in one of the executive suites at Johannesburg's Ellis Park.

'Education reduces the chance of being infected with HIV and AIDS,' he says, staring into the camera. His delivery is a little wooden, and he's clearly not altogether comfortable.

'Can I get a smile?' the director asks. 'If I have to,' Booth replies, smiling.

'This is all a bit new to me,' he says later. 'But we've made a decision to attend functions with a purpose.'

The 'we' is Booth and his wife, Sonia, a former model turned fashion designer. If a media Svengali got his hands on this pair, it wouldn't take much effort to turn them into South Africa's version of Posh and Becks. They could have been created by an ad agency – the white footballer from a middle-class Cape Town family and the black model who lived in two small rooms with her sixteen cousins in Soweto. As Sonia readily admits, their backgrounds are 'chalk and cheese'. They get invited to Johannesburg's glitziest parties and are inundated with media requests. But with two young boys, Nathan and Noah, Booth says they 'can't keep up with the partying circuit any more'.

He finds time for fashion, though. When the pair met (Sonia was babysitting for one of Booth's team-mates), he was comfortable in his sporting gear. Sonia, a one-time runner-up in Miss South Africa, soon tried to change that. Now he rattles off the names of half a dozen South African designers he normally wears and speaks enthusiastically about the state of the country's fashion industry.

Booth first played for South Africa in 1998 and won fifteen caps before winning a move to Russia. But during his seven-year stay abroad he was frozen out of the South African squad. It wasn't until he came back to South Africa to play for Mamelodi Sundowns that he forced his way back into the national team.

'Results were so bad they couldn't ignore me any longer,' he says. It clearly still rankles.

'There was something else to it. Our football team is like a small political party.' Certain agents have too much influence within SAFA, he says. The best players are not always picked.

He's uncomfortable about being singled out as the only white player in the national team – there are usually two or three others in the squad. 'In 1996 there were five white players in the team. Our local Premier League has a very good smattering and fair representation of all races.'

Unlike rugby and cricket, football has never needed quotas to ensure a mix of South Africa's races are represented in the national team. 'I just wish the foreign press would acknowledge this and not make me out to be special.'

In a way he's right. There are thousands of other Matthew Booths – children who went to all-white schools, became adults in a post-apartheid South Africa and flourished. He was fifteen when his school became mixed. 'At that age – I can remember it clearly – there was no attitude change. You didn't really worry about colour.'

Despite players like Booth, Tovey and the former Manchester United goalkeeper Gary Bailey, football has always been seen as a sport played by blacks. That means it has suffered from chronic underinvestment compared to 'white' sports like rugby and cricket. From school level to professional, facilities have always been far better for rugby and cricket. The verdant lawns on which all-white schools played rugby simply didn't compare to the dirt yards that all-black schools had for football.

While it wasn't until 1989 that the first proper large football stadium was built, rugby teams had the benefit of several large stadiums built by the government.

Some of the differences remain today. Big stadiums like Johannesburg's Ellis Park are leased by rugby teams for token prices. Because many football clubs don't have their own stadium they're forced to rent the rugby stadiums, pouring more of football's money into rugby's coffers.

As the new stadiums were being built for the World Cup, the question of what would happen to them afterwards went unanswered. While derbies between Orlando Pirates and the other big Soweto side, Kaizer Chiefs, can easily draw 80,000, none of the teams in the Premier Soccer League has an average attendance of more than 20,000.

When I met Booth, there had been talk that some of the stadiums might be handed over to rugby clubs. 'It will be a travesty if that happens,' he says.

*

Tentative negotiations to bring an end to apartheid had begun secretly in the 1980s, when Mandela was still imprisoned on Robben Island, and gathered pace once he was released in 1990. International pressure on the apartheid regime had become more intense, and once F.W. de Klerk took over as president in 1989 there was a leader who was prepared to negotiate.

The country's first democratic elections took place in 1994. The result was never in doubt, but there were fears that the transition to democracy would be bloody. There had been terrible violence in South

Africa's townships in the early 1990s as the apartheid regime tried to stir up tensions between ANC supporters and the Zulu Inkatha Freedom Party.

Mandela's challenges were many. Ending white rule wasn't as simple as electing a new government. Whites ran almost all of the major companies, they took the vast majority of senior civil service jobs and their children went to the best schools. Transforming the country would be an enormous undertaking.

The victory in 1996 gave South African football a massive boost, and the success continued later that year when Bafana Bafana began their first World Cup qualifying campaign. After beating Malawi home and away, they were drawn against Zambia, Zaire and the Republic of Congo (the smaller Congo to the north of Zaire). The winners would qualify for France 98.

By April 1997 the group had reached the halfway stage, with South Africa on four points and the Republic of Congo on seven. Zaire were nowhere – and they were soon to cease to be Zaire. Laurent Kabila's rebellion was closing in on Kinshasa, and Mandela, cast in the role of African elder, led talks between Mobutu and Kabila aimed at ensuring a peaceful transition. Within a month Mobutu had fled into exile.

With Kinshasa unstable, Zaire were forced to play their matches outside the country. South Africa beat them 2–1 in Lomé, the capital of Togo. The win set South Africa on the path to qualification. They won their final two matches, securing their World Cup place with a 1–0 win over the Republic of Congo in Johannesburg.

In their first World Cup finals Bafana Bafana were drawn against the hosts, France, Denmark and Saudi

Arabia. It was a tough group, but if they got at least a point against Denmark and managed to beat Saudi Arabia, they could scrape through to the knockout stage.

They lost the first match 3–0 against France, and at half-time in the second match, against Denmark, they were losing 1–0. But a Benni McCarthy equaliser gave them a point. Going into the final matches, Denmark were in second place on four points and a +1 goal difference, and South Africa had one point and a –3 goal difference. Bafana needed to win against the minnows Saudi Arabia, and France needed to beat Denmark by enough goals to change the goal difference in South Africa's favour.

Bafana got off to the perfect start when Shaun Bartlett opened the scoring after nineteen minutes. Then things started to fall apart. Saudi Arabia had failed to score in their opening two matches, losing 1–0 to Denmark and 4–0 to France, but they made amends in Bordeaux with two penalties, giving them an unlikely lead. South Africa rescued a point with a last-minute equaliser from Bartlett, but Bafana were going home.

Despite failing to reach the second round, South Africans were proud that their team had managed to qualify for the World Cup at the first attempt. The tournament capped another great year for South African football. At the Africa Cup of Nations in Burkina Faso they had proved their victory at home in 1996 was no fluke, reaching the final before losing to Egypt.

South African football had always believed it was good enough to compete at the top level, and the team's performance post-apartheid proved that they were one of the very best in Africa.

But South Africa's football dreams didn't end on the pitch. The new government wanted to do something no other African country had ever done: host the World Cup.

*

Danny Jordaan is the public face of the South African World Cup. He wears rimless glasses which shade over in the sun and is rarely seen out of his World Cup blazer. We meet outside Soccer City, the Soweto stadium where the Africa Cup of Nations was won. Workmen hammer away in the background, transforming it into a 95,000-seat colossus that's designed to look like a brown cooking pot. The World Cup final will take place here in July 2010, although if it hadn't been for the actions of a seventy-eight-year-old New Zealander, it might have happened four years earlier.

South Africa's first bid for the World Cup was for the 2006 tournament, which eventually went to Germany. FIFA president Sepp Blatter was an enthusiastic backer of the idea of bringing the tournament to Africa, the only continent (Australasia aside) that hadn't hosted it. The vote would be decided by the twenty-four members of the FIFA executive committee, and in the event of a tie Blatter would cast the deciding vote. England, Morocco and Brazil had also bid for the event, but by the time the vote took place in Zurich in July 2000 the two favourites were Germany and South Africa. They duly made it through to the final round of voting.

World Cup votes are difficult to predict. There may be just twenty-four voters, but each one is assiduously courted by all sides, and political calculations and payoffs are weighed up for each option. Some delegates arrived in Zurich under strict instructions about who to choose, following votes by their home federations. Others were still open to persuasion.

Charles Dempsey, the septuagenarian representative of Oceania, was supposed to vote for England until they were knocked out and then switch to South Africa. The decision had been made at Oceania's conference in May. Dempsey, though, hadn't seemed that keen. He had turned down invitations to visit South Africa ahead of the vote, including one made directly by Mandela.

When it came down to the crucial vote, Dempsey decided to defy his executive's wishes and abstain. His non-vote proved vital. Germany won by the narrowest of margins – twelve to eleven. If Dempsey had voted for South Africa, as instructed, Blatter, who had made no secret of his support for South Africa, would have broken the tie.

Such was Blatter's determination to take the World Cup to Africa that he declared his committee would only consider bids from African countries to host the next tournament, in 2010.

South Africa bid again, as did Egypt, Morocco and Libya. South Africa were overwhelming favourites, particularly after having missed out last time around, but it was still close. Lobbying was just as intense as before, and some curious deals were struck to persuade the voters. According to those involved in the South African bid, Jack Warner, the head of the Caribbean region and a FIFA vice-president, demanded a visit from Mandela to the Caribbean in return for his vote.

Mandela and Archbishop Desmond Tutu were in Zurich for the vote and were closely involved in the final lobbying.

It was decided on the first round. South Africa won fourteen votes and were awarded the World Cup.

Celebrations back in South Africa were understandably exuberant. Three months earlier the country had celebrated ten years of democracy. Thabo Mbeki, who had taken over as president when Mandela stepped down in 1999, won a second term on a platform of fighting poverty.

Mbeki's government had been criticised on the left for being too pro-business and not doing enough to help lift the majority of people out of poverty. He had also faced widespread condemnation both inside and outside the country for his stance on AIDS. Mbeki's denialism – he refused to believe the science and argued AIDS was caused by poverty – meant the disease went unchallenged. His health minister, Manto Tshabalala-Msimang, went as far as to suggest that beetroot and garlic were better treatments for HIV than antiretroviral drugs.

For many black South Africans, democracy had not yet brought the gains they had expected. Some hoped that the World Cup would speed up progress. Major investment would need to be made in public transport and roads. Tens of thousands of jobs would be created in the construction industry by building new stadiums.

It didn't take long for concerns to be raised about a South African World Cup, though. Crime remained an enormous problem, with 19,000 murders a year (compared to 850 a year in the UK). Public transport would be a major issue too – South Africa had very little. Some people, both in South Africa and abroad, argued that the money would be better spent on regeneration projects, education or health.

As building work slowly began, people started to ask whether South Africa would be ready. Franz Beckenbauer, the great German defender who won the World Cup as a player and a manager before going on to head the 2006 organising committee, criticised South Africa at the end of the 2006 World Cup. They 'have big problems,' he said. 'African problems.'

There's a real sensitivity to the criticism that South Africa won't be ready. People bristle. They fold their arms. They stand a little bit taller, a little bit stiffer. Every country that hosts a major championship faces criticism in the run-up. Before the Athens Olympics the organisers didn't have time to finish the roof on the swimming pool. But the criticism South Africa faces is a bit different. This isn't just about the organisation of a sporting tournament. According to Jordaan, this is about Africa.

'We want to explode the myth that there's a contradiction between being African and being world-class,' says Jordaan. 'And it is a myth.'

What makes the criticism worse is that much of it comes from inside the country – from white South Africans.

'They assume black people can't run a coffee shop, let alone a World Cup,' said Steven Friedman, a professor in politics at Rhodes University in Johannesburg.

'Mbeki obsesses with this idea that whites didn't think blacks could run a market economy or a stable government,' he told me. 'It's the same with mega events like the World Cup. They are trying to show the world that Africa can do this – that a black-ruled society can run a major event. If it was going to happen in Italy, you wouldn't hear all this.'

Freidman argued that the criticism was stronger because it was football, a game that many whites still hadn't embraced. 'Local football is not something racial minorities get terribly excited about. Black sports fans have a point when they say the whites should care more about Bafana Bafana. They joyously rallied around teams with two or three black guys. When we won the African Nations, I was one of maybe ten white people in the stadium.'

South Africa now has its third black president, Jacob Zuma, but race is still a massive issue in South Africa. The first time I went to the country I met a friend in Cape Town and we went to a bar. It was all brushed metal and mahogany floorboards and full of people more concerned with how they looked than with having a proper conversation. But there was something else strange about it which, at first, I couldn't put my finger on. Suddenly it hit me. I'd been in Africa for a year but I'd never been surrounded by so many white people. Even at the most expat Nairobi party you can imagine (UN types, aid workers, etc.) there were always some black Kenyans. In this Cape Town bar I could count just two blacks. Even the bar staff were white.

In certain parts of the country there was a casualness to the racism that I found shocking. At a guesthouse in Rustenburg the owner apologised because the room hadn't been cleaned yet. 'You know what these blacks are like,' she said to me. A middle-aged white taxi driver in Cape Town recounted how his three children had all left the country and moved to Australia. 'You can't get a job here unless you're black,' he said. 'It's like apartheid in reverse but three times worse.'

In the whiter parts of South Africa I constantly heard the phrase, 'When Mandela dies . . .' The theory is that when the country's first black president passes away the radical ANC leaders will finally show their true colours and set South Africa on a path to anarchy. The people spouting this line – all white, all middle-aged or older – were the same people who claimed this would happen when Mandela stepped down in 1999. And they're the same people who said this would happen when democracy was introduced in 1994 – or, as one Afrikaner described it to me, 'when the blacks took over'.

*

Jordaan tires of answering questions about whether South Africa will be ready. It's not an issue for him – he knows it will all work out fine. But another fear has gripped South African football fans: what if the country is ready, but the team isn't? On the brink of the biggest moment in South Africa's sporting history, the woeful performance of the national football team threatens to spoil the party.

I ask Jordaan about Bafana Bafana. He sighs. A weak smile plays on his lips and he looks away. 'Why do you have to ask about my team?'

No host nation has ever failed to reach the second round of the World Cup. The USA managed it in 1994. Both Japan and South Korea did it in 2002 – the Koreans going all the way to the semi-finals. South

Africans fear their team could be the worst hosts in history.

South Africa has suffered a steady decline since the successes of 1996 and 1998. They qualified again for the 2002 World Cup – once more going out in the first round – but their Africa Cup of Nations performances got gradually worse. A semi-final in 2000 was followed by a quarter-final in 2002. Two years later they didn't make it out of the group stages, and in 2006 they lost all three matches and didn't score a goal.

The nadir was reached in 2008, when they failed to qualify for Angola 2010, the tournament which was set to take place five months before South Africa hosted the World Cup.

It wasn't supposed to be like this. Carlos Alberto Parreira, a World Cup-winning Brazilian coach, had been hired on a salary believed to be around £130,000 a month. He persuaded the mercurial Benni McCarthy, South Africa's best player by far, to return to the fold after a long self-imposed absence, and the team was playing good football.

But Parreira didn't last long. A family crisis prompted him to resign, and he suggested another Brazilian coach, Joel Santana, as his replacement. Unlike Parreira, Santana had no experience coaching a national team, let alone leading one to World Cup victory.

His reign got off to a bad start. Bafana lost twice to Nigeria and lost and drew with Sierra Leone – one of the worst countries on the continent. After failing to qualify for the Africa Cup of Nations, Santana's men enjoyed a five-match winning streak, but the calibre of opposition was mediocre at best. They came crashing back down to earth in February 2009, outplayed and outfought by a good Chilean side.

Much rested on the performance of the side in the Confederations Cup. The tournament is traditionally used as a warm-up for the World Cup host nation. It's a chance to check that the stadiums are okay, the transport systems are fine and all the logistics are in place. For South Africa it was far more important to see if the team was ready.

Bafana were put in a group with Iraq, New Zealand and Spain. The first two were in an even worse state than South Africa, and fans hoped for two comfortable wins before the game against the tournament favourites, Spain. Santana had dropped two of his best players, the defender Nasief Morris, who plays in Spain, and McCarthy, who plays in the English Premier League.

Without McCarthy's pace and power up front, Bafana struggled for goals. They drew 0–0 with Iraq and laboured to an unconvincing 2–0 victory against New Zealand. Spain comfortably beat them 2–0 in the final group stage, but Bafana had done enough – just – to qualify for the semi-finals, where they were due to meet Brazil.

No one gave them a chance against a country that has won the World Cup a record five times. A few months earlier I had met Steven Pienaar, the Everton midfielder, who was one of Bafana's few stars. 'It's a good thing that no one thinks we will do well,' he said. 'We play better when there's no pressure.' And so it proved. For eighty-nine minutes South Africa matched Brazil pass for pass, tackle for tackle – until the final minute, when Brazil won a free kick on the edge of the area. Daniel Alves, the Barcelona fullback, smacked it past the wall and into the top corner, and the game was lost.

Bafana may have been defeated, but they had lost with pride. Three days later in Rustenburg they played Spain again in the third-place play-off. Again, they rose to the challenge, and took the lead with seventeen minutes remaining when Katlego Mphela knocked in a cross from the left. It looked like it would be enough to give them an unlikely victory, but with three minutes left on the clock David Guiza struck from the edge of the area. A minute later Guiza put Spain ahead. But Bafana didn't drop their heads, and in the last minute of injury time they won a free kick about thirty yards out. Mphela struck it sweetly into the top left-hand corner.

Spain won the match in extra time, thanks to a Xabi Alonso free kick, but Bafana and Santana could claim another moral victory. His side had proved that they could compete at the top level, and hopes were raised that South Africa would make it past the group stages at the World Cup.

Within three months, though, the knives were out for Santana again. His team lost three successive matches – to Serbia, Ireland and Germany – making it six defeats in the last six matches. An unconvincing 1–0 win against African minnows Madagascar did little to bolster confidence.

Leading names in South African football were calling for Santana to be sacked. 'The team's got potential, but Santana's not going to bring it out. You need charisma, a sense of leadership. But he's a Fred Flintstone-style goof,' Mark Gleeson, arguably Africa's most respected football journalist, told me.

Rob Moore, a football agent who had been heavily involved in the establishment of one of South Africa's best-run Premier League clubs, Ajax Cape Town, agreed. 'We're star-struck,' he said. 'We think, "Ah, they're Brazilian, they must be good." They're not. This has been one of the worst reigns ever.'

I met Moore at Sun City, the vulgar casino palace built by Saul Kerzner in the 1980s. Sun City doesn't do subtle. The lobby, a grand circular dome, is filled with fake Roman pillars, straight-backed zebra-print armchairs, artificial palms and ostentatious fountains. Perched on the edge of a leopard-print settee, Moore argued that the early success post-apartheid had contributed to the current crisis.

'The victory in 1996 was a great, fantastic, emotional victory. But the reality is that the best team in the continent wasn't in the tournament.' Nigeria would have been overwhelming favourites, but the military regime of General Sani Abacha refused permission for the team to travel after Mandela had criticised his human rights record.

'That early success in 1996 and 1998 was a point where people thought things would be okay. That's when you need to lay the foundations for the future. But the opposite happened.' He likened those first two or three years to the adrenalin and desire that often propel a newly promoted club up the table at the start of the season. Then reality sets in, and they end up struggling to avoid relegation.

No youth structures were set up, and no serious development programme was put together. 'They thought it would fall into their laps, and now we are paying the price. If those players had been prepared when they were younger, they'd be able to cope.

What you are seeing now is a by-product of years of neglect.'

Few clubs have youth teams, and there's no reserve league. Almost all of South Africa's best players of the last decade left the country when they were teenagers, spending their formative years in Europe. Quinton Fortune, once of Manchester United, left when he was fourteen. Everton's Steven Pienaar left at seventeen.

Moore has been involved in South African football for decades. First as the owner of Seven Stars, a Cape Town side which nurtured future stars such as Benni McCarthy, and more recently as a manager and agent for a host of South African footballers.

Moore placed the blame squarely on the game's administrators. 'The guys running South African football don't understand what it takes to organise world-class football. They are world-class marketers, they've brought in a huge amount of sponsorship money, but when it comes to the game of football they don't really have a clue.'

He was not the only one who thought this way. In fact, it was surprising how few people disagreed with what the problems were. Shoes had said the same. 'I worry about what happens after the World Cup. It will be many years before we qualify again unless something changes.'

One of the country's leading broadcasters, Robert Marawa, echoed those views.

'Financially, this is the seventh-best league in the world, but on the field we're seventy-second in the world. We're not even in the top ten in Africa. That tells us something. Had we not been hosts we would not have qualified. It could be really embarrassing.'

Marawa hosts coverage of the Premier Soccer League on Supersport, the pan-African satellite broadcaster, and also presents a daily sports show on Metro FM. As we discuss the state of football in his studio just before his show begins, he gets more and more animated.

'No one gives a damn about development. Administrators have been more interested in developing their bank accounts. It's got very commercialised, but the footballers haven't benefited. It's sad because the potential is there.

'It's jobs for pals at SAFA. You're there for life. There's no accountability – it's non-existent. These guys aren't going anywhere – they'll protect each other. And they'll all get big fat bonuses after the World Cup.'

Marawa nips into the studio next door to start his radio show. Emails and phone calls come flooding in, criticising the most recent Bafana Bafana defeat.

There's one other problem which has plagued South African football: a trigger-happy football association that has gone through twelve national coaches in the last eleven years. Yet while SAFA has sacked coaches who have performed far better, Santana appears to be safe in his job. Coaches like Carlos Queiroz, once assistant to Alex Ferguson, and Stuart Baxter, now managing Finland, have had far better records than Santana yet have been given the boot.

The closer it got to the start of the World Cup the more desperate the situation became. And yet, the harder it would have been to sack him. Eventually, after eight defeats in nine matches, SAFA bit the bullet. Santana left 'by mutual consent' and was replaced by his predecessor, Carlos Parreira. He'd left to look after his sick wife, but she'd since made a full recovery. Parreira, unlike Santana, had some World Cup pedigree.

*

A few days before the grand opening of South Africa's first World Cup stadium, I went along to see how things were going. From a distance, Rustenburg's newly refurbished Royal Bafokeng stadium looked impressive, with its brand-new main stand rising above the skyline.

Up close, it didn't look as good. Construction workers hung from scaffolding, furiously hammering away. The car park was a mess of bricks and gravel. Inside, hundreds of people dressed in blue overalls and yellow hard hats were painting gates, fixing the electronic scoreboard and screwing in seats.

Foremen yelled into mobile phones.

'Of course we'll be ready! Of course!' insisted one as he watched one of his workers run down to the long-jump pit, scoop up a bag full of sand and race back towards a cement mixer.

Bafana Bafana were due to play Norway in the Nelson Mandela Challenge. The former president, now ninety, was too frail to make the journey up to Rustenburg, a mining town in the northwest. Jacob Zuma, who was less than a month away from becoming South African president, would be there to present the trophy instead.

The players trained at a smaller stadium down the road. It would prove to be one of Santana's last games in charge and, as always, he insisted on speaking in

Portuguese at his press conference, frustrating local journalists and also prompting questions over whether he could communicate effectively with his players.

When I spoke to him afterwards, through an interpreter, it was clear that his English wasn't too bad. He understood all the questions but felt more comfortable answering them in Portuguese. His answers were as uninspiring and unrevealing as those of most football managers – except one answer. I asked him if he ever had any regrets about taking the job. On paper, the answer seems upbeat: 'I am very happy here. I have had a great time. I'm not just the coach any more. I am part of the family.' But the tone was anything but cheerful. There was a long pause before he started the answer, a slight sigh, a glance at his feet.

He motioned to the interpreter – interview over – and shuffled off.

*

The last-minute rush at the stadium came off. By match day only the smell of fresh paint indicated that there had been problems.

Zuma was introduced to the crowd and taken to meet the teams. Despite the MC's exuberant welcome – 'our leader, Jacob Zoooooooooma!!!' – the crowd's response was warm, not ecstatic.

The atmosphere was not as lively as I'd expected. The stadium was perhaps three-quarters full, and while the crowd blew their *vuvuzelas* – three-feet-long plastic trumpets – with gusto, the mood was relatively flat.

South Africa were lining up without Benni McCarthy. Santana had picked him for this squad, but he had failed to turn up, citing a hamstring injury. Few seemed to believe him. The headline in one newspaper in Johannesburg read: 'Benni does it again'.

It proved to be the final straw, and Santana refused to pick him again. Fans feared the team would head into the World Cup without their best-ever striker. And judging by the performance against Norway, it would be a struggle.

South Africa looked weak up front without McCarthy. Against Norway they lined up in a 4–5–1 formation, with Pienaar and the similarly slight, creative midfielder Teko Modise pushing forward.

Bafana started brightly. Modise, the local league's newest star, seemed to have a licence to roam, or perhaps had simply taken one. Everyone loved Modise. Gleeson had told me he was the one footballer in the league he would pay money to go and watch. Marawa had been similarly effusive, describing him as the 'shining beacon of hope'.

But Modise's rise also highlighted the problems of youth development. He was now twenty-seven and had only broken into the squad a couple of years ago. Few had heard of him until he was in his early twenties. With better scouting systems and development programmes, a player like Modise would have been nurtured from an early age. 'Can you imagine if Rooney hadn't been discovered until he was in his twenties?' Marawa asked.

Watching him play against Norway, I can see why he's the crowd's favourite. When the ball is at his feet, he looks relaxed as he rolls it under the sole of his boot and tries little flicks. It's from his crossfield pass that South Africa score the first goal. The fullback

Siboniso Gaxa pulls it back, and Bernard Parker, a striker playing for Red Star Belgrade, pokes it past the keeper.

Norway are there for the taking. The heat is sweltering, and the crowd are getting into the game and roaring the home side on. But Bafana sit back. They don't seem to have the confidence to push for a second goal. Somewhat inevitably, Norway equalise.

There are few chances in the second half. Siphiwe Tshabalala, the substitute, blasts well over the bar from thirty yards out. Then, deep into injury time, Tshabalala gets the ball outside the area again. This time his shot is perfect, arrowing into the top right-hand corner.

The stadium erupts, the Norway players collapse, and the match is over. As it's the Nelson Mandela Challenge there's a trophy to be presented. The South Africa players look a little bit embarrassed getting up on stage, and the fireworks when they lift the cup are over-the-top. But they celebrate and smile, a sense of relief coursing through the team.

There would be many more defeats to come. Many more false dawns. But, for a moment, Bafana Bafana were winners again and ready to take on the world.

EPILOGUE

It may have been an international match, but there were little more than one hundred people watching. I sat with Ahmed Nur, vice-president of the Somalia Football Federation, on white plastic chairs in the main stand of Nairobi's dilapidated City Stadium. Eritrea were beating Somalia 3–0 in the 2009 East and Central African Cup, known as the CECAFA Cup.

For Ahmed Nur and the Somali team, what was happening on the pitch was little more than a distraction from the horrors back home. Two days earlier a suicide bomber had made his way into a graduation ceremony for medical students at Benadir University and blown himself up. Three government ministers, two journalists and several would-be doctors had been killed.

The players had hoped a win might lift spirits at home, but it wasn't to be. With twenty minutes left, Mohamed Hassan Copani pulled one back, but despite going close on two further occasions Somalia lost 3–1.

'At least we scored,' said Ahmed Nur. He was heading back to Mogadishu with the team. We hugged and promised to meet up next time he was in Nairobi. On the pitch the Eritrean players were celebrating with the small band of Eritrean refugees who had come to watch. A few days later, after a 4–0 defeat in the quarter-finals, they would join their fans – the entire Eritrean national team failed to board their plane home and sought asylum in Kenya instead.

It was not a surprise. A month earlier I had been in Eritrea and met three footballers in the national league. Like all young Eritreans, they were forced to do several years of national service. The country's autocratic president, Isaias Afwerki – who told me he was an Arsenal fan – had turned the country into a giant prison. Up to 70,000 Eritreans left illegally each year – more than in any other country in the world except Zimbabwe. For these twelve squad members the East and Central Africa Cup provided a way out.

The CECAFA Cup was a tournament for Africa's worst football teams. None of the region's teams had made it to the Africa Cup of Nations, which would take place in Angola a month later. But despite the lack of talent and the lack of interest from Kenyan football fans there were moments – like Copani's goal or the Eritreans' celebrations – which demonstrated how important the tournament could be.

For the Eritrean team, football was the only way they could escape the repression at home, even if it was just for the duration of the tournament. Ultimately, they would use their status as international footballers to escape it for good.

For Ahmed Nur and the Somali national team, the simple act of playing football allowed them to forget the tragedies at home. More importantly, they were able to fly their flag. To show that there was more to Somalia than suicide bombers and pirates. And for the Somali fans back home listening to the commentary on the radio, there was the slim hope of a win, or even just a goal – something small to celebrate.

For ninety minutes, nothing else mattered.

ACKNOWLEDGMENTS

I first had the idea for this book towards the end of 2006, a few months after I arrived in Nairobi. I had been trying – and failing – to fully understand the intricacies of Kenyan politics. It was a confusing world of ever-changing alliances based largely, it seemed, on tribal divisions, money and power.

At the same time, I had taken an interest in the local football league, something Kenyan friends found amusing. They were all far more interested in European football. They spoke about the people who ran football in Kenya in the same way they spoke about their politicians.

The corruption and mismanagement which bedevilled politics in Kenya also appeared to be eating away at the country's football. The more I learned about how Kenyan football was run, the more I understood the problems in government. Was there a way of telling a story about Kenya as a country through its football? And if it could be done in Kenya, what about elsewhere on the continent?

Turning the germ of an idea into a fully-fledged book would not have been possible without the invaluable support and guidance of my agent, Jonny Pegg, who was willing to take a risk on a first-time writer he had never met. Nick Davies at Canongate is an excellent and understanding editor, who provided crucial advice and suggestions throughout the process.

Researching the book has involved conducting hundreds of interviews and watching dozens of matches in more than fifteen countries across Africa. Along the way, numerous people have offered their knowledge, contacts, stories and friendship. In no particular order I am indebted to Ahmad Saied, Khalid Youssef, Al-Siir Sabil, Ahmed Nur Abdulle, Bashiir Mohammed, Farah Blue, Marcio Maximo, David and Juliet Okoth, Bob Munro, Gishinga Njoroge, Mark Ellis Jones, Hez Holland, Matt Green, John and Therese James, Katrina Manson, Isha Johansen, Abdul Tejan Cole, Glenna Gordon, Petros Kausiyo, Fredi and Rita Ruf and Nick Said.

Several people read all or part of the manuscript, offering important suggestions and correcting my errors. I am particularly grateful to Tom Sperlinger and Shashank Bengali.

I also owe a large debt of gratitude to all my editors at the *Independent* and *Monocle*. Leonard Doyle, my first foreign editor at the *Independent*, was willing to fund trips across the continent and was always available when things got hairy, never more so than when I was in Mogadishu.

Andrew Tuck recruited me at *Monocle* and has given me a freedom to report on the continent that few other magazines can offer. I am also grateful to

Tim Lewis at the *Observer*, who commissioned me to write several features on African sport over the last two years.

Words cannot express how much I owe to my parents. My dad introduced me to football, and after much cajoling agreed to take me to Villa Park to see Villa play Liverpool when I was seven. More importantly, they raised me in a household that valued education, and from a young age encouraged me to take an interest in the world around me. Throughout the process of researching and writing this book they were invaluable, asking questions before and after every trip, suggesting themes and making sure I never lost sight of what I was trying to achieve. My sister, Jen, was also a much-needed source of support.

Lastly, this book would never have been written without Dree. She persuaded me to follow my instincts and write a proposal, and then put up with my seemingly endless travel from one corner of the continent to the other. This book is for her.